Average Guy
Meets
Extraordinary God

Average Guy
Meets
Extraordinary God

Frank E. Becker

NORTHEASTERN BAPTIST PRESS

BENNINGTON, VT

Average Guy Meets Extraordinary God
Copyright © 2026 by Frank E. Becker

Published by Northeastern Baptist Press
        Post Office Box 4600
        Bennington, VT 05201

Scripture taken from the New King James Version®.
Copyright ©1982 by Thomas Nelson. Used by permission.

Cover design and typesetting by Leason Stiles

Softcover ISBN: 978-1-953331-78-6

Frank @ Glimmerglass State Park, Cooperstown, NY, 1982

TABLE OF CONTENTS

THE FORMATIVE YEARS:
The Beckoning Hand of God

THE PASTORAL YEARS:
The Anointing Hand of God

THE WANDERING YEARS:
The Preserving Hand of God

ALMOST HOME:
The Reassuring Hand of God

Through many dangers, toils and snares,
I have already come;
'Tis grace hath brought me safe thus far,
And grace will lead me home.

Amazing Grace
John Newton, 1779

DEDICATION

This book describes God's amazing care of our family and is accordingly dedicated to our grandchildren and their wonderful parents.
Every reader will hopefully:

- Find inspiration in the accounts of God's providential care.
- Better understand how world events impacted their own and their ancestors' lives, and how the past affects their futures.
- Be encouraged by learning of the struggles, faith, and accomplishments of average people blessed by our extraordinary God.

The book spans the decades from the First World War to the present, with each chapter focusing on God's miraculous transforming power.
Since every testimony of God's loving care should encourage hope and build faith, it is my prayer that you will profit from these accounts.

A BRIEF PREFACE

As an average guy and a new believer, I saw the Lord as an "Extraordinary God" who was to be worshiped alongside my other idols and ambitions. As time went on, however, and I became more familiar with the Lord through His written Word and personal interaction. I realized that He is the only true God, the wise Creator and all-powerful King. I wasn't to be driven by my own purposes, but by His. My own ambitions and values weren't simply to be subordinated, but were to be established by Him.

Some may call a number of these events "miracles;" while skeptics will call them coincidences, or even fabrications. As eye-witnesses to these arguably miraculous events, and as participants in many of them, my wife, Joy, and I consider ourselves both qualified and obligated to testify to the glory of God. *"For we cannot but speak the things which we have seen and heard"* (Acts 4:20).

This book is not intended as a chronicle, but because these events occurred in the context of our day-to-day lives, and from our human perspective, it is necessarily biographical. To me, these experiences are all the more compelling because I was born with feet of clay and have never been more than an average guy who repeatedly found himself blessed by an extraordinary God.

THE CALL:

THE GUIDING HAND OF GOD

CHAPTER 1

"Defeat the Big Party Spenders"

My father was a true entrepreneur. The year before he passed away with cancer, he was operating five distinctly different businesses in New York and Florida.

One of those businesses consisted of a chain of retail outlets located in New York's mid-Hudson Valley, where he marketed factory-built homes. He had begun by retailing tiny house trailers in Poughkeepsie in 1947, but sales multiplied with the size of the homes, and in his heyday, he delivered over 300 units in one year. He marketed the second ten-foot wide manufactured home in America. It was brought in by rail because such wide loads were not yet permitted on most state highways. He even designed, built, and marketed conventional homes, delivering them on wheels to the building sites.

When I took over that business, however, sales were being strangled by restrictive zoning ordinances and had dropped to about 50 units per year. The business still held promise. We stocked scores of extraordinary homes that were well-designed, precision manufactured—stylish and beautifully furnished—and we had plenty of potential customers. But sales were increasingly restricted to an occasional space in one of the run down "trailer parks" that were already giving manufactured housing a bad name.

In retrospect, my responsibilities demanded far more maturity than I possessed. At the age of twenty-two, I was devoting too little time to a job that a far more mature manager would have found extremely challenging.

Average Guy Meets Extraordinary God

And while I wasn't a playboy, I spent too much time on other interests and devoted almost none to the Lord. My father would have been wiser to have left Ernie Steider in charge, or promoted one of his other employees, like my devoted secretary, Carol Ryan.

I took a giant step forward when Joy MacNiven and I were married in 1964, but I still paid too little attention to either dad's business or to the Lord.

Around 1964, I got my first taste of politics. My dad had purchased a 20-acre tract in a rural area, and I drew the plat plan for an ultra-modern sixty-unit housing development, *Casa de Mobile.*

The plans, which included a costly sewer plant, were approved by the county board of health, but when I mentioned them to the town supervisor, he hinted at a bribe. I was shocked and pretended that I didn't understand what he was suggesting. But when we applied for a building permit, and it was issued by the town's building inspector, he was publicly rebuked by the supervisor, and within a few days the town zoning board of appeals met to rescind our permit.

I then had one of our employees go from house to house around the area where the development was to be located, and without exception, every neighbor signed a petition in favor of construction. Then I wrote a couple of op-eds for the local newspaper, and they evidently helped turn public opinion in our favor.

When it was announced that we were taking the case to court, the building inspector, a fine man, suffered a massive heart attack and passed away. I then became the key witness to support our claim. We won that case in state supreme court, largely because the town was placing restrictions on us that they themselves had not met anywhere else in the township. For example, they required us to build 25-foot-wide concrete roads with curbs. The town had only blacktop roads, mostly sixteen feet wide, with not a single foot of curbing. As a result, the court agreed that they were guilty of arbitrary and capricious behavior.

This was my first taste of politics at the local level, of sloshing through the swamp, and I was immediately disillusioned. But I have always been attracted to lost causes, and in spite of the responsibilities associated with operating my dad's business, I began taking a greater interest in politics.

I had long since concluded that America had slipped her historic moorings. It was obvious to me that we were rejecting the values that had formed the basis for our democratic republic, and as a result, we were floating in a cesspool of pride, greed, and self-aggrandizement.

The world was in political upheaval, and people seemed to be thinking, "Let us eat and drink, for tomorrow we die." We had become a nation where many spurned God, and perverted the Golden Rule by cynically saying, "Do unto others, before they do it to you."

As I grew more interested in moral issues, I concluded that we would ultimately lose the war for our constitutional republic because we were deserting the very God whose grace and favor underlies the self-evident truths "... that all men are created equal, that they are endowed by their Creator with certain unalienable Rights, that among these are Life, Liberty and the pursuit of Happiness."

Although I had not been raised up in the fear and admonition of the Lord, I still understood something of the miracle represented when our founding fathers received the courage and wisdom to agree on those words.

Foremost was the connection they made between faith in God and their ability to secure the ideals of freedom. Those men weren't perfect, but they stood heads and shoulders above most politicians today.

Yet, I made a mistake. I thought that by merely repeating the arguments of the great minds of the past, most people would listen, and we would finally set things right. Of course, we did not. Our nation only slid further toward oblivion, and it is only recently that there has been a glimmer of hope that the Lord might make America great again.

True wisdom and great ideas, as well as the courage and power to exercise them, come only from God, and these ideas have no force unless and until the people yield their will to His will and stand ready to die for their beliefs.

The birth of the United States was a historical phenomenon and a miracle of God. It is doubtful that it will ever be repeated in this world before Christ's return. Despite the fact that every human being is tainted with sin, America experienced one bright shining moment when vainglory was sufficiently set aside, and an incredible political adventure was begun.

Our founding fathers agreed on the words that I quoted, but before affixing their signatures to *The unanimous Declaration of the thirteen United States of America,* they added this fatal statement:

"And for the support of this Declaration, with a firm reliance on the protection of divine Providence, we mutually pledge to each other our Lives, our Fortunes and our sacred Honor."

Average Guy Meets Extraordinary God

They put aside petty differences to produce something that far exceeded their own righteousness. They focused on major issues and did the best they could within the cultural framework of their day to achieve those goals. And that is why it is wrong to "cancel" incredible men like Thomas Jefferson. Their efforts ultimately led to the accomplishment of things like ending the practice of slavery.

God honored their prayers and somehow made their dream of "The land of the free and the home of the brave" a reality. Without God's blessings this nation would never have been born, much less have survived for 250 years.

Fast forward to 1966. In spite of America's problems, my feelings were similar to those of most voters. I might grouse about the nation's problems, but my personal involvement was limited to pulling a lever in a voting booth.

Then some friends challenged me to get serious about my beliefs by becoming involved in politics. Had I been worldly wise, I would have heeded something I overheard my father say when I was a child: "You can't mix business and politics!" Yet, I was troubled by the realization that we should all be speaking up for what we consider right, so I allowed myself to be drawn into regional politics.

Too late I came to realize that my friends, like most people, were looking for someone else to speak up for them. "I'll be right behind you," they promised, but when I looked back, sure enough, some of them were behind me...way, way, way behind me! I was elected co-chairman of the Dutchess County Conservative Party, and later their candidate for the New York State Senate.

During my idealistic and arguably naive political sojourn, I discovered that nearly every politician I met lacked the character of our founding fathers. They were ultimately overcome by pride, ambition, avarice, and/or lust. And if they successfully rose to power, they were certain to become more corrupted by it.

Lord Acton warned us, "Power tends to corrupt, and absolute power corrupts absolutely. Great men are almost always bad men."[1]

Our founding fathers understood this, and so treated leadership as a matter of service, not a license to seize power and wealth. They were de-

---

1   https://www.acton.org/research/lord-acton-quote-archive accessed July 1, 2025.

termined to govern, not rule! Perhaps our greatest example is the "father" of our country, General George Washington, who refused the invitation to become America's "King George." Contrast our founding fathers with the multitude of men and women who seek office today.

And as I stumbled forward into the noisome muck which is politics, I came to see that we are all tossed to and fro by unseen principalities and powers that easily mock our feeble human efforts. And I inevitably learned that, with the exception of the rare person who believes in and fears God, the best of our politicians will at least occasionally feel the necessity to compromise on vital issues. Worse, most lack the wisdom to understand when and where they cross the line.

I came to understand that there are multitudes of ambitious people at every level of society who are vying for wealth and power and are ready to take advantage of those of us who are less aware, weaker, or more complacent. Most of us are challenged to make a living and raise our families and just want to go along to get along. But that is clearly not enough.

Am I unfairly cynical? No, I like to think that my years with Jesus Christ have helped me become more clear-eyed and realistic! That is largely due to the fact that nearly sixty years ago, as a member of New York's fourth largest political Party, I became a candidate for the state senate, running on the Conservative Party line in what was then the 98th Senatorial District—Dutchess and Ulster Counties, with an estimated population in 1966 of 300,000.

I was merely a minor party candidate, a voice crying in a political wilderness, to be swept aside by a growing socialist wave. Less than three years had passed since the consummate politician, Lyndon Johnson, took the reins of power following the still unresolved assassination of President John F. Kennedy. And it had been only two years since Johnson had drubbed conservative Barry Goldwater in the 1964 presidential race.

America's political left had successfully mis-characterized Constitutional conservatives as radical right wingers, crazed and mean-spirited, so that anyone who dared call himself a conservative was continually mocked by the awesome forces of the left—the media, educators, entertainers, and even many religious organizations.

In spite of that, I made a respectable showing. Since our candidate for governor out-polled the Liberal candidate for the first time in history, the Conservative Party moved up to "Row C," the third place on the ballot.

Becker for Senate Billboard, 1966

But we did get something right. Al Salay, my campaign manager, came up with a slogan that still resonates today. Our billboards, bumper stickers, and "Becker Bucks" challenged voters to "Defeat the Big Party Spenders!"

That was over half a century ago, and things are much worse now. Evidence suggests that some "Big Party Spenders" actually have their hands in the till, that many of our elected "representatives" have grown wealthy overnight by using inside information to exploit the stock market, and powerful figures have compromised our interests by making deals with nations that oppose us.

What we did not foresee was how the immoral and unethical actions of our Chief Executive, the Congress, and the Supreme Court might erode the very foundations of our constitutional republic. In 1966, our national debt was $320 billion. By 2024, it was $36 trillion, and our tax revenues no longer cover the interest on our national debt. Because the government lives outside its means, inflation is raging, and we feel the pain every time we fill our gas tank or visit the grocery store.

I remember hearing U.S. Senator Everett Dirksen on TV, mocking his big-spending colleagues: "A billion here, a billion there; pretty soon you're talking serious money."

As I look back, I have to wonder what made me think that I could somehow make a difference, that I could stick my finger in the political dike and help stop the flood of immorality, or slow the ever-increasing flow of tax monies into pork barrel schemes that enriched the unscrupulous while impoverishing our nation.

Forgive me. I have digressed. It was not my purpose to impose my political philosophy. Well, maybe it was. But my real purpose is to share something far more important: how God works through the experiences of Christians to guide us, and how the Holy Spirit helped me—a particularly naive young man—to realize that political action will never save America.

Unless you have become involved in politics, you have little idea of what really goes on behind the scenes during an election cycle. I was a novice, but I learned quickly and painfully, and I can therefore share a couple of examples of dirty politics that I experienced firsthand, and how God used that exposure to help change the direction of my life.

Keep in mind that I was not running for national office. I was only a third-party candidate running for state office, albeit in "The Empire State." Nor was I a major party candidate. I did not have the support of area newspapers, radio stations, labor organizations, or any powerful voting block. So, I had little financial backing. In short, my campaign might have been viewed as a protest—little more than a nuisance. Furthermore, I was only 26 years old!

Nevertheless, the two major parties spent a good deal of time, energy, and money to make sure that their candidate won, and that I lost. Beyond that, they took steps to discourage any future attempts on my part to intrude myself on the political landscape.

I had taken a stand against the very political party that my parents raised me to respect and support, and I soon discovered that that party could and would retaliate against any such rebellion, taking no prisoners.

During the last week of my race for the senate, I made a couple of serious mistakes. First, I prepared a 30-minute speech to be broadcast just one Saturday morning on the area's largest radio stations. I should have bought numerous 15 or 30-second spots and spread them over several stations in Dutchess and Ulster Counties. That's a lesson in not putting all of one's eggs in the same basket.

But my bad decision made no difference. Why? Because when one of the stations aired my speech, the studio engineer turned down the gain, so that I, sitting in my parked car outside their studio, beneath the shadow of their antenna, with the volume on my radio cranked up to its highest level, could barely hear the broadcast. Funny how the station's output rose back to normal immediately after my speech was over.

I couldn't even hire a decent artist to work up our campaign leaflet, which we called the "Becker Buck." It was a mockup of a dollar bill, but with a picture of a donkey and an elephant burning tax money on one side, and my photo on the other, accompanied by a lot of cryptic, but arguably witty, slogans. Dignity was not going to win victory for a third-party candidate. I had to be noticed! But on all the literature was printed, "Defeat the Big Party Spenders." I offer no apology or excuse for being a political neophyte. The money, experienced people, and the influencers were in the hands of the major parties.

You don't have to be a wizard to figure out what happened to my business. It's simple arithmetic. In a two-party system, where many people feel a strong loyalty to a particular political party, a candidate alienates roughly half his politically savvy friends and customers when he supports the opposing side. In my case, I had challenged both of the major parties, which meant that I alienated the vast majority of my potential customers, business associates, and even my own employees. Customers tend to take their business elsewhere, vendors raise prices, and banks raise interest rates. I lost customers.

Campaign Literature

I was beginning to learn the truth of my father's warning, that business and politics don't mix. And though I had no intention of ever again running for office, the opposition was determined to make certain that I would never again have that capacity. I did not foresee the immediate or long-term damage that would be done to myself, my family, and our business. But those who opposed me understood that the health of my business might dictate whether I had the resources to ever again run for any office.

It's a big ego thing to run for office, and a state senate seat is considered important. Later, I would read the words of Jesus and learn that a man should not go forth to war without counting the cost. I had impetuously entered the fray, giving no thought to the price I would ultimately pay. This battle would cost me my business. But neither I nor my adversaries could have imagined the benefits I would ultimately derive because of their attacks.

Was there a conspiracy against me? Not in so many words. But former friends and associates who opposed my political views came to view me as an enemy, and some did not hesitate to say so. Whether they consciously thought about it or whether they worked alone or in concert, they found opportunities to take action against me and my business. Even some of my employees lost the enthusiasm they had once displayed A couple began stealing, using as their justification the need to undermine the business.

Following the election, I returned to a business that I had sadly neglected. I should have been suspicious when several well-dressed men showed up at our offices, introduced themselves as certified public accountants from New York City, and offered to take over our accounting and straighten out our books. But when I retained those expensive CPAs, reasoning that their stature might impress our bankers, I unwittingly opened the secrets of our finances to those who wanted to wreck my business. It was only later, when those accountants began mocking my social values and political convictions and boasted that they practiced sexual relations forbidden by the scriptures, that I realized the mistake I'd made in retaining them.

I began and ended my political career with that senate race in 1966. What I didn't realize was that those who opposed me had taken my campaign seriously, and that they would thereafter take every opportunity to make certain that I would never again run for political office.

They needn't have worried. With my father's passing in 1968, I had other things on my mind. In spite of that, other conservative activists continued to make demands of me. One of them was my former campaign manager's wife. In 1968, she wanted me to become involved in another race, assisting a candidate for the United States Congress.

He was considered a maverick, a staunch conservative running against the establishment's candidate for Congress in the Republican primary. In liberal New York State, he was a knight in shining armor to conservatives, and it was hoped he would somehow supplant the Rockefeller-Republican he was challenging in the primary.

As an assistant district attorney in Dutchess County, he'd gained attention by leading an unsuccessful raid in a search for illegal drugs on Dr. Timothy Leary's estate in Millbrook, New York. During the early 60s, Leary attracted people like actress Elizabeth Taylor to his Millbrook estate where they experimented with LSD and other hallucinogenic drugs.

My first meeting with Helen's friend was brief. I had never met anyone quite like him. During our brief conversation, he told me to call him Gordon. He was very proper, very precise, very buttoned down, and obviously very intelligent; a man who wouldn't suffer fools. And while he expected me to share information about my role in the party, and any plans we might have, he would only share information about himself on a need to know basis.

Gordon asked me to take a train from Poughkeepsie to Penn Station, the terminal in New York City where he wanted me to pick up a couple of heavy cartons packed with IBM punch cards. When I arrived, the woman who met me was palpably angry because I had been sent alone on what was supposedly a secret mission, and I obviously wasn't physically capable of lifting two of those cartons, much less the six that the two men who accompanied her stacked just inside the door of my passenger car. When I turned to ask their help in moving the boxes to a seat, the three of them had already disappeared into the crowd. Since I was unable to move the cartons away from the door, I sat on them for the hour-and-a-half return trip.

I learned later that the cartons contained a quarter-million IBM punch cards which, when read by a computer, would provide Gordon's campaign staff with the name and address of every registered Republican voter in the five counties of what was then the 28th Congressional District. But though Gordon may have had a legal right to the list, the woman who passed the cartons to me was angry because she might lose her job with the state Republican organization if they learned of her part in passing enrollment information to a rogue candidate. At any rate, that's how I understood the incident.

A lot of pressure was brought to bear on Gordon to drop out of the race. It was no coincidence that I happened to be present on one of those occasions, because I too was being coerced. Here's the story.

The president of the bank with whom my father had dealt since the mid-1940s was a silent power in Hudson valley Republican politics. He called me in ostensibly to discuss the application that my father and I had made for a substantial loan to build the mobile home residential development in Hyde Park that I mentioned earlier.

I am sure it was no accident that, within a minute or so of my being ushered to the president's desk, that Gordon was seated at the desk of the senior vice-president, about eight feet away.

My dad and I had requested $100,000 to build our new housing development. Adjusted for inflation, that would be nearly a million dollars in 2024. The project would provide dad with continual rental income, but it would also mean the sale of sixty new homes, a huge boost to my business.

First, he pointedly asked me if I knew the man sitting at the next desk. Why ask me that? I wondered. I had noticed Gordon being seated, and sensed that something strange was going on, but pretended I hadn't. So, I turned, stared for a moment, and then looked back at the bank president, and simply replied, "I've met him." Then he told me that the bank was threatening to foreclose on the mortgage on Gordon's home. I had no idea whether that was true, but it was clearly a breach of confidentiality and none of my business.

Then the bank president told me, "If you run for Dutchess County Executive, we won't loan you the money to build your trailer park. If you don't run, we might loan you the money." You have to give the bank president credit for not mincing words. With his not-so-subtle attempt at extortion, he made it abundantly clear that he would be very unhappy if I were to again run for office. He not only had the power to refuse or approve our loan, but the bank handled all our business, including financing our inventory of fifty homes, as well as underwriting, with no recourse, almost every sale we made. Non-recourse financing was a very unusual agreement, and great for a mobile home or auto dealer. If we had to repossess a home, we didn't suffer any loss; the bank did. We had no financial liability, and in fact could profit from handling the process.

I considered the president's not-so-veiled threat a bit humorous, because I had no intention of running for any office. But his concern with my running for county executive came as a shock. The office was newly created, and people had actually appealed to me to run. I had turned them down.

At that time, there was heated controversy concerning the planned construction of a set of parallel highways through the middle of the city, an east-west arterial that would by-pass Main Street. The idea was unpopular with those who lived along those quiet streets, and several powerful figures opposed the plan. People didn't want their neighborhood streets turned into high-speed roads carrying tractor trailers through the city. Since I also opposed the idea, I might very well win the election, but the bank president did not know that I had already refused the opportunity.

The highway was ultimately built, and the fears of its opponents were fulfilled. Heavy traffic was rerouted through residential neighborhoods, while Main Street, with all its established businesses, became an economic wasteland. Businesses soon deserted the inner city to join the malls on the south road. The irony was that at least one impressive bank building on Main Street would ultimately be shuttered, the one in which I was sitting.

If I had been quicker on my mental feet, I might have recognized an opportunity. I could have said, "Loan us the money by this afternoon, and I won't run." But I didn't, and I'm now convinced that it was because the Lord did not want me to tell a lie, much less build that residential development or again become involved in politics at any level.

And while the bank president was coercing, or "black-mailing" me, Gordon was sitting at the adjacent desk, supposedly being threatened with mortgage foreclosure. The story went that he had fallen behind on payments. Gordon was a realist, a lawyer familiar with local politics and the court system. He undoubtedly knew that the bank could get away with many things. If what the bank president said was true, he was being offered the carrot, a job in Washington, and he was now being shown the stick, financial ruin.

Gordon won the Conservative Party primary and lost the important Republican primary, so he remained in the race for congress as the Conservative Party candidate. His Republican opponent, Hamilton Fish, was concerned that Gordon might prove a spoiler, drawing off enough votes as a third-party candidate to give the Democrat candidate the election. As a result, it was later reported that Fish sought the help of the state Republican leadership. The story goes that the state leader discussed the matter with the Republican Congressional Campaign Committee in Washington, and to entice Gordon to quit the race, they arranged for him to be offered a position with the Treasury Department.

The upshot? Whether what I was told was true or not, Gordon did drop out of the race for congress. He accepted the job in Washington and I have reason to believe that his mortgage was not foreclosed. And though his name remained on the November ballot, he didn't cost the Republican candidate, Hamilton Fish Jr. enough votes to throw the election to the Democrat candidate.

I didn't hear anything more about Gordon until five years later, shortly after I was called to pastor my first church. My wife and I were wandering through a department store when we passed a display of television sets. They were broadcasting national news and talking about the growing scandal surrounding the Nixon administration.

Gordon was at the heart of that scandal and, his name, "G. Gordon Liddy," had become a household name across America. Soon after his arrival in Washington, he had been appointed head of the "Special Investigations Unit" of the Nixon administration—the now infamous "White House Plumbers." The plumbers were caught breaking into the Democrat National Headquarters during the 1972 presidential campaign, allegedly trying to steal campaign secrets. This precipitated the Watergate scandal and led to the resignation of President Richard M. Nixon. It was a huge scandal, but viewed in light of current events, their crime seems tame.

Gordon was later convicted of burglary, conspiracy, and for refusing to testify to the Senate committee investigating Watergate. Because of his loyalty to President Nixon, he refused to turn state's evidence or testify against anyone who might have been involved. It might be said that Gordon was faithful to a fault. For his stubborn loyalty, Gordon spent over four years in prison, until pardoned by Democrat President Jimmy Carter. To his credit, Gordon was willing to pay society for his actions rather than violate his standards of loyalty and it is clear that millions of Americans admired him. He landed on his feet, and went on to become a popular conservative speaker, with his nationwide radio talk show airing on over 160 stations. He passed away in 2021.

Gordon was true to his own standards of ethics and morality and willingly served time to pay society for standing up for what he considered right. Perhaps he felt that he had to use fire to fight fire. Many that I have observed at all levels--in commerce, law, and government-- seem to feel the same way. Far too many believe that "might makes right."

During his incarceration, my friend, Helen Salay, who had supported Gordon during his run for Congress, visited him at the Federal Correctional Institution in Danbury, Connecticut. Her attempts to lead him to the Lord were met with amiable rejection.

It was then that I began to understand that our world will never be saved by politicians, or for that matter, by anyone in any other field of human endeavor. During my brief sojourn in politics, I concluded that most people across the political spectrum lack a spiritual anchor. Many are exigent, choosing what appears the easiest path to their personal ambitions. Since the "first duty" of a politician is to be elected, they are prone to compromise any ideal in order to attain wealth, power, and position. Gordon appeared to be the exception, but that didn't increase my faith in a political solution.

A reading of our Declaration of Independence and the Preamble to our Constitution, makes it clear that the founding Fathers understood and feared these dangers. Our greatest president, George Washington, warned us: "Government is not reason; it is not eloquence. It is force. And force, like fire, is a dangerous servant and a fearful master."[2] It's also clear that most Americans fail to understand why these words are stamped on our coins — "In God We Trust."

No, America is not perfect. In fact, most people would agree that we have slid downhill over the past fifty years. Katherine Lee Bates had a profound understanding of America's condition, and suffered no illusions that our nation was anywhere near perfect. In her song, *America the Beautiful*, she prayed, "America! America! God mend thine every flaw, confirm thy soul in self control, Thy liberty in law." Anyone with a modicum of intelligence must realize that America is now being torn apart by those who lack self control and who spurn the rule of law.

During the French Revolution, 15,000 people lost their heads because they scorned both self-control and law. France was torn apart in the name of "Liberty, Equality, and Fraternity," creating a political vacuum which the opportunist, Napoleon, quickly filled. The socialists of America appear to have resurrected that slogan, but have substituted the words "Diversity, Equity and Inclusion" to tear down the individuals and institutions that made America great. Perhaps their efforts will fail to decapitate our nation?

The events I've described here impacted my outlook on life, but my spiritual awakening wasn't instantaneous. Yes, at the age of eight I had asked Jesus to be my Savior, but it was another twenty years before I began to acknowledge him as my Lord.

Through all the events in between, through all the seeming crises, the Lord never took his hand off my life. Yes, he used both positive and negative coercion, "the carrot and the stick." But unlike the president of our bank, who proved himself dishonest on more than one occasion, the Lord's motives are always pure. *"Let no man say when he is tempted, I am tempted of God: for God cannot be tempted with evil, neither tempteth he any man"* (James 1:13).

That bank president meant his treatment of me for evil, but God meant it for good. And the Lord was guiding me inexorably to a life where I would find blessing, even as I blessed others. God repeatedly steered me away from the wrong courses for my life.

---

2   https://www.goodreads.com/quotes/10292623-government-is-not-reason-it-is-not-eloquence-it-is accessed July 1, 2025/

Unlike the ancient Greek philosopher, Diogenes, I am not going about with a lamp in broad daylight, looking for an honest man. Christ is the only answer to every social, political, economic, or physical problem that any individual or nation may face. America must return to the God who blessed us from the beginning, because *"Righteousness exalts a nation, but sin is a reproach to any people"* (Proverbs 14:34). America will only be as good as her people. We may not Defeat the Big Party Spenders, but one thing is certain: Only God, not politics, can save America!

"For we do not wrestle against flesh and blood, but against principalities, against powers, against the rulers of the darkness of this age, against spiritual hosts of wickedness in the heavenly places."

Ephesians 6:12

Chapter 2

"Daddy, I can't swim!"

*"For You cast me into the deep, Into the heart of the seas,
And the floods surrounded me; All Your billows and Your waves
passed over me. Then I said, 'I have been cast out of Your sight;
Yet I will look again toward Your holy temple.'"*

Jonah 2:3-4

Most people today don't believe in miracles or in the providential works of God. And with the exception of insurance companies and courts of law, most people have stopped referring to natural disasters as "acts of God." As a result, God's marvelous interventions in our lives often go unremarked. For example, if someone survives almost certain death in an automobile accident or is somehow delivered from Stage 4 cancer, most people simply rationalize it away.

An act of Providence is an extraordinary event. It produces unexpected results, sometimes beneficial and sometimes catastrophic. Such acts are difficult and even impossible to explain or rationalize. To a Christian, an act of providence is an expression of God's grace and unmerited favor. A true miracle is the epitome of Providential acts, something that violates what we call the laws of nature, and something impossible to explain in natural terms.

Whether it is the resurrection of a dead man named Lazarus who has been entombed four days, or the survival of a Jonah trapped in the belly of a great fish for three days—a miracle is evidence of God's overt intervention in the affairs of the race to change the natural course of events. It is God piercing the vail of time and space, involving Himself directly in the affairs of the human race.

A miracle is an act of God which alters the course of nature in order to achieve some spectacular end. It may bless the faithful and impress or even bring judgment on the sinful. Raising Lazarus from the dead blessed the faithful, but it frightened the Pharisees so much that they plotted how to kill him in order to bury this living evidence of Christ's power. The deaths of Ananias and Sapphira were the Holy Spirit's judgment on a stubborn couple. Both events clearly testify to God's wisdom, judgment, power, and even love, for it ultimately blessed the Church.

Events that may be considered acts of God include earthquakes, tornadoes, floods, forest fires, blizzards, and hurricanes, each one a potentially catastrophic event that may cause enormous property damage, injury, and death. By referring to them as acts of God, we appear to make God the bad guy. On the other hand, those same words acknowledge God's involvement in the affairs of the race and his immeasurable and frightening power to carry out his will.

Most people fail to credit Providence, or God, for saving them from potentially deadly situations. It's ironic how many ignore or deny God until they face a crisis. They may curse Him as the cause of their problems, then immediately turn around and beg him for deliverance, making all manner of promises that they have no intention of keeping.

But what about occasions when we as individuals somehow survive one of these destructive events? We quickly forget them, rationalizing them away. Few people ever credit any involvement by the Lord who saved them from harm.

Even the disciples of Jesus were guilty of that sin. When Jesus was fast asleep in a fishing boat on the Sea of Galilee and a storm arose, and the boat was swamped, His disciples "... *awoke Him and said to Him, 'Teacher, do You not care that we are perishing?'*" (Mark 4:38). Jesus responded by rebuking the winds and the waves so that they instantly calmed down. Then he chastened his disciples for their lack of faith. As a result, they came to fear Him more than they had feared death by drowning.

Perhaps you can look back on some event in your own life when you were convinced that God saved you from disaster. One such event stands out in my memory. It occurred when I was 29 years old and it was the result of my unwittingly putting four lives in grave danger—those of my wife, our little daughter Sandra, an employee named George White, and myself. Sure, I could claim that we were the victims of an act of nature, but I must confess that I was the one who put us in harm's way.

At the time, I did not recognize any potential danger in my seemingly innocent decision, much less that it might be considered reckless. Nor did they. We were enjoying a weekend at a campground on the shore of Lake Champlain, and when I suggested we take a sail in my little boat, they were all eager to join in.

It was a beautiful morning to go sailing, the sky a beautiful blue, the lake calm, and the wind just lively enough to promise a brisk sail. So we picked up our fifty pound polystyrene sailboat, grabbed the canvas handles of the single cushion that was at that time considered adequate as a life preserver, and headed for the beach.

Our sailboat was a light weight eleven foot long cockleshell, but I had neglected to read the part of the owner's manual that stated it was designed to carry no more than 310 pounds. I later calculated that the four of us had a combined weight of over 525 pounds, well above the limit for which the boat was designed.

When we all tumbled in, I looked over the side and realized that we had no more than five or six inches of free board. Free board is the distance from

Sea Snark
(From manufacturer's website)

the water line to the top edge of the hull. It wasn't much, but I shrugged off any concern because the conditions were ideal.

Apart from my foolishly overloading our Sea Snark, it remains one of the most reliable small boats ever built, outselling anything else in its class. But I knew nothing of the unpredictability of Lake Champlain, which is 120 miles long, and up to fourteen miles wide—several times the length of the capricious Sea of Galilee. Nor was I aware that winds and waves could rise in minutes, of which had swallowed up far larger boats than mine.

And that's exactly what happened. As we slipped away from the shore, the wind suddenly rose and we found ourselves delighted to be racing across the water. It was an exhilarating experience that left us all laughing with delight. But by the time I adjusted the sail and looked up to check our position, we were over a quarter mile from the shore.

Suddenly the waves were two to three feet high, measured from trough to crest, and the wind was pushing us inexorably toward the middle of the lake. Water started splashing over the sides, but I momentarily took comfort in the fact that I had the foresight to tie a bucket to the mast. So I shouted for my wife, Joy, to begin bailing. But the little boat was so crowded that she had almost no room to dip the pail.

I knew that if I attempted to turn the boat toward shore, not only might someone be struck on the head by the swinging aluminum boom as the sail swung wildly across the hull, but we would very likely be swamped by the mounting waves. I turned to look for the shore, but we were down in a trough, and all I could see was what seemed like a massive wave of gray water sweeping toward us.

At that moment, bailing became an exercise in futility because the wave swept over the side, filling the boat with water and completely swamping us. I can't imagine what little four-year-old Sandra felt from her seat next to the mast, but when our eyes met, I heard her plaintive cry clearly enough; "Daddy, I can't swim!"

Even as I shouted for everyone to hang on and stay with the boat, the pressure of the wind against the sail caused the boat to lay over on it's side, so that the mast and sail now lay flat on the surface of the lake.

It wasn't necessary for me to shout to Sandra to hang on to the mast. The boat was now on it's side, more than half submerged, and she was standing chest deep in lake water, her arms desperately grasping the base of the mast, her little feet obviously resting on the inside of the hull which lay about two feet beneath the surface.

As I recall the fear I felt, Jonah's words seem appropriate, "For thou hadst cast me into the deep, in the midst of the seas; and the floods compassed me about, all thy billows and thy waves passed over me" (Jonah 2:3).

The irony is that Jonah's foolish refusal to obey God brought terror to those around him. But after prayerful struggling, the sailors finally regretfully cast him out of the ship in order to save themselves. Meanwhile, my foolishness was about to result in our all drowning.

I had to trust the brochure that described our eleven foot expanded polystyrene hull as "unsinkable," but I couldn't help remembering that a deckhand on the Titanic once declared, "Even God cannot sink this ship."

I had only an instant to glance at my wife and George, but so far they seemed okay, clinging desperately to the "unsinkable" hull as it rose up and down with the waves. Sandy was the most helpless, and had my attention. Joy and George were hopefully able to fend for themselves. None of us wore life vests, and Sandy's buoyant seat cushion had floated away unnoticed.

All of us, Sandy excepted, were now in the water outside the boat, We desperately held on to the edges of the hull, me on the downwind side, and Joy and George on the side facing the oncoming waves. Working together, the three of us tipped the boat back level, and Sandy resumed her seat, her arms still wrapped around the thin aluminum pole that served as the mast, The buoyant hull was still slightly submerged, the mast and sail again pointing to the sky. Sandy was sitting in water up to her little chest. She didn't cry or panic, but looked steadily at me, waiting for any instructions while waves threatened to again roll the boat onto its side.

I cried out, "Lord, help us!" and was somehow suddenly reminded of how, years before, while at Boy Scout Camp, I was taught how to empty the water from a swamped canoe. It seemed a forlorn hope here, where waves were alternately lifting and dropping the submerged hull, but I was heartened by the idea that the boat was supposed to be unsinkable, and was obviously very buoyant. The harsh reality was that the boat might be unsinkable, but we were not.

I shouted to the others what I planned to do, and they braced themselves to follow my instructions. "Sandy," I shouted, "Take a deep breath and hang on tight, because we are going to tip the boat on its side real fast, then flip it back level."

She wrapped her little arms around the thin aluminum pole that served as a mast and hugged it to herself. I centered myself on the downwind side of the hull, and the moment we were in the trough of a wave, I pushed down on my edge of the hull, thrusting myself up out of the water as high as I could to hold it down. At the same time, George and Joy, on the opposite side, pushed their side up high out of the water. Gravity carried me back down into the water, and I continued to yank down on my edge of the boat, while they momentarily held up their side. With the highly buoyant hull on its edge, it seemed to almost leap up into the air as the enormous weight of the water it contained poured out. My head was underwater momentarily, and I hung desperately to my edge of the hull as I kicked hard in an effort to push it up again, while Joy and George pulled down on the opposite side. And the vessel, now nearly empty, returned to level.

Praise God, it worked! Most of the water had been dumped out of the lightweight hull. I immediately looked for Sandy, fearing that she had been swept away, but she was again seated on the thwart next to the mast, amazingly calm. George hung on to the bow, while Joy somehow crawled back aboard. She immediately began bailing out the remainder of the water. Then I laid my weight on the port side to balance the craft, while George clambered aboard on the starboard side. And finally, I somehow dragged myself over the stern in order not to again upset the boat.

I looked out over the water and was amazed to realize that the waves had diminished, and concluded that we had a reasonable chance of returning safely to the shore. As I reached for the end of the light rope that controlled our sail, we heard someone shouting. I turned to see a big inboard motor boat cutting across our bow. The campground owner, his face suffused with anger, shouted that he was about to throw a rope, and we were to take it fast. George caught it and tied it to the ring bolt in the bow, and we were towed to shore.

As we dragged the boat up onto the sand, our rescuer told us not to put our boat into the water again or he would throw us out of the campground. He followed that with, "Maybe I will anyway." I assured him that we would not, but he simply turned and strode away.

Looking back, I consider our survival to be a miracle. If the wind and the waves had not died down when I cried aloud to God, our efforts would have been in vain. The boat would have again filled with water, and it's likely that one or more of us would have been swept away long before any rescuer could reach us. And the fact that none of us—even little Sandy—were drowned, was remarkable. So I have no doubt that God was involved in turning that impossible situation from death to life. Our survival was indeed providential.

Was I at fault? Certainly! I exercised poor judgment by overloading what was a great little sail boat. I might be excused for not providing life vests, because they were not readily available until the federal mandatory wear law was passed thirty years later. Some might say it was an "Act of God," because the winds and the waves arose. Others would agree that it was a miracle because, when we prayed, God delivered us. The point is that God delivered us!

Should our survival be defined as an authentic miracle? Rationalize it, if you must. Joy and I are satisfied that the Lord saved our lives that day. And with that act of grace, God did a bit more to draw my attention to him. It's not enough to say, "All's well that ends well." God intervened, and we all survived, and I will praise Him forever for His mercy.

And Sandra? In spite of my foolishness, she grew up to have a family of her own. Perhaps that experience inspired her to learn to swim long distances. A few years ago, I followed her in a rowboat as she swam back and forth across a mile wide lake.

What of George White? He was a likable guy with a great line of gab, but my hiring him was another error in judgment. He proved to be an alcoholic, and he actually stole a travel trailer from our inventory and left town. This was another of many experiences that the Lord used to motivate me to enter the ministry.

And what about Joy and me? In 2024, our four children, with their families, surprised us with a wonderful party to celebrate our 60th wedding anniversary.

Does God have a plan for you and me? His mercy and grace certainly helped lead me to repentance and left me eternally grateful. Consider this question:

"...despisest thou the riches of his goodness and forbearance and longsuffering; not knowing that the goodness of God leadeth thee to repentance?"

Romans 2:4

CHAPTER 3

Burning Bridges

"But Jesus said to him, 'No one, having put his hand to the plow, and looking back, is fit for the kingdom of God.'"
Luke 9:62

In 1970, I was determined to serve Jesus, but being tossed to and fro seemingly by circumstances, I was not always wise in how I pursued my goal. It's obvious that God also had my future in mind, otherwise I would not be sitting here writing this. And though I lack the spiritual quality of the great men and women of the Bible, perhaps my beginnings were not so different from theirs, for they, like me, had feet of clay.

In 1970, I was persuaded to foolishly place my signature on a document without even reading it. The things my signature authorized irrevocably altered many lives, and ultimately sealed my own fate, breaking me free from my past and sending me whirling about like an autumn leaf, tossed about on the winds of change.

But God is, of course, involved in every aspect of our lives and, as it turned out, this event was more than a mere turning point for me. Some opportunists were temporarily enriched by my action, while others were harmed. I have no idea whether they looked to God for help or leaned on their own understanding, but God used the situation to guide me. I have concluded one thing: when people respond to God's call, they should expect dramatic changes in their lives.

Average Guy Meets Extraordinary God

For example, after the Lord commanded the prophet Elijah to anoint young Elisha to serve in his place, Elijah searched for the younger man and found him plowing a field. Elijah threw his mantle over Elisha's shoulders to indicate that he would now have the role of prophet.

But Elisha asked permission to go and kiss his parents goodbye, to which Elijah responded, *"What have I to do with thee?"* Young Elisha's response sounded much like the replies of those whom Jesus later criticized in a parable, three individuals whose affections were still fixed on this world and made excuses to turn back (Luke 14:16-20). But in the end, Elisha did not return home. Instead, he proved his commitment!

So Elisha turned back from him and took a yoke of oxen and slaughtered them and boiled their flesh, using the oxen's equipment (the wooden yoke and plow), and gave it to the people, and they ate. Then he arose and followed Elijah, and became his servant. (I Kings 19:19-21).

When Elisha burned his plow, he was doing more than making a statement to Elijah. He was destroying his connections with the past, and leaving himself with no alternative but to serve God. So Elijah burned his plow, leaving himself without the means to return to his former life.

History tells of other determined leaders who destroyed things in order to keep themselves and their followers from turning back. Homer's Iliad tells how King Agamemnon burned his fleet so that his army could not return to Greece. He would either conquer the people of Troy or die. Similarly, Julius Caesar burned the bridges behind his army as he crossed into enemy territory, also making victory or death their only options. And when Hernando Cortes reached the New World, he burned his boats to keep his followers from returning to Spain.

But when Elisha slaughtered his oxen, and used his plow as firewood to boil their meat, he ended his career as a farmer. He even gave the meat away instead of selling it, so he not only destroyed his means of making a living, but gave away his remaining equity, thus doing away with any possibility of replacing them and returning to his former occupation. Elisha made certain that he could not turn back!

Something similar happened to me. I had no intention of changing my mind about closing my business in order to serve Jesus, but I was increasingly concerned that I must do so in an honorable way, so that there was no stain on my reputation as a Christian. I became particularly anxious about paying all corporate debts.

And when my best friend, Al Salay, suggested that I might put off attending Bible college in order to continue operating the business, I gave it serious thought. His idea had merit, but I stubbornly clung to my intention to start school that fall, and I began to ask God to give me direction. I am now convinced that the Lord set up a situation where, figuratively speaking, I wound up slaughtering my oxen and burning my plow; creating circumstances under which I would be unable to turn back, and might even cause myself embarrassment.

I had set a deadline. We needed to be finished and ready to move to Pennsylvania in less than two months, and I began to realize that was an impossibility. In fact, In my haste I committed a foolish act that was equivalent to burning my plow. Once again, the president of my local bank was involved in unwittingly directing my path.

Looking back, I can't imagine how I forgot the treatment we had received from those bankers in the past, nor my determination that I would never again trust them. But I was focused on doing the "right thing," and I wanted to believe that my bankers were also men of honor, so I continued to credit them with undeserved integrity, burying memories of their dishonest manipulation.

The summer selling season for recreation vehicles was nearing its end, and I still had about fifty RVs in stock, spread over two locations. As a young Christian, I was prone to take decisions out of God's hands, and not seek or wait for His infallible direction. I was in a hurry to close the business and began trying to think of a way to quickly liquidate the stock.

We financed our stock of RVs using a financial device that the bankers call "floor planning." Our bank extended us a line of credit for one hundred thousand dollars, which would be close to a million in today's money. When an RV arrived, we'd cut a check to pay the manufacturer and then the bank would loan us back 90% of the purchase price which we would repay when the unit was sold. If one of the RVs didn't sell within 90 days, the bank charged us interest. When we sold the unit, we paid back the original loan.

Our bankers, of course, expected us to encourage buyers to finance the purchase of their new RV through them at five or six percent interest, thus producing significant income for the bank. Then the bank put a small part of that interest income in a special account on our behalf.

We enjoyed an enormous advantage over other dealers because we had a great credit rating, paid lower interest rates, and enjoyed non-recourse financing. That meant that if a purchaser failed to make their payments, the bank repossessed and owned the RV, not us. They would pay us for repossessing the unit, plus any costs for reconditioning and reselling it. So, we never took a loss. This was possible because we had great credit and were well respected. At that time, our reserve fund with the bank was over $25,000. Again, adjusted for inflation, it was equivalent in buying power to a quarter million dollars today.

I wanted to clear out our inventory, and I wasn't greedy. I reasoned that if I could get another dealer to take the inventory at our cost, and we also gave them our 20% equity, they'd get the entire stock at a bargain basement price, and would make a substantial profit. We would still have our $25,000 in reserves at the bank to pay our creditors, and would be able to close out with honor.

So I explained to one of the vice-presidents at the bank my desire to close the business so that I could enter the ministry. He seemed very helpful, even suggesting that he might have a local competitor who would take our inventory, thus enabling me to close much sooner. The next time I visited the bank, he handed me a piece of paper, and told me that, if I signed on the bottom line, he'd have all our stock moved to another dealer and I'd be home free. As with most things that seem to good to be true, this was! When I started to read the paper, he assured me that there was nothing to worry about, that we had known one another for a long time, and I could trust him. And I, who'd been a hard-headed businessman, foolishly believed him. Now I shake my head. "Who doesn't read the fine print?" I didn't even read the large print!

I don't think I need to tell you the rest of the story. The bank immediately transferred my stock to the competitor. Not only did they take our RVs, and our 20% equity for the dealer, but they kept our $25,000 reserve fund. And my appeals to the bank president fell on deaf ears.

With that, I had virtually nothing to work with, except about five thousand in our checking account. There was no way in the world that I could raise additional money because I had signed away our entire RV unit inventory, worth well over $120,000. Months later the bank took our real estate, but by then I was in Bible college, and never did learn how they accomplished it. I never received a single legal notice, not even a tax bill. And there were no bankruptcy proceedings.

When I placed my signature on the bottom line that day, I'd sealed my fate. I'd already given away a bulldozer, a bulldozer trailer, and a pickup truck to Teen Challenge Institute, and had few assets left. Figuratively speaking, I had slain my oxen, burned my plow, destroyed my boats and burned my bridges. There was no turning back, no way to pay any remaining creditors, and no way to assuage my shame.

Yes, I thought of taking legal action against the bank. But the law firm that had represented us for many years had been among the first to turn their backs on me when I made my run for the state senate. And I had no money to begin what was likely to be an extended and losing legal battle with the bank.

My decision was suddenly made for me. I'd surrendered my company, and I could either look for a job somewhere or attend Bible college. But I couldn't help anyone who might have been hurt by our abrupt closing. What was ironic was that the bank offered me a job handling repossession of cars, trailers, and real estate.

Months later, after we sold our manufactured home, Joy and I returned to the bank to pay off our loan. We had a large cashier's check from the buyer, and we were waiting for a clerk to deduct the mortgage balance and return our equity. As we waited, the vice-president, who had convinced me to sign that fatal document, walked over and boldly suggested that I turn over our equity from the sale of our home to the bank. I quietly refused, and continued waiting for my money.

A moment later, the insurance salesman who'd been our agent for many years rushed in and confronted me. His complexion gray, filled with anxiety and anger, and looking like he'd aged a decade, told me that the vice-president had just called him to alert him to my presence. He asked me to pay the balance on my defunct company's insurance bill. I pointed at the vice-president, and described how he'd cheated us of our inventory, our equity, and our reserve fund, and was therefore unable to repay him.

There was no question that he believed me. He looked at the bank's vice-president with shock in his eyes, but instead of defending himself, the vice-president turned and almost ran across the carpeted lobby, disappearing through a door marked "Staff Only." My former insurance agent turned away and without a word stumbled out of the bank. I was sick with shame that I had failed him, and can only imagine the harm done to the bank's reputation when this man told others.

I understood that my reputation had been irreparably smeared. "How," I wondered, "will I now be able to serve God?" One thing was certain: I'd never again live in that town. I'd burned my plow. There was no going back! My experience may sound a bit melodramatic, but I now realize that I was being hedged in, and like someone trying to find their way through a maze, I was inevitably guided from place to place by the invisible hand of God.

Everyone who is called to the work of God faces difficult challenges. They might have second thoughts, and they will certainly be discouraged by the enemy. But they are to follow the Lord!

Elijah had no interest in Elisha's desire to return home to kiss his father and mother goodbye. He expected immediate submission. And, Elisha, to prove that his face was set like flint, took just enough time to burn his plow, and then never looked back.

Nor are we to turn back! Matthew 4:18-22 tells how Peter, Andrew, James and John, the first four disciples, immediately responded to Jesus, and walked away from their boats and nets to become *"fishers of men."* But after our Lord's death and resurrection, they didn't immediately go about fishing for men. Instead they returned to their former occupation, perhaps because they needed the money, but more likely, because they were like sheep without a shepherd, and simply didn't know what else to do.

"Simon Peter said to them, 'I am going fishing.' They said to him, 'We are going with you also.' They went out and immediately got into the boat, and that night they caught nothing." (John 21:2-4). Then the resurrected Jesus appeared to them on the shore, and broiled them some fish to fill their bellies. But it wasn't until Pentecost that his promise was fulfilled, and the Holy Spirit fired up their souls, and they truly became fishers of men. Elisha burned his plow and sacrificed his oxen. I signed away my business. In each of these situations, subsequent events reveal that God was always in control and that's a miracle!

"But Jesus said to him, 'No one, having put his hand to the plow, and looking back, is fit for the kingdom of God.'"
Luke 9:62.

CHAPTER 4

"Man proposes but God disposes"

"A man's heart plans his way, But the LORD directs his steps."
Proverbs 16:9

It's both instructive and encouraging to look back and realize how God directs our steps.

Take my own case. My dad passed away when I was twenty-eight. If my dad had lived, would he have discouraged me from entering the ministry? I think so, because I was the only one of his four sons that continued working for him during his last years.

All four of us hungered for his approval, but rarely received it. And approval wasn't the only thing we felt shorted on. He often gave us the unpleasant jobs, and then paid his other employees more money than he paid us for work that we often did better, faster, and with more loyalty and enthusiasm. But there were extenuating circumstances.

Dad's generation was shaped by the concerns of the day and the hardships faced. He was six when the U.S. entered World War I, and he assisted his father as he treated those stricken with Spanish flu, the pandemic that killed an estimated 21-million to 50-million people worldwide. He was nineteen, and attending college, when the stock market crashed and the Great Depression began. And he was thirty-one when we entered World War II.

Many Americans had been poor and hungry for much of their lives, and were clearly driven to make certain it never happened again. They pinched every penny, carefully invested every dime, treated every minute as though it was gold, and when World War II arrived, took every opportunity to improve their lot.

My oldest brother, John, was born in 1935, when the Great Depression had reached its low water mark, when over twenty percent of American workers were unemployed. Franklin Roosevelt's New Deal was a failure, and employment only began to rise as the storm clouds of war swept over Europe. Thousands of Americans were provided opportunities to work in defense industries or enlist in the military where they could get three square meals a day. And the depression didn't end until after we were deep in war.

Shortly after America entered World War II, I was a toddler, but I remember two men coming to the back door of our home on Greenbush Drive, begging for something to eat. My mom gave them each a sandwich, then told them to please not return, nor to tell anyone else where they had gotten the food. I didn't understand until later, when I learned that word would get around, and hordes of homeless would eat us out of house and home. It wouldn't take long to exhaust what little food we had on hand. Lend Lease was enacted in 1941, and Roosevelt's "illegal" shipments of food, oil, and war material to our allies in the United Kingdom, the Soviet Union, France, and the Republic of China, were finally dignified by law.

Two months before my birth, and just fifteen months before the Japanese attack on the U.S. naval base at Pearl Harbor, the United States instituted the draft, and countless young Americans donned uniforms as they either volunteered or were conscripted into various branches of the military. American industry was suddenly called upon to produce huge numbers of ships, tanks, and planes, as well as oil and food, and Americans had to tighten their belts even as they were being blessed with jobs and income they never before imagined.

My brother John, who was six when we entered the war, was always dad's favorite. Perhaps it was because he was the first born, or perhaps for other reasons that need not be explored here. As a child, John was the only one allowed the use of dad's shop and machine tools, and he was given authority to dictate our access, lording it over us three younger brothers. Typical of the favoritism shown him, John was privileged to sit in the front seat of the car next to dad and mom until he finally left home for college. Bill, Bob, and I always shared the back seat. And dad once admitted that he might leave his entire estate to John, in the manner of European monarchs. John worked for dad on and off through the years, but at the time of dad's passing, he was a mainframe computer engineer at IBM. John was short and slight, probably because he lacked enough nutritious food early on, but he sometimes exhibited a mean streak. Yet, in spite of the suffering that a bullying older brother imposed, as well as typical sibling rivalry, John was an amazing brother, and we were proud of him.

During World War II, when I was just four, I remember John making a crystal radio that picked up our local radio station, WKIP. And in 1947, when gas powered lawn mowers were still a new innovation, John somehow managed to scrounge a gasoline engine and mounted it on a go-cart frame that he welded together from scrap metal, using drawings in a Popular Mechanics magazine. John regularly used both dad's acetylene torches and his arc welder. He also made a water gun that would shoot twenty feet or more, and a foot tall guillotine with which he decapitated wasps.

Like all frustrated geniuses, John was a bit eccentric, but as a teenager, he did some amazing things. For example, he designed and oversaw construction of two soap box derby racers that won the local soap box derby, one in 1952 and the other in 1954. The trophy for the 1954 Derby, with my name engraved on the nameplate, stands on a shelf in my office.

But his crown jewel was the miniature brass cannon he turned on dad's metal lathe. He mounted it on a wooden carriage that had tiny brass wheels and he ground up match heads to produce the powder to fire his lilliputian "cannon balls." They were actually BBs, the 4.5 mm diameter ammunition used in Red Ryder BB guns.

The cannon was a near disaster, because when he set it on our dining room table, and fired it through four inches of Montgomery Ward catalogs, the BB struck the wall just inches behind my mother's head. She just happened to be leaning over the kitchen stove, and the BB smashed a hole a half-inch deep in the concrete block wall just behind her head. I know; I was there! But while dad would punish one of us by taking such an offending thing away, whether a hunting knife or a BB rifle, John always got to keep his.

John went on to design and build many unique and beautiful things in his lifetime, from custom field stone fire places, to a 1/10th working scale model of a Civil War cannon. He even did most of the design work for our seven-hundred square foot underground bomb shelter during the Cuban Missile Crisis, photos of which appear in my 2005 book, *You Can Triumph Over Terror.*

Average Guy Meets Extraordinary God

John was nearly seventy years old when he cut two wrecked automobiles in half, and joined the two good ends, producing an entirely new car. In 1957, John graduated from Rensselaer Polytechnic Institute (RPI), America's oldest technological research university, located in Troy, New York. He was immediately commissioned an officer in the U.S. Navy, and never entered the field for which he had prepared—petroleum geology. As children, John often bullied us, but after I entered the ministry, I benefited from his generosity and kindness.

Bill was the second born. He was born a year after John, and always lived in John's shadow. Bill was called a day-dreamer. His teachers complained that he sat gazing out classroom windows, as many intense men had done before him, men who were poorly understood by those who had less lofty thoughts. One of Bill's favorite songs was "The Happy Wanderer," perhaps because he loved to spend hours walking through the woods, exploring the wonders of God's world.

One day I heard dad criticize Bill for singing:

> I'm always chasing rainbows
> Watching clouds drifting by
> My schemes are just like all my dreams
> Ending in the sky
> Some fellows look and find the sunshine
> I always look and find the rain
> Some fellows make a winning sometime
> I never even make a gain, believe me
> I'm always chasing rainbows
> Waiting to find a little bluebird in vain

I'm Always Chasing Rainbows
Music by Chopin, adapted by Harry Carroll, lyrics by Joseph McCarthy
1917 and in the public domain

Early on, I was there when Bill committed some questionable acts, perhaps to win attention, but I never had anything but love for him. During my childhood and teen years, Bill was the closest of my brothers. We hiked, camped, and hung out together. I think that Bill was frustrated because, while people attempted to force him into a mold, his creative talents, sensitivity, and unique skills were largely overlooked and went unappreciated by others. Mom's brother, Larry Klaus, a farmer and outdoors man, wanted to adopt Bill. It would have been a perfect place for Bill to grow up, but my parents refused.

If John needed something for one of his projects, he would simply ask dad, and he would generally receive it. Not so for we three younger sons. Bill wanted materials for his wood-working projects, and it seemed serendipity to him that, while he was wandering through the woods that surrounded what was then the Hudson River State Hospital, he discovered a remote garage that sheltered stacks of the very highest quality lumber, clear, straight, and knot-free.

The following day, he asked me to take a bike ride with him, but didn't say where or why, and I wound up following him through unfamiliar woods to that garage. There sat a big stack of lumber, seemingly forgotten, and free for the taking. Bill tied about twelve of the boards together, bundled them across the handlebars of his bike, and somehow got them home.

Those boards may have been knot-free, but pardon my pun, Bill soon realized they were not free! He hid them in the back corner of the garage beneath an old tarp. I know that he suffered pangs of guilt because he told me he thought he should return them, and I agreed. But I refused to to go with him this time. I think that I refused because I was too small to actually assist him, and I was afraid of getting in trouble.

When he returned home, Bill told me that when he returned to the garage, he found it empty, so he carefully stacked the boards he was returning, and got out of there as quickly as he could. I was happy that he made his decision without any adult input, and that he returned home without being caught.

A few days later, we breathed a sigh of relief when we heard by the grapevine that the hospital police had been looking for the thief. They had received a report that a teenager on a bicycle was seen leaving the woods with a stack of lumber, but they gave up the search after the boards were inexplicably returned. Bill later returned to the scene of his crime, and found the doors chained and padlocked.

The important point here is not that a boy succumbed to a temptation, but that—without any human guidance or coercion—he recognized his sin and rectified the matter. As I look back, I realize that our very busy father did the best he could to instill values of honesty and integrity in us, but he was rarely around. We sort of stumbled our way through those years, somehow learning right from wrong.

Average Guy Meets Extraordinary God

Christmas day, 1956, Bill gave each of us—John, Bobby and me—beautiful leather-bound, gold-embossed Bibles. Bill had found religion, but he had not yet found Christ. Fourteen years later, I would carry my copy to Bible college. It is well-worn now, and has a place of honor on my study shelf.

I especially recall that Bill made a beautiful lamp that won first prize in a competition between students from various high schools in the mid-Hudson valley. After graduating high school, he went to the Hobart Trade School, in Ohio, where he spent sixteen weeks learning to weld. Bill worked for Dad for a few years, but Dad gave him many of the unpleasant jobs, and little reward or praise. Bill finally quit and moved his family to Tampa.

My youngest brother, Bob, was born on the 4th of July, 1941, five months before the Japanese attacked Pearl Harbor. Even as an adult, he was always the adored "baby" of the family. In 1957, dad and mom had a house built overlooking the Hillsborough River, in Tampa. Bill, Bob, and I drove straight through from New York to Tampa, and were the first to move in. Bob became a true Floridian, and apart from one or two visits to New York, he never returned. And he never worked for Dad. But in the years that followed, I continually moved back and forth between our New York and Florida homes,

After attending Florida Southern for a couple of years, Bob transferred to the University of Florida. He dropped out and took an entry level job at Eckerd Drugs, working directly for the founder, Jack Eckerd. Bob ultimately reached management's celestial heights when he was appointed Vice President of Advertising at Jack Eckerd Corporation. Eckerd became a devout Christian, but his example didn't seem to rub off on my brother Bob.

I was born in March of 1940 and eight years later raised my hand to receive Christ as my Savior. Like John and Bill, I worked for Dad on and off during high school and college, and it is pretty clear to me that Dad wanted me to remain on board.

And I might have done so, because I loved the variety and excitement of managing the business. Dad was so eager to retain me that, just prior to the events described below, he sold me ninety percent of the stock in his New York operation for one dollar, retaining the remaining shares for my mother.

But things didn't work out the way we had planned, for both our worlds turned upside down. As Thomas à Kempis, the medieval Christian monk, wrote, "...man proposes but God disposes; neither is the way of man in his own hands."[3]

Thomas may have based his observation on Proverbs 16:9: *"A man's heart deviseth his way: but the Lord directeth his steps."* William Shakespeare's Hamlet seemed to agree, when he conceded that "There is a divinity that shapes our ends." The words of the Apostle James are particularly appropriate: *"Come now, you who say, 'Today or tomorrow we will go to such and such a city, spend a year there, buy and sell, and make a profit;' whereas you do not know what will happen tomorrow"* (James 4:13-14).

Things certainly did not go the way my father hoped or envisioned. I think it was in January of 1968 that he called me from Florida and told me to come south for a personal meeting as soon as possible. This was unprecedented because, as a rule, he only called me to receive updates on the New York business, and to make his wishes known.

I, on the other hand, had coveted the idea of living and working at one of his sunny Florida enterprises, but it was never to be. He needed someone he could trust in New York, and never wanted me to take time off, let alone spend time in Florida. But this time he said that he had something urgent to discuss. So Joy and I packed up our little family for what I hoped would be a brief working vacation, and headed for Florida.

As I remarked earlier, Dad was a true entrepreneur. He had begun his first business about 1934, during the Great Depression, and continued to manage and diversify even while working at Bendix Aviation in New Jersey during World War II. At the time of the stock market crash in 1929, Dad was nineteen years old and studying electrical engineering at RPI. It was a fine school, but he was ultimately forced to drop out because his roommate stole his tuition money to pay fraternity bills. I have many of Dad's old documents, including hand-written receipts from the RPI business office for payments he made toward his school loan. Those payments were typically two dollars, a far cry from the tens of thousands that students now pay.

His apparent reason for leaving was a lack of money, but I suspect he may have been eager to drop out to marry my mother, Loretta May Kathleen Klaus. According to a clipping published by the Troy newspaper at that time, Loretta was the winner of a beauty contest, chosen above

---

3   Kempis, Thomas a. *The Imitation of Christ*. Accessed online July 1, 2025: https://www.gutenberg.org/ebooks/1653

other young women from villages surrounding her home in nearby Grafton. About the time they married, Dad opened an auto repair shop in what had been a blacksmith shop in rural Clinton Corners, New York.

He obviously prospered, because in 1939 we find him operating a gas station and garage on an acre of land at the northwest corner of Greenbush Drive and Violet Avenue in the town of Poughkeepsie. Violet Avenue was named for the violets that grew in huge glass greenhouses that ran along the east side of the highway for miles, and were sold in abundance in New York City. That corner property was just down the street from what is now 6 Greenbush Drive, the house in which his father, Doctor John Isaac Becker, MD, lived and had his office until his death in 1939. It is also the home of which I have my earliest memories.

The green bush, for which our street was named, was actually a fairly large pine tree which grew in a hollow in the center of Greenbush Drive, at its intersection with Violet Avenue. When I was a teenager, that tree was finally removed. As the story goes, teens were smoking and engaging in other questionable activities beneath its low hanging branches, so the place where it grew has long since been filled in and paved over.

At the beginning of the war, Dad's gas station was little more than a small unheated shack that stood on the southeast corner of his property, just north of the intersection. That shack provided the attendant with shelter from wind, rain, and snow. He kept from freezing by using a small portable kerosene heater. As a four-year old, Dad took me to see it. I found it fascinating. It was set back from Violet Avenue perhaps twenty-feet and was shaded by large maple trees on either side. The floor area was about 6x10 feet, with its long wall facing Violet Avenue. Looking from the highway, the door was on the left, with a window on the right. The single gas pump was just to the side, and a few feet closer to the highway.

The interior was unfinished, with exposed wooden studs. A single bare light bulb was screwed into a porcelain fixture that was mounted to a rafter above. There was a chair, a single pedestal desk, and a boxy cabinet on legs, insulated with Celotex which, during hot weather, held glass bottles of Nehi soft drinks immersed in ice water. The bottles of Nehi were five cents, and there was a two cent deposit on each glass bottle. In the back corner, there was a 30 gallon steel drum, with a hand pump protruding from the top, from which the attendant pumped motor oil into quart glass bottles that had metal funnels screwed to their tops.

Soon after our entry into World War II, the manufacture of automobiles for civilian use ended. Because of their scarcity, any cars built before the war became quite valuable, but they required a lot of tender loving care. Owners of driving machines built during the 1920s and 30s frequently had to add oil to their engines, grease the fittings in the suspension, and make costly repairs.

For a short time, oil was still available in quart cans, but savvy drivers were wary of the dishonest operator who would simply flip an empty can over, hide the existing hole with the palms of his hand, then pierce the undamaged exposed end, and pretend to pour its non-existent contents into their engines. But when Dad's customers saw the full quart of oil gurgle out of the glass bottle into their engine, it helped secure his hard-earned reputation as an honest businessman. Aside from the fact that the reusable glass bottles were ecologically superior—a word rarely heard and even less understood at that time—the sheet metal that would have been required for oil cans was soon directed to the manufacture of ships, trucks, tanks, and planes.

We who are used to driving thousands of miles on one change of synthetic oil can't imagine the idea of having to change oil every two thousand miles. However, automobiles during that period were not built with the precision of those today and engine parts wore out quickly. And some of those engines were pretty primitive. For example, on Dad's 1942 New York State registration for his tow truck, he had to check a box indicating whether the engine was gas, electric, or steam.

The single gas pump out front supplied leaded gas only. It had an inverted five-gallon glass bottle mounted at the top. The attendant would turn a crank to pump the desired number of gallons from a storage tank up into the bottle. The bottle had markings down its side, so that the attendant and the customer could see the actual number of gallons of gasoline it contained. When it was filled with the desired quantity, the attendant would insert the metal spout at the end of its rubber hose into a vehicle's gas tank, turn a valve, and the pre-measured quantity of gas would flow by gravity from the bottle at the top of the pump down into the vehicle's gas tank.

The attendant would then multiply the number of gallons by the going price of 18 cent per gallon, and charge the customer the appropriate amount. For example, five gallons of gas cost a hefty ninety cents. A federal tax of one cent per gallon was levied in 1932. Today, the federal tax is more than my Dad charged for a gallon of gas, and both Pennsylvania and California charge more than 50 cents per gallon in taxes on a single gallon.

That little "gas station" left a permanent impression on me. But that was eighty years ago, and I was just a toddler, so I had only vague impressions of life around me. I learned a great deal more about Dad's real estate when I recently found some old newspaper clippings dated 1943. What I did know was that, on the northwest corner of the property, behind and to the right of that little gas station, stood a brand new masonry garage, including an office and a shop, all built of cinder blocks. I wouldn't visit it for another year or so, but I would ultimately live in that garage for ten years.

What I do remember is a red metal bucket, filled with sand, that sat on the floor in the shop area. It was required by regulations of the United States Civil Defense organization. The sand was to be used to smother an incendiary bomb in the event that a German bomber, with a maximum range of 1,850 miles, somehow flew 3,900 miles across the Atlantic from Berlin to Poughkeepsie, successfully evaded our fighter and anti-aircraft defenses, then arbitrarily dropped an incendiary bomb on my father's garage.

I also found a hand written contract that Dad prepared in 1944. He had contracted to build a six car garage, with a shop out back and an office and bathroom along one side. The contractor was to lay up the eleven foot high walls of cinder blocks, including materials and labor, for $1,100. Dad used blocks made with the coal cinders, because he couldn't get the stronger concrete blocks. The materials used to make them were rationed.

What I didn't learn until recently was that this new garage replaced one that had burned to the ground on November 10, 1943 because an employee was carelessly welding near the gas tank on a customer's car and set it afire. Instead of pushing the car out of the garage, both mechanics panicked and ran away, and the entire building, including the three automobiles that were in for repairs, burned to the ground.

The fire then spread to a large four-family house, also owned by my father. The good news was that none of the families who lived there were injured, but many of their possessions were lost. The nearest fire hydrant was 2,000 feet away, and by the time the local volunteer fire departments from the area were able to gather and connect enough hoses to reach that distance, they found that the water pressure was so low that it was hopeless. Both the house and garage were total losses. The house was partially insured, but the garage, with those three private automobiles, was not.

As children, we boys did not see our father for days at a time. When we awoke, he was already gone for the day, and when he returned at night, we were fast asleep. When the war started, Dad kept the house on Greenbush Drive, but our entire family moved to New Jersey where he now worked at Bendix Aviation. We seldom saw him because he took every opportunity to return to Poughkeepsie to oversee his business and to get a head start on his post-war plans. Before the war ended, he had a store under construction, with an apartment above, where his little "gas station" once stood on the corner of Route 9-G and Greenbush Drive. Today it's a pizza parlor.

But that was all ancient history. It was now 1967, and over twenty years had passed when I received that phone call to travel to Florida. I still thought of my father as a human dynamo. He was financially secure, yet he never ceased to worry about money. But he truly loved his work, moving from one kind of job to another, always busy, always sought after for advice and any opportunities he might provide. I heard people say that every thing he touched turned to gold. That was far from the truth, but what he did earn came by dint of hard work and no small genius.

One moment I would see him in the office helping close a sale. The next, lying on his back in the garage under one of his trucks. Then, he'd be leaving for the bank, now decked out with an old necktie under the collar of his signature plaid flannel shirt.

When Joy and I traveled to Florida to see him, he was operating a variety of businesses. He had three mobile home retail outlets in St. Petersburg and Clearwater, owned a beachfront motel on the Gulf of Mexico, had just earned his Florida Realtor's license and opened his own real estate office, and was negotiating the purchase of an existing mobile home park. The day I arrived, dad took me to lunch, and while I was stuffing my mouth with tossed salad, he blind-sided me with the shocking news that the doctors had told him he had cancer and had only six months to live. I choked down the lettuce and stared at him in disbelief. He looked fine to me.

Those were increasingly dark days for our family, as we saw evidence of the cancer eating into his body, and watched as the destructive radiation treatments literally bruised and burned his flesh and sapped his strength. And always in the back of my mind was the nagging concern that my mom, as well as my brothers and me, were going to have a hard time getting along without him.

Average Guy Meets Extraordinary God

During the next six months, I returned to Florida a couple of times, the first with my family because we wanted to be near Dad. But he insisted that I was useless there and needed to get back to New York. The second time, shortly before his passing, I traveled to St. Pete to pick up a big Ford truck for use at our business in New York. In the meantime, I was stumbling along, planning how I might transition the business from marketing manufactured homes to selling recreation vehicles, a truly foolish decision.

And during that time, perhaps because of Dad's declining health, I began searching for God. I remember standing by Dad's bed during one visit and asking how he stood with God. He replied that a couple of men had come to visit him, prayed for him, and he thought he was okay. What a tenuous question. What an uncertain reply.

After he passed away, I came to realize how much I had come to count on his presence in my life. I coveted his rare praise. He was the one I always imagined would rescue me if I had a problem. Now he was gone and there was a void in my life that I couldn't fill. I no longer had my Dad's powerful personality to keep me focused on worldly activities and I began to realize how feeble is the help of any man or woman. So I began a search for the real meaning in life, and I began to direct my questions to God.

As long as my earthly father kept his businesses alive, I remained focused on the things that he valued. I honestly found much satisfaction, and lost myself in the complexities of running of a business. But as Dad liquidated most of his enterprises in anticipation of his death, I was forced to consider change. I could either continue as I had been, or look for another career path. Dad would no longer be there to pressure me, but I realized that God had a purpose for both of us, and he was drawing us toward him in different ways. Although I had received Christ as a child, I had not immediately taken up my cross to follow him. At the age of eight, Jesus had saved me, but it took twenty years before I finally became his disciple.

I now see these events as evidence of God's love, and of how our Lord guides us through periods of peace and joy, as well as pain and sorrow, in order to get us to where we belong. He is the One *"Who hath saved us, and called us with an holy calling, not according to our works, but according to his own purpose and grace, which was given us in Christ Jesus before the world began"* (2 John 1:9).

It's impossible to fully comprehend and appreciate these concepts, even after a lifetime of study, but it is possible to grasp their essence. As the verse above states, we were given eternal purpose and value by God!

Dad passed away in July of 1968, and I trust that he went to be with the Lord. Left behind, I was passing on in a different way, struggling to reconcile my worldly values with those I was discovering in the Word of God. My earthly Dad was gone, but my heavenly Father was coming alive in my life.

Jesus told Saul on the Damascus Road, "It's very hard to kick against the pricks." Our Lord was comparing Saul, the Pharisee, who ultimately became the Great Apostle Paul, to a dumb ox who had to be pricked with a goad in order to get him to turn in the right direction. If Saul required such treatment, why should it be any different with me? And speaking from experience, the sharp end of that ox goad can really smart, while the knobbed end can produce quite a headache.

As I began to discover the truths of God's Word, my values and ambitions changed. We disposed of almost everything that we owned or controlled. What little we didn't give to the poor, we set aside to pay for Bible school and as a result, Joy and I entered college in August of 1970. When we finished, we didn't have any money, but we were rich in the things of God.

I have often pondered the events that led to my closing the business and committing my life to Christ's service. Looking back, I can see a pattern that provided me with the opportunity to say "yea" or "nay" at every turn in the road. But the Lord offered me the choice, and I somehow exercised his grace to follow him.

I have never had cause to doubt God's presence in my life, though I have at times foolishly questioned his purpose. As Thomas à Kempis wrote, "Man proposes, but God disposes!"[4]

---

4   Kempis, *Imitation*. Accessed online July 1, 2025: https://www.gutenberg.org/ebooks/1653

Chapter 5

"Wisdom is justified by her children"

"For I know the plans I have for you, declares the LORD,
plans for welfare and not for evil, to give you a future and a hope."
Jeremiah 29:11

How would you respond if someone you respected suddenly told you that they had a message for you from God? That happened to me when my best friend's wife, Helen, called me one day at work.

I met Al and Helen Salay in 1964, and in spite of the fact that Al was ten years older, we became best friends. "Brother Al," as he was later known, served as the manager of my campaign for the New York State Senate, and later supported my preparation for the ministry. We remained close friends for nearly sixty years, when he passed away during the Covid Pandemic.

Al and Helen's marriage weathered some terrible storms, including an auto accident in 1965 which took the life of their six-year old son. As a result, they began searching for any eternal truths that might govern our world. They both subsequently received the Lord Jesus Christ as Savior, and became enthusiastic followers of the Lord.

I was happy for them, but it was months before Joy and I considered accepting their invitation to visit their church. When we did, I found myself sometimes blessed and frequently convicted by the sermons, but I felt inexplicably compelled to continue attending.

Average Guy Meets Extraordinary God

Joy and I had been attending several months when a very excited Helen called me at my office. I was in the midst of a staff meeting, but since she had never called me before, I was concerned that someone in her family might be ill or injured. When she told me that God had spoken to her about me, and that she wanted me to know what He had said, I was immediately on guard.

She persisted, however, and I realized that unless I listened to her earth-shaking revelation, I wouldn't be able to get off the phone without offending her. And as I listened, I realized that Helen's prophecy for me could not have been further from the realm of possibility.

She told me that God had told her that I was to enter the ministry. Then she said that she wanted to help me prepare. And while I sat there dumbfounded, she went on to say that she felt I could begin that preparation while I continued operating my business and that she was ready to invest in helping me toward the fulfillment of her vision.

I immediately began to tune her out, but Helen was a very persistent woman. I had a great deal of respect for her, so I tried to let her down gently, and not express the near contempt that I was feeling. There I was, managing a good sized business, and she was talking about my leaving everything that I knew and loved in order to enter a profession in which I had no interest and even less, knowledge. But she wasn't content to merely share the message that she said she had received from God. She proceeded to outline the steps she planned to take to help me.

First, she told me that she had spoken with the president of the Teen Challenge Institute of Missions, located twenty miles north, in Rhinebeck, New York, and had arranged for me to take evening Bible classes at no charge. Helen went on to say that she realized my business might suffer from my absences, and since she had once been an executive secretary at General Electric, she would be happy to work several hours a week at my office, both to help with the business and to transcribe and type any papers required for my studies.

She also said that she was aware that my studies would result in travel expenses, so she had spoken to her husband, and that Al had agreed that she could give me ten dollars a month toward expenses. That would come from savings she planned to make on her grocery purchases. That small amount might sound laughable, but your perspective may be skewed by the incredible inflation that America has experienced over the past fifty years. In 1969, ten dollars was not an insubstantial sum. It was a day's pay for many people, and taxes were low. For example, the IRS collected a dollar a week in federal tax on my weekly income. A gallon of gasoline was twenty-eight cents, less than a tenth of what we pay today. In fact, Joy and I ate very well on less than ten dollars per week for groceries.

But I considered Helen's idea ludicrous. I remember thinking, "I love you, Helen, but you're nuts!" However, I didn't say it aloud until after we got off the phone. I remember sitting there, holding the phone away from my ear, my hand over the mouthpiece, with a mocking grin on my face as I indicated to my secretary that I needed a few more minutes to complete the call. And all the time, I was wondering how to terminate the conversation.

Helen had gone overboard, but I tried to respond without offending her. I decided to show appreciation for her interest while going my own way. Hopefully her zeal would cool, and she'd forget about the entire episode in a week or two.

I reasoned that, "If God has something to say to me, let Him say it to me!" But, of course, I didn't have much of a dialogue with God at that time in my life. Nor was I aware of the fact that the Bible describes numerous occasions where the Lord commanded one individual to instruct another. On one occasion, God even used a donkey to rebuke a man. Apart from that, I had an overweening pride in my abilities, judgment, and strength, and I didn't think that I could count on a remote God to guide me through life. Since then, however, I've come to realize that Pride is the Prince of Liars.

I saw Helen's intervention as a judgment of my lifestyle, but I was nevertheless touched by her concern for my welfare. The problem was that I was living a life of confusion. Although my words and actions denied it, I was a believer. I had received Christ as a child, and in spite of the fact that I had little subsequent exposure to the things of God, and had followed a zigzag path ever since, it was becoming obvious that the Holy Spirit, whom Francis Thompson described as the "Hound of Heaven,"[5] was intent on chasing me down.

Helen's call made me wonder why she would risk our friendship in order to share such outrageous ideas. And it ultimately made me grateful that she and Al cared so much about Joy and me. As the Bible observes, *"As iron sharpens iron, so a man sharpens the countenance of his friend"* (Proverbs 27:17).

---

5   http://www.houndofheaven.com/poem Accessed online: July 1, 2025.

No, I didn't accept Helen's prophecy concerning my future, though I was baffled. Al wasn't at all surprised with my reaction to his wife's phone call, and understood completely my determination to ignore her. I'm sure that my rejection to Helen's phone call stung her, but when someone is the real deal, as she was, the Holy Spirit will help them handle rejection. He obviously helped her.

As time went on I began to feel a sense of gratitude for her concern, but my thoughts remained confused. She had obviously spent time in prayer on my behalf, and in planning how she could help fulfill God's will. Yet, it would be quite some time before I considered that the Lord might actually have been involved.

Helen's words, however, went far beyond someone trying to help me on the path to salvation. She had claimed to know God's will for my life, and she had not hesitated to predict my future. In fact, she went beyond fore-telling, and attempted to actually facilitate the fulfillment of the prophecy.

What's more, I might have been susceptible to such a suggestion, for those were admittedly challenging and confusing times in my life. My father had passed away a year earlier, at age 57, struck down by cancer. I was recently married, and had become the father of two wonderful little girls. And, apart from my business, I'd even co-chaired the county's Conservative Party and made an unsuccessful run for the state senate. But I was a long way from being confused as a Christian saint. Why would God single me out for ministry?

I never did study at Teen Challenge. Nor did Helen ever give me ten dollars a month for gasoline or come to work in our office. After the call, I laughingly told those in the office what she had said, and shared my initial reaction, "I love you, Helen, but you're nuts." I couldn't begin to imagine that God had actually told her any such thing.

Yet, despite my doubts, I actually had more faith in God's ability to intervene in the affairs of individuals than many reprobate seminary instructors. In fact, I had only recently visited Teen Challenge Institute of Missions for the first time. It was New Year's Day, 1969. The Salays had invited both my brother John's family and my family for an elaborate New Year's lunch. After the meal, Al got a phone call from the president of the institute, John Q. Kenzy, asking for his help.

I had avoided Helen's invitation to take classes at Teen Challenge, but Al had become involved. He had set up an audio production studio, and was helping with repairs around the property. The school occupied a rundown mansion that was owned by descendants of one of the stupendously wealthy families—like the Vanderbilt dynasty—who had built summer retreats along the east shore of the Hudson River during the 19th Century.

Al agreed to drive to the campus that afternoon and invited my brother and me to go along. Evidently, there was some sort of problem with a three-car garage that the school was trying to convert to a men's dormitory. As it turned out, the basement was flooded to a depth of five feet. During the week following our visit, my brother John drained the basement, repaired a broken water pipe, and volunteered to install a hot water heating system in the new dorm.

We both became involved because we were impressed with the work the school was doing. The mission of the Institute was to prepare born-again and rehabilitated alcoholics, drug addicts, and prostitutes who had come through the Teen Challenge program with practical and biblical knowledge to reach others with the love of Christ. Both my brother John and I were inspired with their truly amazing testimonies.

My exposure to John and Carol Kenzy, and the Institute they directed, profoundly impacted me. It represents one of a series of amazing events that saw me divesting myself of my business and entering Bible college in August, 1970.

Now, over fifty years later, Joy and I are still serving the Lord, and are thoroughly convinced that our friend Helen was right. God had indeed called us to the ministry. Helen's was not a mere self-fulfilling or self-serving prophecy, for God had to guide us through many difficult challenges, while both she and Al proved themselves ready and willing to make great personal sacrifices to assist us.

Some might interpret this as a latter day fulfillment of Joel's prophecy: *"And it shall come to pass afterward That I will pour out My Spirit on all flesh; Your sons and your daughters shall prophesy, Your old men shall dream dreams, Your young men shall see visions"* (Joel 2:28) Helen's prediction was validated, not because I entered the ministry by dint of her words or efforts, but because God did indeed call me, and his grace has sustained me. Which proves, indeed, that, "Wisdom is justified by her children." (Luke 7:35)

Chapter 6

Brother Al's Last Cigar

It's just like Jesus to roll the clouds away,
It's just like Jesus to keep me day by day,
It's just like Jesus all along the way,
It's just like His great love.

Edna Randolph Worrell, 1903[6]

From the day I met brother Al, he always seemed to have a cigar. There were exceptions, of course. When he was at home, Al only smoked in his study. But if we were driving somewhere, out would come a cigar, and he would light up. At one point, I actually bought a small package of cigars and tried joining him, but the allergy problems that I suffered in those days, and my dislike for the taste of tobacco, caused me to quit after a couple of cigars.

In those days, tobacco products, especially cigarettes, were ubiquitous. They were advertised via magazines, newspapers, radio, and television. During World War II, cigarettes were packed with candy and gum in military K-rations, and GIs were required to have a pack in their foot lockers. If they wanted more, they could buy cigarettes for just a nickel a pack. Needless to say, because of it's addictive properties and low cost,

---

6   Accessed online July 1, 2025: https://hymnary.org/text/a_friend_i_have_called_jesus_whose_love_

tobacco consumption skyrocketed during the war. Al joined the Marines in the early 1950s, during the Korean War, and joined the ranks of those who smoked cigars.

By 1954, the American Cancer Society was claiming that there was an association between smoking and lung cancer. And less than fifty years later, experts would claim that big tobacco companies had genetically engineered their crops to double the amount of nicotine. These critics pointed out that the death rate from lung cancer had doubled in spite of the fact that the number of people smoking had been reduced by half.

During the 1940s and 50s most of my father's employees were GIs, and virtually all the employees smoked. I grew up breathing second-hand smoke because Dad's offices were occupied by people puffing away. Sadly, most of those employees, including my own secretary, ultimately succumbed to cancer or heart disease.

One of our employees, "Whitey" Grenville Boddy, would come into the office every morning, light up a cigarette, begin coughing, and joke, "I can't wait 'til they make 'em bigger and better." Then, about 1980, while I was pastoring in Troy, I felt led to call that old friend. When I reached Whitey on the phone, he told me he was ill with heart disease, so the next day I drove the seventy-five miles to Poughkeepsie, and met him at a restaurant near his home. His wife was an active Jehovah's Witness, but he was willing to hear about Jesus. I answered his questions and prayed with him.

The next day, Whitey called my office, but I was in a meeting. My secretary relayed my message to him to take confidence in his new relationship with Christ. I have never forgiven myself for not speaking with him. Whitey passed away that same day!

As I remarked earlier, Brother Al was a cigar smoker. The myth was that, since the smoke had to pass through more tobacco before it was inhaled, it would filter out more of the toxins. It didn't! But one day, while Al and I were driving somewhere together, I noticed that he wasn't smoking his perennial cigar. I was surprised and concerned. After all, no one finds it easy to break the nicotine habit, and I wondered what had caused this radical change in his behavior. But in the interest of friendship, I had learned not to probe. If and when Al was ready, he would offer an explanation.

In the meantime, I became increasingly concerned that he might have been told that he had heart disease or lung cancer. Finally, one night when we were visiting his home, and he and I were sitting alone in his office, I blurted it out.

"Al, why did you give up cigars? Do you have cancer?"

"No," he replied in his quiet voice.

"But you loved your cigars. I don't understand. Did you quit because the people in the church frown on smoking?"

"Well, I heard a few criticisms," he said, "but I didn't care."

I sat there, waiting for an explanation.

"I didn't care what people thought," he repeated. "but I wanted to please God, so one day I prayed, 'Lord, if you want me to give up cigars, you'll just have to take them away from me.'"

"And?"

"And a few days later, I realized that I hadn't had a desire to smoke since I had offered that prayer."

"Just like that?"

"Just like that!" he replied. "I didn't even notice that I had lost the desire, or that I hadn't smoked, and I haven't smoked since. God just took the desire away."

On the night Brother Al was baptized, he was asked if there was a particular hymn he'd like sung. He chose a gospel chorus: "It's just like Jesus to roll the clouds away." But it wasn't just the dark clouds of life God rolled away away; it was the smoke from Brother Al's last cigar.

CHAPTER 7

David Wilkerson's Inadvertent Blessing

The New Testament book of Acts describes contention that arose between Barnabas and Paul, illustrating how a difference of opinion between two great men of God may change the course of many lives, and yet be used of God to further His purposes. You are probably familiar with that biblical account. Earlier, Barnabas had rescued the Apostle Paul from seeming obscurity and brought him to the attention of the Apostles. Later, the two of them took John Mark with them as their assistant on their first missionary journey. But Mark soon quit the team, and returned home. After Barnabas and Paul returned from their mission trip, they decided to make a second journey.

The Bible states:

> *"Barnabas was determined to take with them John called Mark. But the Apostle Paul insisted that they should not take with them the one who had departed from them in Pamphylia, and had not gone with them to the work. Then the contention became so sharp that they parted from one another"* (Acts 15:37-39).

Perhaps the Apostle Paul and Barnabas did not act in the ideal manner, but the Holy Spirit made things work out for the best. Among other things, there were now two evangelistic teams—one led by Barnabas, the other by the Apostle Paul—traveling to vastly different mission fields. In addition, those two men of God could no longer lean on one another for counsel and comfort. So, as undisputed leaders of their own mission teams, they had no choice but to grow in faith and wisdom. The Apostle Paul, for example, was able to recruit and train godly young men like Silas and Timothy to become fellow laborers in Christ.

In 1970, I had not yet learned about that disagreement between Barnabas and Paul, but I found myself at the heart of a similar conflict. Like John Mark, I was the cause of a misunderstanding between the leaders of two Christian ministries. As a result, the direction of my life was altered dramatically. In my case, however, a "Barnabas" did not take my side. Instead, a rocky relationship between the two men survived, while I was set adrift.

It seems strange, but it all started months before, when my father, in anticipation of his death, arranged to sell our flagship sales location in the mid-Hudson Valley. A year or so earlier, I had launched Traveland, a recreation vehicle dealership with locations in both Highland and Kingston, New York. Our buildings were identified by yellow roofs, cream-colored walls, faux leaded-glass windows, and topped with our distinctive sign, a stylized version of the word "Traveland." That logo was also printed on our literature, painted on our vehicles, and even embroidered on the shirts worn by those in our service department.

But despite any creative ideas I may have introduced, my father had wisely disagreed with my decision. He argued that the recreational vehicle business was too seasonal, that profit margins were too small, and that competitors were too numerous. Dad was right! At that time, there was a multitude of manufacturers springing up who were competing for dealers to handle their RVs. So anyone with access to a little highway frontage, who possessed minimal skills, and had a few dollars, could find a manufacturer eager to place a few units with them on consignment, with not a dollar out of pocket.

My father instead wanted me to expand our marketing of the new factory-built, FHA approved, sectional houses. Those beautifully designed homes were precisely engineered and efficiently manufactured on assembly lines for far less money than comparably sized stick-built houses that had to be erected piece by piece on building sites.

Many people are familiar with the old double-wides trailers. They were essentially two mobile homes, with the common inside wall of each unit removed. The two open sides were joined together, thus creating a "double-wide." But visionaries soon saw the potential for manufacturing traditional houses on an assembly line, and it wasn't long before market pressures and clever innovation saw the double-wide morph into a beautiful, factory-built, FHA approved, conventional house.

Competition between manufacturers meant that these assembly-line houses were built of high-quality, innovative materials that were purchased in bulk, thus further reducing costs. They had space-efficient floor plans and because they were built on assembly lines with precise controls, they were built to rigid standards. In many cases they were better constructed than houses built with semi-skilled workers on site.

Because of mass purchasing and assembly line efficiency, they cost far less. When someone purchased one, it could be moved to their prepared home site, set on a conventional foundation, and connected to utilities in as little as a day.

I shared my father's enthusiasm for these homes, and I would later recognize that his counsel was better. It was only better, however, if I was destined to spend my life as a businessman. When I chose not to follow Dad's counsel, and instead entered the RV business, I suspect I did exactly what God wanted me to do.

Did the Lord engineer the events I faced, or did he simply allow them? How do I explain it? I cannot. As Isaiah wrote, *"For as the heavens are higher than the earth, So are My ways higher than your ways, And My thoughts than your thoughts"* (Isaiah 55:9). The Apostle Paul put it another way, stating that, *"... the foolishness of God is wiser than men, and the weakness of God is stronger than men"* (1 Corinthians 1:25). All I can say is, I was searching for God's will for my life and, by what seemed a circuitous route, He led me to it.

This was one of my earliest brushes with the Apostle Paul's profound declaration that *"...all things work together for good to them that love God, to them who are the called according to his purpose"* (Rom 8:28). I was rushing to serve God, but to some, it seemed as though I was irresponsibly running from my obligations. God was directing me into paths of righteousness, for I seemed hopelessly caught up in events I could not control, while he was teaching me my first major lesson in humility.

Figuratively speaking, I did the same thing that Peter, Andrew, James, and John did. Jesus *"... said to them, 'Follow Me, and I will make you fishers of men'"*(Matthew 4:19), and they simply walked away from their nets to follow him. There is no indication that they showed the least interest in what happened to their boats, their employees, or their families.

I ultimately left retailing to do the same. I was a bit like Elisha, who killed the oxen that had pulled his plow. I left the career path I had followed for eight years and burned my bridges behind me. There was no going back!

But what if I had experienced great success in the recreational vehicle industry in the late 70s instead of following Jesus? What of my future? At that time, the RV industry was flourishing. Americans were on the road, roaring down the new Interstate Highways to vacation spots in Florida and California. Many of them preferred to travel with their own RVs, sleeping each night in their own beds, cooking their own meals, and freed from reliance on public facilities. The industry was thriving, and several manufacturers were already listed on the New York Stock Exchange.

Yet, just a few years later, most of the manufacturers and dealers who had prospered during the late 60s were wiped out by the Arab oil embargo of the early 70s. People could not buy gasoline to drive to work, much less to haul an RV. I can remember sitting in long lines at the pumps, just to purchase my limit of two gallons of gasoline at an exorbitant price. Ironically, millions of us wasted much of those precious two gallons while making the round trip from home to the rare gas station that had gasoline. But by then I was a pastor, not an RV dealer with a sales lot full of unsold motor homes. In hindsight, my decision to quit the RV business to serve God cost me nothing, and won me everything.

It was during this time of turmoil in my life—my passing through one crisis after another—the death of my father, the transition of our business, national political upheaval, the betrayal of my bankers, my marriage to a wonderful young woman, and the birth of two daughters—that the Lord touched my heart. I realized that I would never again be content with operating a business because I needed to be serving God. But I wasn't viewing life as I do now, with the clarity of hindsight. I knew little of the Word of God, and I was struggling to find my way spiritually, while trying to care for my family.

The period between 1968 and 1970 was a time of general prosperity. The unemployment rate was an incredibly low 3.4 percent, and I found it nearly impossible to hire responsible, adequately skilled, and honest individuals. At the same time, I found myself becoming disillusioned with activities that had formerly energized me.

I hired a couple of young men who were students at John Kenzy's Teen Challenge Institute, in Rhinebeck. I was intrigued by their work ethic, as well as their testimonies of God's saving grace. While they insisted that they worked honestly to glorify God, they were clearly motivated by the pay checks as well. They could have helped me make a great success of my business, but they were limited to part time work because John Kenzy properly insisted they have adequate time to study and pray. John told me a couple of times that, when he saw a student cutting back on their prayer time, he knew they were about to backslide.

John Q. Kenzy became one of my mentors, and he remained my close friend for over fifty years, until he went to be with the Lord in 2019. During his college years, John ministered at the Brooklyn Teen Challenge center, which was followed by 57 years of ministry to reclaimed human beings, first through Teen Challenge and then Youth Challenge. He and David Wilkerson co-founded the Teen Challenge Institute of Missions in Rhinebeck in 1970. John served as President through its closing about 1975. He then went on to found a similar educational program at the Youth Challenge Institute in Sunbury, Pennsylvania where he ministered for the rest of his life. Observing these two heroes of the faith, I came to realize that I too wanted to be involved in work where God was dramatically saving souls and changing lives.

Joy and I celebrated my thirtieth birthday by inviting John Kenzy, and his wife Carol, along with our pastor, Ralph Midgett, and his wife, to dinner. That night I announced my plan to close the business and search for the niche in which Jesus would have me serve. After dinner, we all joined in a game of Monopoly. Although it is just a game, Monopoly tends to ignite competitive spirits, and while most people believed that they could be cutthroat in their dealings with other players, honesty was still expected. But I saw our pastor snitch several of those little orange $500 bills from his wife a couple of times during the game, and his behavior made me uneasy.

Soon after that dinner party, as I began closing the business, I became excited about John Kenzy's invitation to join his staff at Teen Challenge. I would serve as his director of maintenance, a position that desperately needed filling, not merely repairing and upgrading the facilities, but building a mobile home park for staff and student housing. I would also sit in classes, as Helen Salay had suggested earlier. I thought that, by starting part-time in this program near my home, it would permit an easy transition from business to ministry. But God had something else in mind.

I was very naive concerning Christian leaders. I hadn't yet read the Apostle Paul's warnings about false teachers. and I naively believed that all of God's servants would be essentially honest. I did not realize that "ministers of the gospel" also have feet of clay. I expected people of "the world" to be what they are, people of the world. But I mistakenly believed that all those who claimed to have given their lives to serve Christ were more than a cut above the rest. Many are, but not all. And in my ignorance, I was blind to the bad feelings that existed between our pastor and John Kenzy.

On the night of my birthday party, I was operating RV sales outlets at Kingston and Highland, with over 50 units in stock, and I was in the throes of closing the business. Since the two outlets were on the west side of the Hudson, and Teen Challenge was on the east side, at Rhinebeck, I sought any excuse to cross the river to visit the school. During those visits, I became increasingly concerned with the near poverty in which both the staff and students at Teen Challenge lived.

I was deeply impressed with the sacrifices they made and couldn't understand why God's people weren't doing more for the school. I mentioned this to my pastor, not realizing how manipulative he was, and he suggested that I write David Wilkerson and appeal for more funds from the Teen Challenge program to be diverted to the Bible Institute in Rhinebeck.

David Wilkerson, who passed away in 2011, was one of my early Christian heroes. He had traveled to New York City's Bedford Stuyvesant area in the late 1950s, accompanied by John Kenzy, and enjoyed significant success in reaching violent gangs with the message of Christ. In 1962, Wilkerson wrote *The Cross and the Switchblade*, a book that sold over 50-million copies in thirty languages. It tells of his confrontation with gang leader, Nicky Cruz. When the two met, Cruz drew a knife and threatened to cut Wilkerson into little pieces. Wilkerson's legendary reply was: "Yeah, you could do that. You could cut me up into a thousand pieces and lay them in the street, and every piece will still love you." Nicky Cruz ultimately became a Christian leader, and wrote his own successful book, *Run, Baby Run!*

David's involvement with the gangs in New York led him to begin the Teen Challenge program, with its mission to rescue addicted individuals. And now John Kenzy was presiding over their Bible school.

I was intensely involved with my business, but still took time to design a 30-unit mobile home park for the Institute, then successfully interceded with the Dutchess County Board of Health to approve its sewer system. John Kenzy secured sufficient funding to have the acreage leveled, and I wanted to find a way to get professional help to actually install the water and sewer lines, and run the electrical supply lines for each mobile home. I was certainly too busy to take a hand in the actual work of running a backhoe and installing plumbing, so I tried to think of someone who could help.

An answer came to me, and I wrote to the retired CEO of IBM. Thomas J. Watson, Jr. was a philanthropist and had served as the national president of the Boy Scouts of America, and U.S. Ambassador to the Soviet Union. Under his leadership, IBM had become one of the dozen largest industrial corporations in the world. And I had the boldness, born of ignorance, to write and ask him to arrange for one of IBM's' employees—specifically, my brother John—to be given two paid weeks off to build the mobile home park at Teen Challenge Institute.

And Watson replied, sending me his response on engraved note paper. As a consequence, my brother John, figuratively kicking and screaming, was given two weeks off from his wonderful clean office job to grovel in cold, muddy ditches at Teen Challenge. My brother John's greatest frustration was the ignorance of the student volunteers who John Kenzy sent to help him. My brother is with the Lord now, and I hope he's finally forgiven me for volunteering him for that dirty job. It seems I have an incurable propensity to match unwilling saints to unsavory tasks.

In light of my success in writing to one of the most powerful men in the world, I figured that I ought to have equal success by following Pastor Midgett's advice, to write a great man of God like David Wilkerson. About a week after I sent him my heartfelt request that he consider sending more support to the Institute, I received a phone call from John Kenzy. It was a busy work day at Traveland, but he demanded that I drop everything and drive to Rhinebeck immediately.

When I arrived at his office, John was sitting behind his desk, and his anger was palpable. He left me standing there like a truant school boy while he told me that a furious David Wilkerson had called him that morning, and had accused John of persuading me to write my letter, which, of course, John had not done. In fact, I had told no one that I had written it, reasoning that, if David Wilkerson wanted to ignore my appeal, nobody needed be the wiser, and if he wanted to assist the school, he should be the one to announce it. My name never needed to be mentioned. Above all, if it did come to something, I wanted John to be happily surprised.

He was surprised all right! Perhaps I should have foreseen that possibility. After all, if Nicky Cruz had threatened to cut David Wilkerson up into little pieces, I should have realized the sort of people that David was forced to deal with on a regular basis. But I never expected him to question my motives, much less John's character or actions. Nonetheless, John Kenzy and David Wilkerson were not to be separated as the Apostle Paul and Barnabas were.

Looking back, I suppose that it should have been no surprise that David concluded that I was merely a selfish, immature Christian who wanted the Institute to prosper so that I would have a more comfortable life there. I knew the privation in which they lived. I remember one occasion when the entire staff and student body basically survived for an entire week on the squash they harvested from a nearby field. And I don't like squash! But improving the Institute's financial situation for my own sake was not my motive. I was willingly relinquishing a business in which I had enjoyed a great lifestyle, as well as the respect of many in my community, in order to enter a life of relative poverty in a ministry that was anything but prosperous.

It seemed to me that a little additional income from David Wilkerson's ministries might help pay to replace the water heater in the main building, but it wasn't going to significantly improve the quality of life for the staff. And it certainly wasn't going to improve the lot of this new maintenance manager.

As I stood there, feeling like the dog in a "kick the dog" scenario, John echoed David Wilkerson's view of my character, then accused me of being impulsive like the apostle Peter. I remained silent, but in retrospect, I would prefer to think of myself as an Apostle Paul, bold and faith filled. But wouldn't we all?

This criticism went on for several minutes, but it was clear that John wasn't finished, and he soon dropped the other shoe. He told me that David Wilkerson didn't want me anywhere near Teen Challenge, much less serving as a member of the staff. I was to get my office equipment off the property as soon as possible. But, John added, maybe I could leave my bulldozer and other equipment around for them to use, and if I stopped by once in a while to help out, maybe no one would notice.

When I later told Pastor Ralph Midgett what had happened, he didn't seem at all surprised. In fact, he told me that he expected that response. Up until then, I had no idea of the animosity he felt toward the school, or that he felt he was competing for funds that some members of his congregation, like Al Salay, were giving Teen Challenge.

What's more, he seemed delighted that I'd been given my walking papers. I realized that he had used me, but when he suggested that I might apply to his alma mater to study for the ministry—and I realized that I didn't have any other options—I decided to pray about it.

Subsequent events would reveal more of our pastor's shortcomings. He ultimately disgraced himself, and lost his family and his ministry. But in my case, he was used of God to point me in the right direction.

The years have flown by, but a short time before David Wilkerson passed away as the result of an automobile accident, I wrote him a second letter, reminding him of my original message, assuring him that John Kenzy had nothing to do with my writing the letter to him, and asking his forgiveness. His reply was gracious.

And that's how Joy and I wound up at Bible college instead of at Teen Challenge Institute.

CHAPTER 8

"Jesus loves the little children"

"See that you do not despise one of these little ones. For I tell you that their angels in heaven always see the face of my Father in heaven".

Matthew 18:10

———————

Joy and I are blessed to have four adult children, two of each gender, male and female, faithful to God's plan. As children, each of them was unique and ingenious. Each brought us great joy, but also presented unique challenges. I thank God that I married a woman of amazing commitment and inherent wisdom, for she often met their needs when I failed.

As a young man struggling to support a family while finding my own place in the world, I had no idea how much pride and how little wisdom I possessed, Being intensely involved in business and politics, I can only look back and try to recall bits and pieces of my own family's history. And when I do, it is with amazement that I realize how our children's lives were shaped and preserved, not by us, but by God. When we failed, the Lord was looking out for each of them—mentally, physically, and spiritually.

One of the first things that parents should learn is that they are ill-prepared to be parents and should therefore pray for God's guidance and protection, then act accordingly. Another thing that few people understand is that we, and our children, are often saved out of life's-threatening situations without our even recognizing how close we have come to disaster. We rarely recognize the scope of the deliverance, much less offer thanks for it.

Our younger daughter, Cheryl, was, and is, an incredible individual — a born adventurer. She is a dedicated wife and mother, but much more. She is a professional educational writer, as well a gifted musician, vocalist, and lyricist. Like most artists, she is a romantic, but also a thoroughly rational woman, whose faith leaves her undaunted by adversity and determined to explore every possible opportunity.

As a toddler, Cheryl went far beyond repeatedly asking us "Why?" and put one foot in front of the other in an effort to satisfy her curiosity. She had an insatiable appetite to explore her world, and this attribute could have cost her her life.

We lived on a heavily wooded three-acre parcel south of Highland, New York. Our unpaved driveway ran downhill from our home for nearly two hundred yards, crossed a stream, then twisted serpent-like up a steep hill where it met the very busy state highway, Route 9-W.

Before the New York Thruway was built, 9-W was the main thoroughfare on the west side of the Hudson between New York City and the state capital at Albany. There were so many head-on accidents along the stretch that passed our home that the state had reduced the dangerous three lane highway to two wider lanes. Eighteen wheel tractor trailers raced along its blacktop surface, and there were frequent accidents and occasional deaths.

That highway was at the center of our little world because our home was on one side, and one of our RV sales locations on the other, just a hundred yards north. And while our home was far back in the woods, and we felt safe letting our two little girls play in our small grassed yard, we were concerned about the potential dangers that the highway represented.

For example, I recall standing in our RV store one morning when traffic was relatively light, looking through one of the picture windows as an eighteen-wheeler labored slowly up the hill in the north bound lane. Its old stake body trailer was heaped with what looked like scrap metal, and hundreds of the small pieces were tumbling over its sides to spill in a windrow of razor sharp steel across the uphill lane. The driver actually stopped and got out of the truck, looked over the scraps he had lost, looked across the street toward me, then climbed back in his cab, and continued up the road a short distance, where I saw him pull off by a public phone booth.

As I continued watching, a car came up the highway, swerved to avoid most of the scrap, and blew a tire. The driver continued driving slowly up the highway toward a gas station. Curious, I looked both ways before running across to the far side. When I examined the things spread along the blacktop, I realized that they were not junk scrap metal. Every one of them was stamped out of 1/8" thick steel and was precisely the same. They were odd shaped pieces of steel, perhaps five inches long, with four incredibly sharp little serrated "legs" that pointed in different directions.

There were hundreds of them, and I realized I couldn't clean them up, so I grabbed a couple and ran back to my office, thinking I would call the police. I sat down behind my desk, studied the devices for a moment, and tossed them in the bottom drawer. As I picked up the phone, a New York State Department of Transportation dump truck, followed by a tractor with a front end loader, came up the hill. A half dozen men began sweeping the scrap metal onto shovels before tossing them into the bucket loader, and the tractor in turn raised the bucket and dropped them into the dump truck. Within five minutes, there was no trace of the strange little gadgets, and I marveled because I had never witnessed such a rapid response from any state bureaucracy. It's as though they'd been standing by for just this purpose.

The clean up crew had just departed when a state police car pulled up in front of my store, and a trooper rushed into my office. He was curt and threatening, and he demanded to know whether I'd seen whatever it was that had fallen off the truck, and whether I'd picked anything up, or had anything in my possession. I don't know whether I lied to him or not, but I did not tell him that I had a couple of the objects in my desk drawer. Then he told me that this was a matter of national security, and if I were to say anything to anyone about this matter, I would be arrested and probably imprisoned. Then, without another word, he left.

1969 was the height of the Vietnam War, and we had over half a million troops on duty there. I had read about how the Vietcong guerrillas had been setting up booby traps made of sharp bamboo stakes, often coated with feces or other poisons, to impale our troops. What the media was not reporting was that a startling two percent of our troops were injured or killed by these traps that were laid for them in the thick jungles.

The Vietcong were not signatories to the Geneva Accords, so they could be as savage as they wished. But we had accepted those rules of warfare, and therefore any similar activity on our part was illegal, and any violations would arouse America's highly vocal anti-war activists. Indeed, there had been suggestions in the media that, in violation of the Geneva Accords, we might be retaliating. So it was obvious that the current administration would struggle to keep any violations secret.

I had immediately recognized those hundreds of pieces of scrap iron that dropped from the back of the truck, and had ripped a hole in the tire of the passing car. They were caltrops, little steel devices with wickedly sharp spikes, crafted so that no matter how they landed on the ground, at least one spike would always point upward. They were cheap to stamp out, and could be dumped in streams and across the fields of Vietnam to pierce the feet of the enemy.

It is not so much that I was opposed to the use of this atrocious weapon. After all, countless bullets and bombs, were being expended by both sides to injure and kill multitudes. But I wasn't about to to risk my future and my freedom by making any statement to a state trooper who acted like one of Hitler's Storm Troopers. Americans were still paying a little attention to our Constitutional rights, in this case the 5th amendment, and I had no intention of incriminating myself for an innocent act.

I did support our efforts to stall the spread of communism, but I was angry that our government was being dishonest with the citizenry. That smacked of totalitarianism, and I wanted to give a little thought to the matter. Soon after, however, someone did leak that story to the press, and the media was again alive with controversy. Such was life in the 60s, and such were the perils along Route 9-W, whether from fast-moving 18-wheelers, spilling caltrops, or drunk drivers, or officers of the New York State Police.

Although not nearly as sensational, our daughter's adventure is a case in point. Late one morning, my wife Joy was surprised to receive a phone call from our occasional baby-sitter, a lady who operated a small mom and pop store about a quarter mile south of our home, on the opposite side of Route 9-W. Our little girl had somehow made her way, over six-hundred feet, from our little front yard to the end of our driveway. Then she had toddled south along Route 9-W, keeping to the narrow grass shoulder that lay between the guard rail and the pavement. She later told us that a few of the big trucks slowed down, and the drivers waved to her. Others blew their horns, which frightened her, and the wind of their passing almost blew her over. But she finally crossed the highway to reach the little store, and attempted to negotiate the purchase of candy with some pennies she carried in her pocket.

That very concerned store keeper—who was also our occasional baby-sitter—called Joy, and promised to entertain our little girl until we could get there to pick her up. Joy then called me at work, I raced home, and we were at the store in minutes. We were horrified by what had been a near tragedy, and thankful for our little girl's survival.

The point is that our adventurous little girl left the safety of our yard, survived her walk down that hill and across a highway heavily traveled by tractor trailers, by speeding police cars, and even by the occasional truck carrying things like caltrops. Feel free to judge us for our carelessness, for we relied on our distance from the highway to serve as a buffer, but don't forget the point of this story. When you consider the worst that could have happened, it is remarkable that our toddler survived that walk.

In some ways, our daughter has never changed. Cheryl is still a bold adventurer, an explorer, and a risk taker, but with the prudence that maturity brings. But when she was a little one, lacking such maturity, I am convinced that someone special was watching over her. Remember the words of Jesus: "...their angels in heaven always see the face of my Father in heaven."[7]

---

7   Matthew 18:10b

CHAPTER 9

The Broken Spark Plug

"But it happened that as one of them was cutting down a beam, the ax head fell into the water; and he cried out and said, 'Oh, my master! It was borrowed!' Then the man of God said, 'Where did it fall?' And when he showed him the place, he cut off a stick and threw it in there, and made the iron float".

2 Kings 6:5-7

The year that followed my father's death was extremely busy. God continued to work in and around me to narrow my options and ultimately guide Joy and me to Bible College. To me, our experiences were like looking at the back of a tapestry—just a riot of colored threads zigzagging over one another in every which way—making no sense. It was a chaotic scene, and I wouldn't be privileged to glimpse much of what God saw until many years later.

But the Lord was looking at the picture that He was creating on the opposite side of that tapestry. And so it is for those of us who follow the Lord. Sometimes we seem to stumble around in relative confusion, but we stubbornly hang on to his promises because that is the character of faith.

The Lord was going ahead of Joy and me, preparing our hearts, and shaping the course of our lives. And in spite of the various trials, he somehow kept bringing us back to one ultimate purpose—to serve him. The conviction grew in me that He had called me. I had no idea in what capacity or where I would serve, for the situation was fluid, my perspective continually changing, and He had not yet planted that purpose in my heart, but I came to believe that if I toughed it out, He would show me the way.

We faced many challenges, large and small, and one seemingly small event stands out. I recall a particularly bitter cold and windy March day in 1970 when my friend Al and I drove to Teen Challenge to pick up my office furniture.

I loved the students at TCIM, and was almost in awe of them. They had been the wretched refuse of New York City—alcoholics, drug addicts, and prostitutes who had been redeemed through faith in Christ—and they seemed to glow with thanksgiving for their deliverance. But early in their walk with Christ, they were very susceptible to temptations. So David Wilkerson and John Kenzy had contrived to move them out into the country, far from the temptations of the Big Apple, for as new Christians, preparing to serve as missionaries to their former associates in sin, they had to be protected from predators.

Drugs, alcohol, and sexual addiction severely damage the body, and actually "rewire" the brain, and only the blood of Christ and the Word of power can repair them. No matter who you are, it is only immersion in the Bible, accompanied by prayer and meditation, that will restore your mind. And I never ceased to be amazed by the stubborn faith of those who were overcoming.

In practical matters, however—for example, caring for motor vehicles—those survivors from the Big Apple were untutored and often less than useless. A little background will be helpful. When I decided that I was to close the business and take some sort of role in God's work, John Kenzy invited me to move to Teen Challenge and take charge of their facilities. Since I had spent much of my life building things, but had little knowledge of the Bible, this seemed a wise move. I could repair and maintain their facilities, while they introduced me to the Living Word which would repair and maintain my soul.

I had already designed a 30-unit mobile home park for the staff and students, over which my brother John had assumed the roll of general contractor. And John Kenzy had allotted me some space in the administration building where I had set up an office area to begin my work. I'd even begun transferring ownership of valuable equipment to the school, including a bulldozer, a flatbed trailer, and a pickup truck.

But when God used David Wilkerson to make it clear that I was not to be part of the Teen Challenge program, and I began making preparations to attend Bible college, I was told to retrieve my personal office equipment. That cold March morning, Al and I planned to use a pickup truck I had loaned the school to cart my office furniture away. But we discovered that a student had abandoned the truck in the middle of the six acre field where we were building the mobile home park. That field had been leveled by bulldozers, and subsequent rains had turned the surface into a quagmire of mud, clay, and rock. Now it was frozen, and the pickup had been abandoned there, its front passenger tire flat.

Someone had pulled my gasoline powered air compressor out onto the field, obviously intending to reinflate the tire, but they had never completed the job. When we checked the engine, we discovered why. The spark plug had been broken in two, with the top half of the plug hanging from its electrical cable, and the lower half screwed into the engine.

I looked at it and realized it was useless. It is difficult enough to start a one cylinder gas engine with a good spark plug in the summer, but when the temperature is freezing, it's a real challenge. I'd spent too many winter days trying to get stubborn engines to start, and was ready to walk away in discouragement.

But Brother Al had another idea, and it was immediately obvious that he was taking the possibility of miracles far more seriously than I. He picked up the broken end of the plug, with the wire clipped to its tip, and balanced it atop it's damaged base. Then the man of God said, let's lay hands on the compressor and pray. So we did. I don't remember Al's exact words, but I do remember that he reminded God that we were trying to get the tire inflated so that we could use the truck to move items in preparation for my moving to Bible school.

After Al prayed, he yanked the starter cord, and instead of his violent motion causing the top of the spark plug to topple off its base, the engine started. The vibration of the running motor immediately caused the spark plug to topple off its base, and it dangled there at the end of its electric wire, but the engine continued to run. And run! The compressor pressurized the storage tank with air, and continued running while I knelt down on the frozen ground, pressed the nozzle of the air hose against the valve, and inflated the tire on the pickup truck. Then we shut the motor down.

"Let's try it again," Al said. "Now that it's warmed up, the motor should start just fine." So we again carefully balanced the top half of the broken spark plug atop its bottom and pulled the starter rope. After repeated tries, the engine wouldn't start.

The purpose of our prayer had been to get the air compressor running so that we could inflate the tire on the truck. That job was accomplished. We really had no more need for the compressor, and our amazing experience testified not just to God's faithfulness, but to His accomplishment of His specific goals.

The Apostle Paul once asked the rhetorical question: "*Who shall separate us from the love of Christ? Shall tribulation, or distress, or persecution, or famine, or nakedness, or peril, or sword?*" He went on to assure us: "*... in all these things we are more than conquerors through Him who loved us*" (Romans 8:35-37). We now had another example of something that wouldn't separate us from the love of God...a broken spark plug. What we did have was an inflated tire.

A miracle? You be the judge. But one thing is certain. That freezing cold March morning, Al Salay and I witnessed a remarkable event, one so stunning in its timeliness that we never forgot it. It not only increased our faith, but it reassured me that I was heading in the right direction. For that morning a man of God prayed and the Lord added a little spark to our lives!

THE FORMATIVE YEARS:

THE BECKONING HAND OF GOD

CHAPTER 10

The Seed is Planted

"The seed is the word of God. ...the ones that fell on the good ground are those who, having heard the word with a noble and good heart, keep it and bear fruit with patience."
Luke 8:11, 15

I have discussed some of the experiences that convinced me I was called to prepare for full-time ministry. Now I want to point out some of the unusual events that resulted in my receiving Christ in the first place.

I celebrated my eighth birthday in March, 1948. Just seventeen days later, without realizing it, I made the most momentous decision of my life. It occurred not far from my childhood home, in New York's mid-Hudson Valley. I had spent the early afternoon with my older brother Bill, wandering around the winding macadam roads of our hilly neighborhood.

Of my three brothers, Bill was always the better influence. But that day, without realizing it, he opened the door to the greatest experience of my life. It would be nearly seventy years before I would be able to repay him.

"Hey," he said, pointing to a house on our left, "the lady that lives there, Mrs. Roberg, has a Bible story time today. Want to go with me?"

I didn't know much about the Bible, but I had been warned that some people taught things that were bad. So I replied, "Mom might get mad if we go there."

But Bill persisted, searching for arguments that would sway me, and he began laying them out. "They tell Bible stories."

When I shrugged my shoulders, he brought out the heavy artillery.

"And they give away cookies and punch."

Well, that did it! Although the Second World War had ended nearly three years earlier, I had enjoyed few sweets in my brief lifetime. Why? With America's entry into the war, rationing was introduced, and sugar was the first food to be rationed. I was two years old at the time, and it would be five years before sugar was removed from the ration list in many parts of the United States. So I was almost eight years old before candy was regularly found on store shelves across America. In fact, my three brothers and I had enjoyed virtually no sweets during the war years.

I remember two exceptions. My grandfather had been a medical doctor, but when the war began, the part of our house that had served as his office was converted to an apartment for an elderly Jewish couple. They were very fond of me, and one day gave me a slice of white bread, spread with oleo, and liberally sprinkled with white sugar. They were shocked when they realized that I didn't like the taste. My mother was also shocked that they'd wasted so much of their sugar ration on me.

The second occasion was toward the end of the war when my mother received a jar of home-made blueberry jam in the mail. Blueberry was her favorite, and she again marveled that someone had sacrificed their own precious sugar ration for her. Mom allowed each of us a taste, again on a piece of sliced bread. But when she later opened that precious jar to enjoy some for herself, she discovered that Billy had almost emptied it. Mom had a special place in her heart for Bill because he was often the only son to help her in the kitchen. So instead of biting into jam on bread, or biting Bill's head off, our mom bit her tongue.

Incidentally, in January 1943, the War Foods Administration established a nationwide ban on the sale of sliced bread. No one ever explained why. There was plenty of wheat. Commercial bakeries already had the slicing machines. Was there a shortage of waxed paper? I remember my mother making her own sourdough bread, and we didn't like the taste. Sugar and coffee were already rationed, and America's housewives rebelled. The ill-conceived ban lasted just two months before the rationing board was forced to rescind the order. Sliced bread was the only food removed from their rationing list during the war.

And that's why, when Bill used free cookies and punch as his argument for visiting the Bible story time, I changed my tune.

"Well, okay," I replied, trying to sound indifferent, but obviously failing.

"You need to promise that you won't tell mom," he said.

"Okay, I promise."

So he led me up across the shale embankment that lay in front of Mrs. Roberg's newly built house. Millions of troops had come home, so there were several new houses in the neighborhood. As we approached the front door, I hung back as a shy little boy concerned about the reception we might receive. But Bill confidently knocked, and I began to wonder whether this was his first visit. The door was opened by a smiling woman who welcomed him by name, and invited us in. So I was right; it was definitely not his first visit. I was a veritable Sherlock Holmes. I was still timid, but Bill had been here before, so I figured I would survive the experience. My resistance was already broken down by the promise of cookies.

My fears were completely alleviated when I spotted a number of children I knew, who were seated in the living room watching another woman tell a story. She was standing before an easel, pressing colorful pieces of felt onto a black flannel background, and I was intrigued when she pressed a picture of a big wooden boat against the background, then added various wild animals walking up to its door. I was spellbound, for I had never heard the story of Noah and his ark. And I was mesmerized by the vibrant colors of the images she was pressing to her flannel board.

Remember—with the exception of the comics in the Sunday newspapers and an occasional magazine advertisement—every newspaper and magazine was printed in black and white. Those were the days before commercial TV, and with the exception of blockbuster movies like "Gone With the Wind" and "The Wizard of Oz," most films were still produced in black and white.

Perhaps, because I was a child during the war, and had heard how our soldiers died to save the world from evil, I was able to understand when the lady explained that Jesus was put to death on the cross to suffer for our sins. At least I understood enough to raise my hand to indicate that I wanted Jesus to forgive me for the bad things I had done, and to come into my heart and be my Savior.

Many people, even among Christians, mock the idea that a little child can understand enough to be saved, but I have come to believe that

God adapts his message to our unique needs, reaching us where we are, at almost any age or mental capacity, and that he helps our understanding and our appreciation to grow from that point. Jesus Himself warned his disciples, *"Let the little children come to Me, and do not forbid them; for of such is the kingdom of God"* (Luke 18:16).

It may be argued that we hadn't reached the age of accountability and could not be saved, but that decision isn't up to us. It's up to the Spirit of God. Yet, to the self-righteous and those who believe that it takes special knowledge or wisdom to begin a walk with God, Jesus told a crowd, *"Unless you change and become like little children, you will never enter the kingdom of heaven"* (Matthew 18:3).

So, in childlike faith, I raised my hand to accept Jesus as my Savior. Afterward, our hostess gave me a little book with a red leather cover. Its title was picked out in gold leaf: The New Testament. The symbol of The Gideons was pressed in the lower corner. Then she handed me a fountain pen, and made certain that I personally scribbled my name and that day's date inside before I left her house. The funny thing was that the cookies and juice had all been given away before we arrived. But I didn't miss them... much.

In spite of my promise to my brother, I told my mother about our experience that day, and she didn't seem upset. But she did say I wasn't to return. I still thank God for the ministry of those two women. That Gideon New Testament has a special place of honor in my office today; I can see it from where I'm sitting. As I was writing these words, I opened the cover of that little book, and realized that I received Jesus Christ as my Savior seventy-seven years ago.

Please note that I referred to him as my "Savior," not my "Lord." That's because any meaningful understanding of His sovereignty, and my subsequent commitment to Him, did not come until decades later. There was a gap of about twenty years between my receiving his Word *"... with a noble and good heart,"* and the time I began to *"...keep it and bear fruit with patience"* (Luke 8:15).

But my salvation is a matter of record, and my commitment is revealed in the scribblings of an eight-year-old boy in the front of his little Gideon New Testament. Is it any wonder that the enemies of God want to remove Gideon Bibles from hotels and other places? Or that they hate public school "released time teaching," as well as Sunday schools, and other outreaches of the church. Oh, that we might have more godly women like Mrs. A. Sidney Roberg to influence our children!

The idea that God can and does touch the hearts of little children has grown on me as the years have passed, and certainly had a part in my later leading a ministry whose Sunday School grew from zero to an average of nearly 300 in sixteen months. One thing more. To those who argue that people like Mrs. Roberg shouldn't conduct Bible studies in their homes, please keep in mind that most of the real work of the Church has always taken place outside the walls of purpose-built church structures, and much of it by women. What's more, for the first two hundred and fifty years after Christ's resurrection, the early churches did not meet in purpose-built structures. They met in homes!

"So what?" someone asks. "So a skinny little kid like you thinks he got saved. What's the big deal?" Well, looking back over the past seventy-seven tumultuous years, it's a big deal to me. A very big deal! Because, at the age of 85, I'm getting ready, as they say, to meet my Maker. And I'm glad I will be able to meet Him on His terms.

If you want to understand how big a deal it is, you need to understand what followed. Perhaps you can explain how I wandered around this world, involving myself in a multitude of activities, exposed and even succumbing to temptations and sins and yet, God never let go. I am pragmatic, and when I consider all the events that I describe in this book, I find it impossible to deny that the relationship I have enjoyed with Jesus Christ began the very afternoon that I received Jesus in childlike faith. And the Lord has kept the promises recorded in that little Gideon New Testament and has never let go of me.

Through all the ups and downs, through all the ins and outs, the Holy Spirit of God persevered in my life and caused my faith to grow. So that today, nearly eight decades later, my confidence in God and my peace of mind, is greater than ever. Whatever your age, you too may experience the greatest miracle of all, and that really is a big deal!

Earlier, I mentioned that it would be nearly seventy years before I could knowingly repay my brother Bill. At that time, he was in the early stages of Alzheimer's Disease, so while I was driving him from Tampa to Clearwater for what would probably be the last get together of us four brothers, I asked him if he would like to receive Jesus as his personal Savior.

He replied, "Why not?"

So I pulled off the highway, and prayed with Bill as he asked Jesus Christ to forgive him for his sins, to come into his heart, and to be his

Savior and Lord. While the disease my have caused Bill to later forget his prayer of commitment, God's Holy Bible assures us that the Lord Jesus Christ did not. *"For I am convinced that neither death, nor life, nor angels, nor principalities, nor things present, nor things to come, nor powers, nor height, nor depth, nor any other created thing, shall be able to separate us from the love of God, which is in Christ Jesus our Lord"* (Romans 8:28-29).

I am looking forward tomeeting both my brother Bill and Mrs. Roberg in heaven.

CHAPTER 11

"He will keep thee...."

"You will keep him in perfect peace, Whose mind is stayed on You, Because he trusts in You."

Isaiah 26:3

———————

At the height of World War II, when I was just three-years old, my family moved to New Jersey where my father was employed as an engineer at Bendix Aviation. While in New Jersey, Dad continued to employ mechanics at his auto repair shop in New York. One of those men set a car afire while welding near its gas tank. Then, instead of pushing the burning auto out of the garage, the two mechanics panicked and ran away, and the garage, with three cars under repair, burned to the ground. The building was not insured, but despite the loss, Dad somehow raised the cash to build another garage on the northwest corner of his property.

As the war drew to a close, the United States had a surplus of 270,000 warplanes, and since we only needed a fraction of that number, the military destroyed most of the planes. Manufacturing plants were closed, and workers like my father were laid off.

So we returned to our home at 6 Greenbush Drive, in Poughkeepsie, and before VE (Victory Europe) Day, Dad completed his new garage, and began construction of a retail store at the corner of Greenbush Drive and Violet Avenue. He sold the house on Greenbush Drive to finance the store where he sold commercial refrigeration equipment, and we moved into the apartment above. But when he was almost killed by a leak of hydrogen sulfide gas, he closed that business.

He then opened a forerunner of today's 7-Eleven. Most of the floor area was used to stock groceries, but there was also a small luncheonette in one corner, and two Sunoco gas pumps out front. Dad refused to spend money to blacktop the driveway. I remember raking cigarette butts and gum wrappers out of the crushed stone around the gas pumps. The store did fairly well until the traffic between New York and Albany was shunted from Route 9-G to a newly widened Route 9.

Then Dad bought a couple of tiny house trailers, parked them under the Maple trees on the north side of the store, and stuck "For Sale" signs in their front windows. These little eight foot wide, twenty foot long house trailers were smaller than most RVs on the road today, but there was a shortage of housing and millions of returning veterans eager to marry. So, those tiny homes were an instant success. And with prices well under a thousand dollars, they sold like the proverbial hotcakes. Dad began to pour every cent into increasing his inventory and locating additional sales locations.

To get the cash he needed, he sold the store, including half of the land he owned on the corner of Greenbush Drive, and our family moved into the big garage which he built during the war.

In spite of dad's growing income, we wound up living in that "temporary home" for ten years, from 1947 to 1956. In view of his growing income, some wondered why my mother tolerated living there. They were married during the depression, and dad promised mom that if she'd do without the things most women coveted—from nylon stockings to a house of her own—he would one day buy her anything she asked for.

That garage was far from a conventional home. It was an ugly commercial structure with high unpainted cinder block walls, an oil-stained concrete floor, and a Celotex ceiling. It was a crude facility designed for the servicing of cars and trucks, nothing like the multi-million dollar architectural showplaces where cars are sold and serviced today.

Four cars could easily be parked on the main floor, with space for tool benches and machinery around the perimeter. In the left rear corner, there was a big rectangular cavity in the floor. It was about three feet wide, twelve feet long, and five feet deep, where a mechanic could stand beneath a car and reach up to make repairs, change the oil, and lubricate the chassis. Because of the risk of our falling into that pit, dad had it filled with dirt and capped with concrete.

There was an office area that extended off the south side of the garage, and he converted that into an apartment. It was divided into three rooms: an eleven by eighteen main room, plus a small bathroom and a tiny excuse for a kitchen. That improvised apartment served as our living room, dining room, and my parents' bedroom.

We four boys would spend the next decade sleeping in a dormitory above the garage. The rear half of the attic was partitioned to create a twelve by twenty foot dormitory. The low knee walls and peaked ceiling were covered with large sheets of Celotex, a highly flammable material similar to that used in today's suspended ceiling squares. The only good feature was a beautiful solid oak floor.

To reach our dormitory from the garage below, Dad had a massive plank stairway built in the rear corner. He refused to pay to have a railing placed on the outside edge, so my five-year-old brother, Bobby, was afraid to climb the stairs. Dad threatened him with a spanking if he didn't comply, so I went first, staying as far from the edge of the stairway as possible. Soon enough, however, Bobby and I were carelessly running up and down those stairs.

Not only was the staircase open, but Dad's employees stored combustibles beneath it, and there was no fire door at the top. In fact, there was no door at all, which meant that we were very hot in the summer and very cold in the winter. We once had a bird fly through the garage and up the stairs into our bedroom. He finally escaped through the small window at the end of the room near the stairway.

That window permitted a little circulation and supposedly served as a fire escape. However, Bobby and I were too small to climb over the radiator that was installed beneath it and were therefore, unable to reach the window. Dad assured us that our older brothers would lift us through the window if there were ever a fire.

We did have fire fighting equipment of sorts. It consisted of a soda-acid fire extinguisher that stood in the corner of our dorm near the top of the stairs. All we had to do was flip it over to rupture the cartridge inside and that would initiate an uncontrolled chemical reaction which would expel a foam extinguishing agent. We would just need to aim the little hose at the base of the fire, which would presumably be downstairs. It wasn't the best device, and Underwriters Laboratories Inc. discontinued their use in 1969. But I have a special memory of that fire extinguisher.

Average Guy Meets Extraordinary God

I was probably the only one of us four boys who ever cleaned our dorm room. I remember undertaking that thankless task one afternoon, leaving the room gloriously clean and well organized. I even carefully positioned that fire extinguisher against the wall near my brother John's bed, for he, being oldest, was to take charge of our survival in the event of a fire. Regrettably, around 3 am he somehow knocked it over, and when that fire extinguisher hose began its snakelike undulations, it sprayed foam on the walls, ceiling, floor, and the adjacent bed, which happened to be occupied by a sleeping John. His reaction was something to see, and I regret I missed it, for I felt it prudent to keep my eyes closed.

Wow! Those old soda-acid extinguishers could sure make a mess of a room! And John never forgave me, stating that this 9-year old intentionally placed it by his bed so that he would knock it over. My mother heard his ravings from their downstairs apartment, and ran through the garage and up the stairs to learn what had transpired. Poor Mom; she was frequently left wringing her hands, asking God why He'd given her four sons.

For my part, I kept my eyes tightly shut and faked sleep, while she tried to calm him as they cleaned up the mess and changed his sheets. But he continued screaming that I was awake, and of course he was right. No one could sleep through that racket, but I was counting on Mom, and she came through. He threatened to kill me, but she warned him to leave me alone. He was still muttering dire threats long after the lights were turned out.

The dorm itself was about twelve feet wide and twenty long, and had a gabled ceiling, with thirty-inch-high knee walls on either side. It was like living in a big wall tent. Dad set up two double beds against one long wall, while a single 4-drawer bureau on the opposite wall served the needs of all four of us boys. We each had one drawer, which was sufficient for our limited wardrobes. Johnny built a closet at each end to hang our Sunday-go-to meeting outfits, Boy Scout uniforms, and winter coats. We each had one set of school clothes, one set of play clothes, one pair of shoes, and a pair of cheap canvas sneakers for gym class and after school play. We wore khaki slacks to school; denims were not allowed.

The small window was about thirty inches off the floor at the back of the dorm, near the top of the stairs. At the opposite end, a flimsy door provided access to the attic. John later built a small darkroom for processing photographs just outside that door, in the attic.

Beneath our little window was the roof of the one-story workshop that extended beyond the back of the garage. In theory, if there was a fire, we were to climb through the window to reach the nearly flat tar paper roof, then jump ten feet to the ground below. But as I remarked, there was a small cast iron radiator beneath the window which made it difficult for little Bobby and me to climb over. As we grew older, we had little trouble getting in and out, but Dad refused to let us sleep on that roof on hot summer nights because we might puncture the tarpaper or roll off the slightly sloping roof.

To reach the bathroom, we had to walk down the stairs, across the concrete floor of the garage, passing mom's laundry sink and ringer washer. If it was after bedtime, we had to knock on the door for permission to enter the apartment. It was two steps up from the garage floor to the old office level, and the bathroom was immediately to the right as we entered the "great room." The bathroom was small, with just enough room to walk alongside the tub before reaching the toilet in the left rear corner, and the little porcelain sink hanging in the right-hand corner on the cinder block wall.

To those of us today who consider two bathrooms an absolute minimum, this must sound primitive. Keep in mind that in 1940, only 55% of Americans had indoor plumbing, and few plumbing improvements were made to homes until after the war. With the convenience of indoor baths, plus the availability of piped hot water, many people even began to bathe more than the customary Saturday night. If we managed to get ourselves especially dirty, Mom sometimes made us take an extra bath during the week.

Those post-war years saw advertisers promoting detergents that would remove "Ring around the collar," and the ring around the inside of the bathtub. I remember Mom complaining about the dirty ring around the inside of the tub that remained after we were finished with our baths. Bob and I hated the fact that we had to share the same bath water.

I remember the little sink in the corner, because Dad took me there after he happened to hear me utter a foul word in the garage. I watched him as he thoroughly washed his hands with Ivory soap, but instead of rinsing and drying them, he got a thick layer of soap on his fingers, then ran those soapy fingers around the inside of my mouth.

If you think the threat of having one's mouth washed out with soap is fictional, I can assure you it is not! It was a memorable experience, but not as unpleasant as when I committed what he must have considered a felony, and he removed the wide belt from his slacks, made me drop mine, and applied the rod of correction a half dozen times to my seat of understanding. He seemed to be just warming up about the time I thought he should be finishing.

I recall Bob being in line for a spanking, but Dad and Mom always had a tender spot for their baby, and didn't insist he drop his drawers. They really couldn't keep from laughing when they discovered that he had put several layers of newspaper inside his underwear.

Today, such means of discipline might see the parent prosecuted and jailed, and their abused child removed from their home by some government agency, only to be placed in a group home where he or she can experience all sorts of evil. But in my day, folks correctly believed, "Spare the rod and spoil the child."[8]

Sometimes, corporal punishment is the only means of correcting a recalcitrant child's stinkin' thinkin'. You don't agree? Consider this: during the 1940s, children received fine educations in our public schools. We weren't experiencing 70% truancy, we didn't have kids shoplifting or shooting one another, our jails weren't overflowing with criminals, and multitudes weren't living on our sidewalks, high on drugs.

We've sown the dragon's teeth of permissiveness, and we are reaping a harvest of frustration and hatred. America's decision to reject the Bible's wisdom, and instead follow John Dewey's erroneous advice for the last generation, has resulted in a nation of rebels who run the spectrum from the effete intellectual, anti-Semitic, anti-Christian, self-aggrandizing pro-communist snobs in our "Ivy League" colleges, to the anti-social mobs who run amuck through retail stores, injuring the clerks, and destroying what they don't steal. Worse are those who break into homes to terrorize, rob, rape, and murder.

The Bible states that, *"Foolishness is bound up in the heart of a child; the rod of correction will drive it far from him"* (Proverbs 22:15). There's no question in my mind that my brothers and I were better for the correction we received, and it certainly did no harm.

But most people who strike children today are not interested in their welfare. They don't do it to correct, but to punish or vent their wrath. That's not discipline. True discipline must be tempered with love, and that's what a father is to do: love his sons. Fathers who fail to lovingly correct their children are raising kids who will ultimately be terrible parents.

---

8   This was a common statement in western Christianity throughout the 20th century. The statement is an application drawn from Proverbs 13:24.

There was another room built on that back of the garage. It was Dad's shop where he kept his metal and wood lathes, anvil, table saw, grinder, drill press, acetylene torches, and work benches. The electric welder was out front.

This was the age of "Use it up, wear it out, make it do!" Dad was an inventor and improviser. I remember watching him and another man attach baby carriage wheels to the bottom of a wooden platform, then mount an electric motor on the top, fasten a sharpened length of band iron to the motor shaft that extended beneath the platform, and attach old lawn mower handles, thus creating an early electric lawn mower. It worked, but was dangerous because the operator was prone to run over the electric cable that ran from the mower to the nearest 120-volt electrical outlet, cutting the cord and potentially electrocuting himself.

My oldest brother, John, was the envy of the neighborhood boys because Dad gave him free run of the garage, and John took full advantage. Using scrap iron and old auto parts, he built one of the earliest gas-powered go-carts in America. He also designed three soap box racers, two of which won the local soap box derby.

Through the years, John produced things as diverse as a small working guillotine and a tiny cannon so powerful that it shot a BB through multiple Sears Roebuck and Montgomery Ward catalogs. Those big mail-order catalogs had over 650 pages of product pictures, descriptions, and prices, from mittens for sis to an electric range for mom. Those catalogs were my generation's Amazon and e-Bay. Years later, Mom confessed that the pages from outdated issues had served as a substitute for toilet tissue in outhouses across America. Rags and even leaves also sometimes served.

We lived in that garage ten years, while Dad reinvested every dime he could get his hands on to build his businesses. By 1947, he had three mobile home retail outlets in New York and had built a trailer park in Florida. By 1953, he had five outlets in New York. We still lived in that garage, but Dad now parked a Cadillac beneath our attic dorm, and was financing John's freshman year in college.

My brothers were given a basketball rim our first Christmas there, and the high ceiling in the garage suddenly became a blessing. That winter, the neighborhood boys came by every day to shoot baskets until Mom put put a stop to it because of the racket they made.

Although my older brothers had access to tools that enabled them to create amazing "toys," and were the envy of the boys of the neighborhood, our social opportunities were limited. My younger brother and I were able to play with our neighborhood friends, but few came to our garage. One winter, we invited them over to play marathon Monopoly games at a card table in the middle of the garage, but that ended when one mother concluded that a fully equipped garage put her little boy at risk.

Getting dates with girls posed a different problem. Mothers in the neighborhood thought of us as "Those Becker Boys;" poor folks who lived in a garage. We discovered that we were not destined to take any of the neighborhood girls to a high school sock hop.

Enough was enough. At some point, my mother told my father, "If you don't build me a house, I'm going to leave you." So he built her a house. Two of them.

In 1956, Dad built a beautiful ranch house in Hyde Park, and a year later, he built a pool home in Tampa, Florida. But to our dismay, the house in Hyde Park lay just outside the school district where we grew up, so while my two older brothers were able to graduate from F.D. Roosevelt High School, Bob and I had to transfer to a small rural free school.

Bob accommodated well to the new environment, but during that first semester, while entering the eleventh grade, I came down with a severe case of mononucleosis—the so-called "kissing disease." I took a lot of ribbing, but to my regret I didn't even have the consolation of being infected by a kiss. Worse, it cost me an extra semester in high school.

Because my mother was prone to bronchial infections, my parents decided to spend the winter of 1957 at their new home in Florida. And since I couldn't be left alone in our New York home, I was sent to live with an aunt and uncle near Kingston, where I attended a very large high school. With winter almost over, I was slowly regaining my strength, while trying to adjust to my third high school in a six-month period.

I was trying to catch up on my schoolwork when I suddenly found myself dealing with a somewhat painful lump on the left side of my chest which felt hot to the touch. I was at first too embarrassed to mention it, but finally confided in my uncle. To my surprise, he seemed very concerned, and my aunt immediately called my parents. With winter over, they had returned from Florida to oversee their business activities in New York. The plan was for me to return to our Hyde Park home at the end of the school year, in late May.

At this point, my memory is a bit foggy, but I do remember clearly the morning of April 19, 1957. It was Good Friday. I had celebrated my 17th birthday a month before.

I was awakened to both good news and bad. The good news was that I wouldn't be attending school that day. The bad news was that I wouldn't be allowed breakfast because my uncle was driving me twenty miles to a hospital in northern Dutchess County, where we would be met by my parents, and I would undergo surgery. When my aunt asked how I was feeling, she seemed near tears.

I don't recall much about the trip to the hospital, but I recall lying on a gurney and being prepped for surgery. I didn't have time to feel perplexed or concerned about the cause of my problem. The idea that I might have cancer never entered my mind, but that was what everyone else feared.

I was being operated on to remove what they thought might be inflammatory breast cancer. When the biopsy later revealed that it was a non-malignant cyst, everyone was relieved. Everyone, that is, except me. I was still unconscious. The anesthesiologist couldn't wake me up!

They had put me under for what they thought would be a very brief procedure, but they used Thiopental Sodium, or Sodium Pentothal, a barbiturate, as the anesthetic. I have since learned that Pentothal is very effective for minor surgeries, and patients generally regain consciousness quickly. The drug causes unconsciousness within thirty to forty-five seconds, and a surgeon can proceed almost immediately.

Consciousness generally returns in less than ten minutes, but nowadays, if unconsciousness needs to be extended, they generally switch to a different anesthetic. In 1957, however, they frequently injected more of the Pentothal, which could result in long periods before consciousness was regained, if ever. That may help explain why—after being put to sleep on the morning of Good Friday—I didn't wake up from that "relatively minor surgery" for nearly 48 hours; not until Easter Sunday, the third morning.

I, of course, had no idea of the passing of time, but my mother, who was sitting at my bedside when I finally awoke, was visibly relieved. She blurted that they were worried that I wasn't going to wake up at all, but for me, the entire period was one of absolute unconsciousness. There was no past, no present, no future. I was not asleep. I simply didn't exist.

You can imagine my surprise when I awoke from surgery on Easter Sunday, and was told that I had been talking in my sleep. I didn't learn until later that sodium pentathol is also used as a "truth serum," and that I was likely to have honestly answered any questions my mother put to me while unconscious.

But I did realize that, if I had talked in my sleep, I might have somehow embarrassed myself. I recalled how, at age twelve, I had played hooky from sixth grade, and foolishly written about it in my diary. My mother found my diary, read the account, and later asked me, "Frank-E, is this true?"

Mom called me "Frankie" when things were okay, but if she was upset with me, it was either "Frank-E" or "Frank Edward!" Is that why mothers frequently add a middle name, so that they can use it to emphasize their indignation and anger? Does formalizing a name make it more potent?

Anyway, when she asked whether I had played hooky, I prevaricated. I liked that word, "prevaricated." It seemed to dignify my lie. And that's what I did. I promptly replied, "No."

But formalized or not, it was clear to both of us that I was flat out lying. She surprised me. All she said was, "You won't do it again, will you?" And with great relief, I said, "No, Mom." And I never did play hooky again, but I also never made another diary entry until I had reached adulthood. And then I was very careful about what I included.

When my mother told me I talked while unconscious, I asked, "Did I say anything bad?"

"No," she replied, and I wondered whether she was now the one prevaricating. Then she surprised me. "But you prayed a lot."

Me? Prayed a lot?

I can rarely remember ever praying, except in company with others, bowing my head and closing my eyes in church or over a holiday meal.

As I mentioned earlier, it was shortly after my eighth birthday that I asked Jesus to come into my heart. But I don't know if there was any visible change in the way I lived. In fact, that was pretty much it. The day I accepted the Lord was the end of any significant spiritual activity for nearly a decade. I lived as my family lived, decent enough people, but scarcely ever attending church, much less establishing any sort of a meaningful personal relationship with the Lord Jesus Christ.

On the other hand, unlike the children of this generation, who are exposed to all manner of filth everywhere they turn, I was an incredibly innocent teenager. But I was no goody-two shoes. Like everyone else, I was born to sin. But the evil my feet were quick to run to would be considered pretty tame by today's standards, and it didn't leave very dark stains on my shoes. But sin is not relative, and I did not have, nor shall I ever have, an occasion to boast of anything good that came out of my life, except through Christ.

My mother told me that I had prayed a lot during that period of "nothingness," during that time when I'd had no awareness of my own existence, when I certainly didn't have any conscious control over my words or actions. I would not even have been aware that I had prayed had not my mother told me about it that Easter morning. And what possible motive would she have for making up such a story?

Me? Praying? What an extraordinary idea!

It's true that she was the only parent who ever encouraged church attendance, but through the years my parents had done little to promote spiritual growth. And despite Mom's express desires, Dad argued that he was working seven days a week and was too busy to attend church, so we rarely went. We didn't even pray over meals except at Christmas and Easter.

But time and distance have brought hindsight. By the grace of God, I have lived 85 years, and hopefully I now have a better understanding of our world than I did in my youth. Yet, even now, my understanding is laughably limited.

Isaiah made it clear, "*...as the heavens are higher than the earth, so God's ways are higher than our ways, and his thoughts than our thoughts*" (Isaiah 55:9).

It doesn't take a genius to see that the human race, for all its boasted accomplishments, has not made itself any better. Everywhere we look in the world today, there is perversion, division, strife, hatred, murder, war, hunger, disease, pride, selfishness, lust, malice, and greed. Consider how the world repeatedly faces the same crises, and continually responds with the same ageless errors.

We may have achieved incredible technological advances—many of which enable us to kill one another more efficiently—but the human race hasn't improved at all. Whether or not we accept the fact that each of us participated in Adam's fall, the fact is that all of us exhibit Adam's fallen nature.

Sin seems to dominate, and our pathetic boasts of knowledge and wisdom are little more than mole hills compared to God's mountains of omniscience and power. We desperately need anything that God is willing to share with us.

Over time, I learned that things change when we begin to walk with Jesus. Our thinking and attitudes are refocused by the Holy Spirit. We begin to notice God's hand at work in and around us, and we come to understand things as we never could before salvation. We welcome truths we formerly denied, and even the trials we experience help us to develop spiritual maturity.

My mother told me, "You prayed a lot." I did not see how I could have prayed at all. Nor why. But God doesn't leave us where we are. He wants us to become mature, perfect, and complete. And when we stop short, He is prepared to move us on or move us out. When we are ignorant, He is determined to inform us. When we exalt ourselves, He will humble us. And, if we follow him and fall down, He will pick us up. He's the perfect Father.

God exposed more of my ignorance just a few days before I sat down to write this chapter, and I realized that it has only taken me a mere sixty-eight years from the time my mother told me, "You prayed a lot," to realize the significance of her statement. I happened to be reading through the Apostle Paul's letter to the Romans, and I had an epiphany—instantly and without my seeking it—as God's wisdom often comes. It was really very simple.

Back in 1957, while I was lying unconscious in that hospital recovery room—helpless, hopeless, and hapless—my Savior was looking out for me. He was making intercession for me because I was one of His kids—a King's kid. I was infirm, but not dead; I was down, but not out. It's a scientific fact! I was in a coma! I was helpless! The doctors thought I might not regain consciousness. Yet, I prayed aloud. How could that be?

The Apostle Paul put it this way:

"...Likewise the Spirit also helps in our weaknesses. For we do not know what we should pray for as we ought, but the Spirit Himself makes intercession for us with groanings which cannot be uttered" (Romans 8:26).

What I have come to understand is that the Spirit is not limited to our consciousness to exhibit His grace and glory. Lazarus was dead and his corpse was rotting when Jesus commanded, *"Lazarus, come forth!"*[9]

The Apostle Paul wrote, *"The Spirit also helps in our weaknesses"* (Romans 8:26). I was so weak that I was incapable of praying at all, let alone as I ought to, but the Spirit Himself made intercession for me with groaning which I, without Him, could not utter. But I uttered something. My mother heard me.

Now, 68 years and several actual life-threatening diseases later, I am far better able to understand. For there may be times when we are unable

---

9   John 11:43b

to pray: times when we are utterly helpless, times when we are asleep, when we are ill, when we are injured, or confused.

The Holy Spirit prayed through me with words I was unable to consciously verbalize, indeed I was unaware of my existence; but the Holy Spirit dwelt within me. And those unconscious prayers of a rambunctious teenage son certainly served as a testimony to my mother.

If you don't consider yourself very religious, but you once found yourself in a place where you were so desperate that you turned to prayer, you may wonder why you still remember that particular moment. Perhaps the Spirit prayed through you. He was certainly convicting you of sin, and righteousness, and judgment.

The world speaks of "the power of prayer." I don't believe in that dubious unfocused phrase—"the power of prayer." Prayer can be perfunctory, or a matter of hard and painful persistence, but prayer is still only a means of communication. It is the Object of our prayers that is important, the Person to whom we pray. Christians know that the Object of our prayers is the Mediator between God and man—Christ Jesus! We pray because we believe in the power that the Lord will wield in answer to our prayers.

Prayer is our means of communicating with God. He has infinite knowledge, wisdom, and power! Prayer is conversation with God. It can consist of worship, adoration, petition, or thanksgiving. It is how we ask God for help, and how we thank Him for answers. And best of all, it is one way we can express our love to Him. That's why we are commanded to come boldly to the throne of grace and make our requests known to God.[10]

But even those who are fervent practitioners of prayer are sometimes forced to acknowledge their occasional inability to touch the heart of God. Sometimes they simply don't know what to pray. Sometimes the heavens seem like brass, and their words come ringing back, seemingly unanswered.

They are unable to conceptualize their needs. They can't identify, much less express their true and honest feelings. They can't imagine an answer that would suffice. They may even find themselves called upon to judge the conduct of others, and cannot decide who is right or wrong, much less what to pray for or how to express it in words.

Many Christians have trouble believing that the Lord will hear their prayers, much less that He has the power and the will to answer them. At

---

10   Hebrews 4:16

such times, some people simply say, "The Lord's will be done." And while that may sometimes be a satisfactory way to handle a problem, it can become an evasion. It can even be an act of negligence that plants the seeds of doubt to fester in their lives, in the lives of their loved ones, and in the Church.

We need to "pray through." We need to persist, until we are satisfied that we have prayed enough, or perhaps until the Spirit prays through us. We dare not fall short. *"Therefore, to him that knows how to do good, and doeth it not, to him it is sin"* (James 4:1).

Prayer can be hard work. It takes time from life's responsibilities and pleasures. It often seems non-productive. Prayer requires confidence in God that He will do what is best for us.

There is no boast here. I make no claim to being a great prayer warrior. Quite the contrary. And on that Easter weekend in 1957, this worldly teenager was lying there unconscious. If I was praying, it was not I, but Christ in me, for I knew and felt nothing!

If you think that I babbled, or spoke gibberish and nonsense, then my words here will hold no meaning for you. But my mother told me that identifiable thoughts came out of my mouth! Something from my subconscious? Unlikely. The computer programmer will tell you, "Garbage In, Garbage Out!" I had not been feasting on God's Word but on the ideas and ideals of the world around me. Yet, something good did come out, and I'm certainly not going to take credit for speaking something good. I can only conclude that the Holy Spirit spoke through me.

As I look back, what occurred seems clearly the providence of God. Some might even call it a miracle. Isn't it a miracle when the Holy Spirit intercedes through us, or speaks through us, sharing some idea or concept that is so sublime and glorious that we could never have thought of it or expressed it on our own?

My mother thought it was a miracle that I woke up. I think it was a miracle that I prayed while I was unconscious.

"In peace I will both lie down and sleep, For You alone, LORD, have me dwell in safety."

Psalm 4:8

CHAPTER 12

Grandma Had
the Last Word

*"I thank God...when I call to remembrance the genuine
faith that is in you, which dwelt first in your grandmother Lois
and your mother Eunice, and I am persuaded is in you also."*

2 Tim 1: 3, 5

Where did the journey begin that finally led me to the ministry at age thirty? Surely it was a matter of God's calling. Yet, while God determines our paths, He obviously works through those around us, using them as His instruments to help guide us.

I entered kindergarten as World War II was ending, and to me, even teenagers seemed old and wise. And why not? Those teens were sobered by the labors, the privations, and the fears that had been thrust upon them by the war, and would forever bear the memories of the deaths of friends and loved ones.

Some teenagers, in patriotic fervor, rushed to the enlistment offices to risk their lives for "Mother, Apple pie, and the American Way of Life." I understand that my cousin, Bill Herman, who stood six feet, five inches tall at the age of fifteen, tried answering the call. Being underage, he was caught, and sent home. Not to be denied, he enlisted in another branch of the service, and survived the war.

Some teens today, as well as many adults in the so-called X, Y, and Z Generations, seem so childish by comparison. Regardless of diverse backgrounds, their actions reveal that many are spoiled and full of self, and self-pity. Their sense of entitlement reveals a complete lack of understanding of how and why America became a rich, free, and productive nation.

Consider both the symptoms and the results of their spiritual malaise. As a result of the breakdown of faith, morality, and patriotism, America—which was once the "breadbasket of the world" and "the land of the free and home of the brave"—has become rife with crime, immorality, perversion, and homelessness. As a result, our nation is beginning to receive its recompense. We are experiencing trials that will force everyone to either grow up or give up; to bear the responsibility for their actions, or lapse into servitude.

As difficult as things were during World War II and as divided as we sometimes found ourselves politically, there was a spiritual cohesiveness that bound the diverse people of our nation together. Today, everywhere we look, there is hatred, division, and strife. Much of it is provoked by evil people who encourage and exploit division in order to profit from it, and even to destroy our way of life. But the flames are growing more intense because of the sin that is in the hearts of so many.

Compared to the dangers that little children face today—such as parental neglect and abuse, kidnapping and child trafficking, immorality and sexual perversion, poor educations and ignorance of God's Word—most of the things my peers worried about during World War II now seem relatively laughable. In Europe, of course, there was hunger and homelessness, the threat of slave labor camps and the gas chambers. And while millions of Jews perished, millions of non-Jews were also enslaved, starved, tortured, and executed.

Children in America didn't require much protection because society was constrained by strict rules of behavior, and curbed by the threat of the law. Yes, my mother worried about us succumbing to many of the things to which children are prone, whether being run over by a car because we played in the road, or contracting some fatal disease, or even possibly being harmed by a beggar or criminal.

But the worst danger I can remember is laughable. It occurred sometime during 1944, when two of our aunts—Dad's twin sisters, Evelyn and Ethelyn—were scheduled to visit our home. My younger brother Bob and I shared bad memories of an earlier meeting with those aunts, and we tried to find a place to hide. But Mom rooted us out from our hiding place in the back of a closet, and insisted that we say "Hello." It was as we feared. While saying how cute we were, they both pinched our cheeks so hard that they left bruises.

Bob and I were born before the United States entered World War II, so we weren't war babies or "baby boomers." And during those years of bitter conflict, our mother made sure we remained innocent and ignorant toddlers.

After our family returned from New Jersey to the house on Greenbush Drive, we discovered that we now had elderly tenants living in the west side of our house, in what had been my late grandfather's medical offices. On occasion, I was permitted to pass through the French doors that separated our living room from theirs, and visit with Mr. Benjamin. He would turn down his radio, tap the tobacco out of his pipe and hang it on a rack, then ask me to do something like count backwards from one hundred to one. I still remember the fragrant odor that clung to his clothing. He insisted that I count from one to one hundred, and then reverse the process. But, at my mother's insistence, when the war news came on the radio, he dutifully sent me back through the French doors to our part of the house.

Our trials of life were pretty bland, while those around us bore the burdens of war. But it was a different America then. Yes, there was prejudice and hatred and crime, but it was still a far kinder and gentler America. There was little risk of some pervert molesting us, much less a public school teacher attempting to groom us or physically alter our sex.

Our aunts took what pleasure they could find in life, which evidently included pinching their nephew's cheeks. But their mother—our grandmother—was different. Elina Becker was Dad's mother, and she was not frivolous like her daughters. In fact, both of our grandmothers seemed very serious, focused on their love for God.

My mom's mother, Martha Klaus, and my dad's mother, Elina Becker, came from very different backgrounds, but both were nonetheless devout Christians.

My mother, Loretta May Klaus, was born in 1914, near the beginning of the 20th century. She was born only about a month before the assassination of Archduke Franz Ferdinand of Austria, the event that triggered World War I. She was the only daughter of Martha Odell and William Klaus.

Grandpa Bill was an infantryman in World War I, and I have a fading photo of him in the "doughboy's" uniform of the American Expeditionary Force. Cavalrymen used the term "doughboys" to deride foot soldiers, because the brass buttons on their uniforms looked like flour dumplings or dough cakes called "doughboys", and because of the color of their uniforms.

Mom had three brothers, Harvey, Larry, and Ansley, whom they called Andy. They lived on a small hard-scrabble farm atop Grafton Mountain, about fifteen miles east of Troy, New York.

Mom often told the story of how she walked her youngest brother, five-year old Andy, to his first day at school. Since it was five-year-old Andy's first day at school, he was unaware that students were not permitted to speak without raising a hand to receive permission. Andy asked a question, and the teacher decided to make an example of him by holding his hand down on a desktop and striking his knuckles ten times with a ruler.

District No 5 School House, Grafton, New York

My mother was outraged. She defied the teacher, warning him that he was not to touch her little brother. Then she took Andy by the hand and stormed out of the school, walking the child back home. I assume that Andy ultimately returned to the school, but my mother ended her formal education that day—her first day in the fourth grade. My mother was anything but ignorant, however, and I remember her as a voracious reader with an extensive vocabulary. Mom proved that a person could become very knowledgeable without access to a formal education.

My first memory of Mom's mother consists of a visit we made to her childhood home when I was perhaps four years old. I remember grandma giving me permission to go get the two cows at milking time. I still recall struggling up a narrow rock strewn cow path that was overhung by weeds, and stopping to remove cockleburs from my corduroy slacks.

Suddenly I was aware of the tinkling of a bell, and then of being lifted bodily off the pathway. Someone held me in his arms as I watched what seemed to be an enormous cow, a bell swinging back and forth beneath her neck, making her way imperiously down the narrow path on which I'd just been standing. I had been unaware that one of my uncles was just a few steps behind me, watching over me to keep me safe.

During the Great Depression, Mom's father, William Klaus was blessed with the meager income of a forest fire spotter. He kept watch from atop the Dickinson Hill Fire Tower, at the top of Grafton Mountain, now a historic landmark. His three sons were hard workers, not merely caring for the family livestock, but actually building a barn, and even moving hundreds of large boulders to form a causeway across the swampy area that lay between their house and the dirt road that fronted their property. When I drove past that property in the 1970s, a professor from Rensselaer Polytechnic Institute had set up several big radio antenna on the property, and was reliably communicating with ham radio operators around the world.

My grandparents were among millions of poor and hard-working American farmers who struggled unceasingly to pry their livings from the rocky soil. But because they raised their own livestock, grew their own crops, canned their own fruits and vegetables, churned their own butter, and bartered for what they couldn't themselves produce, they survived the Great Depression far better than many city dwellers.

They cut their own firewood, yet except for the kitchen, the house wasn't very warm. I remember a Christmas visit when Bobby and I were tucked into a bed beneath icy cold sheets and blankets because the house was so cold. Nor was it much fun being carried through deep snow to reach the "three holer" outhouse, an experience that does not bear description. But I also remember watching grandma stirring the coals in her big kitchen range in preparation for preparing an incredible Christmas dinner.

Two of Mom's brothers graduated from Ivy League colleges, Harvey from Harvard and Larry from Cornell. Andy's education would take place on the islands of the South Pacific during World War II, and would terminate with his tragic death in an auto accident less than two weeks after he returned home from the Pacific.

While my mother's mother lived a simple farm life, my father's mother, Elina Tabor, came from a well-to-do family. Unlike Grandma Klaus, my father's mom was privileged to attend a "finishing school," and became a talented landscape artist. One of her brothers was a New York lawyer and the other a New York architect.

Grandmother Tabor married John Isaac Becker, MD, a medical doctor, and their family dwelt in large homes wherever his practice took him. They had six children. Elizabeth, their first born, passed away at age sixteen. Her siblings, were Frances; followed by the twins, Evelyn and Ethelyn; then my dad, John Sanford, and finally the baby, Charlotte.

Consider the contrast in the lives of the two families during the Great Depression. While my mom's mother had four children, and toiled as a dirt-poor farmer's wife, Elina had six children, and was a country doctor's wife. If Dr. John was fortunate enough to be paid for his services, he might be compensated with poultry or produce, rather than hard coin. As a result, both grandmothers were often challenged to put sufficient food on the table, but Elina enjoyed a far more gentile lifestyle. Yet, in spite of their different backgrounds, they were both devout Christians.

I have several century-old Christian chorus books that belonged to Dr. John, that he used when he was a member of various Christian men's vocal groups. His grave is in a church cemetery in Clinton Corners, New York, and carved into his headstone is this quote from a hymn by Philip Bliss:

> Dare to be a Daniel,
> Dare to stand alone!
> Dare to have a purpose firm!
> Dare to make it known. [11]

I never met my dad's father because he passed away a year before I was born, and I didn't know either of my grandmothers very well. But it appears that both of my grandmothers took special interest in me. Perhaps that was because I was polite and willing to sit and listen to them, while my brothers always found excuses to run off and play.

I was five-and-a-half years old when World War II ended. Grandmother Klaus was in her sixties, and had remarried. She was a robust woman, but she and her second husband, who then owned an Oklahoma truck farm, grew weary of their struggles with droughts, floods, and tornadoes. He passed away, and she moved back to New York. I recall seeing photographs of the incredibly large cantaloupes they grew in Oklahoma.

Grandma Klaus worked long hours all her life and took a fundamentalist's view of the Scriptures. During the 1970s, shortly before her death at age 93, I met her for the last time. She expressed delight that I had entered the ministry, told me that she prayed for me daily, and gave me a

---

11   Accessed online July 1, 2025: https://hymnary.org/text/standing_by_a_purpose_true

copy of a Bible that she treasured because it had been signed by evangelist Oral Roberts. Sadly, I gave that family heirloom away.

Grandmother Becker may have had a sophisticated childhood and attended a young lady's finishing school, but as the wife of a country doctor and the mother of six, she didn't enjoy much leisure. But some of her ancestors did. One book I read stated that Grandma Becker's ancestors, the Tabors, once owned two castles on fifty square miles of land in Flanders. During the 17th Century, Flanders was a southern province of the Netherlands, but disappeared as a political entity during the French Revolutionary Wars. It is now part of Belgium.

On Grandpa Becker's side, one of our ancestors, Cornelius Melyn, was the Dutch Patroon who owned New York's Staten Island. He led an exciting life, even surviving shipwreck on his way back to Holland to expose the crimes of his adversary, the scheming Peter Stuyvesant. Another ancestor was secretary to the governor in Fort Orange, now Albany, while a third was exiled into the wilderness at age 70 because he was considered incorrigible. So, I have sort of a checkered ancestry.

As a young woman, Grandma Becker painted beautiful landscapes in oils. One of her paintings hangs today in the home of Sharon Becker, widow of my brother John. When I met her, Grandma Becker was almost helpless, blinded by cataracts.

Though both of my grandmothers were Christians, due to her early involvement in my life, Grandma Becker had the greater impact on me, though, I wouldn't realize it until many years later.

In the 1940s, Grandma Becker lived with the family of my father's youngest sister, Charlotte Hunt. They lived on a farm that had been in her husband's family for nearly a century. They operated a summer resort, or boarding camp, popular with New Yorkers during the first half of the 20th Century, and they were initially well to do. Shortly after World War II ended, I even rode in their new Cadillac.

Evidently my Aunt Charlotte complained to my dad that she was overworked and needed a break, so in 1946 Grandma Becker came to stay with us for a short time, in our apartment above my dad's new store. But her visit was difficult for all of us. My older brothers, John and Bill, shared one of two small bedrooms, while Bob and I shared the other, and Mom and Dad had the master. At the Hunt farm, Grandma had her own bedroom, but in our small apartment, she had to sleep on the sofa in the living room, and had little privacy.

The living room had been our gathering place in the evenings, and we boys often lay on the carpet and listened to the radio. I remember Dad's' jubilation when we went to bed after hearing the radio commentator declare that Dewey had defeated Truman in the 1948 presidential election, only to awaken and learn that the opposite was true. But we all enjoyed listening to "The Lone Ranger," "The Shadow," and "Fibber McGee and Molly." These activities ceased when our blind Grandma arrived.

But whenever we were in the same room, she would ask if one of us would please read the Bible to her. It was a book that she always had close at hand, but when she asked, the older boys quickly made themselves scarce. I was just learning to read, but I did try once. I stumbled over the difficult language of the King James Bible, and as I tried to sound out each word, she would pronounce it for me. It was obvious that she pretty much had it memorized, and I soon gave up.

The next time she visited was the winter of 1952, when we were spending the winter in Florida. We lived in a tiny cottage that Dad had converted from a two-car garage. It sat on the front corner of his Sunset Bay Trailer Park, an eight acre parcel located at 4013 West Shore Boulevard, on the west shore of Old Tampa Bay. Grandma was again forced to sleep on a sofa in the living room because we had only two bedrooms. Mom and Dad had one, and we four boys slept on double bunks in the other.

Grandma, now completely blind, again asked us to read her Bible to her, and again I was the only one willing. I remember reading from the book of Luke on a couple of different occasions, but then I too quietly rebelled, and escaped to play with the other kids.

Looking back, however, I realize that my wily old grandmother had more than her own spiritual edification in mind. And her motives are at the heart of this chapter. She knew that if I read God's Word, it might not seem to have an immediate impact on me, but it would have an enduring one.

Grandma Becker tried to do what I believe my parents often tried to do, *"Train up a child in the way that he should go, and when he is old, he will not depart from it"* (Proverbs 22:6). She believed the words of the great prophet Isaiah: *"So shall my word be that goeth forth out of my mouth, it shall not return unto me void, but it shall accomplish that which I please, and it shall prosper in the thing whereto I sent it"* (Isaiah 55:11).

It is impossible to evaluate your life, even when you are old, but as I look back, I am astounded at the Truth of the Scriptures, for as a formerly belligerent and blaspheming heretic, I am living proof that God's word is

"*...quick, and powerful, and sharper than any two-edged sword, piercing even to the dividing asunder of soul and spirit, and of the joints and marrow, and is a discerner of the thoughts and intents of the heart*" (Hebrews 11:1). The Bible that my grandmother introduced me to continues to discern my thoughts and shape my intentions. It also shows the way to the peace that passes understanding, to the end of earthly anxieties, and leads to joy indescribable and full of glory.

The Apostle Paul spoke of "*...the genuine faith...*"[12] which first dwelt in Timothy's grandmother. The same applies to my two grandmothers. Thank you, Grandma Becker and Grandma Klaus for introducing me to God's living Word. You truly had the last Word!

---

12   2 Timothy 1:5

Chapter 13

Christian Mythologists

"But the natural man does not receive the things of the Spirit of God, for they are foolishness to him; nor can he know them, because they are spiritually discerned"

1 Corinthians 2:14

———————

After I lost a semester in high school due to illness, I wound up graduating from Tampa's Hillsborough High School in the same class as my younger brother. It was 1959, and Disney World was probably just a twinkle in Walt Disney's imaginaneering eye. Orlando was only a backwater city, and our college town was even smaller, about a third of its size.

Bob and I chose the same college. He had an ambition to become an architect and I was impressed by *The Fountainhead*, by atheist Ayn Rand, and by the architecture of Frank Lloyd Wright. The college we chose was originally established to prepare young men and women for the ministry, but preparation for Christian ministry is notably absent from its current website. Instead, it now states that the college, "maintains its commitment to academic excellence through 70+ undergraduate programs and graduate programs ...."[13]

———————

13   Accessed online February 5, 2026; Florida Southern College, https://www.flsouthern.edu

Nor was the profession of ministry emphasized when Bob and I enrolled there over six decades ago. Yet, ministerial and missionary training were precisely the reasons the school was founded, and the reason why my roommate, Steve Wise, and I signed on in 1959. We both planned to enter the ministry.

It didn't take us long to have our minds changed. We knew little of church politics in America during the first half of the 20th Century, or how the old mainline denominations were substituting socialism for salvation, turning to so-called "higher criticism" of the Bible, thus infecting the minds of their adherents and future leaders with error, and effectively rejecting the Bible's divine origin, its inerrancy, the virgin birth, the divinity of Jesus, the resurrection, and the atonement. Their sort has been around a long time. In fact, the Apostle Paul actually cursed them: *"As we have said before, so now I say again, if anyone preaches any other gospel to you than what you have received, let him be accursed."* (Galatians 1:9).

Nor was Steve or I aware that our mainline denomination, as a member of both the National and World Council of Churches, had become, not just a voice for the left, but was diverting huge sums from the donations of believing Christians to support leftist and even communist causes. Both Steve's parents and mine had raised us in the same denomination, assuring us both that it embraced the most accurate biblical interpretations and values. They were wrong!

When I was about twelve years old, my three brothers and I were baptized in a private ceremony at our large local church. Its supporters included wealthy and influential members of Dutchess County society. The church boasted that they had just raised $25,000 to refurbish their impressive pipe organ, an amount equivalent to about $300,000 in today's dollars. The emphasis was no longer on aggressive efforts to reach the world's lost and to edify the saints. Instead, efforts were focused on "bricks, butts, and bucks," and the subsequent potential for political influence.

Seventy years have passed, and so has that impressive brick church building. Today, as is the case with thousands of other church structures built during the late 19th and early 20th centuries, that building is gone, wiped from the surface of the earth and from most people's memories. All that remains is a grass-covered corner lot with a small commemorative plaque to mark its former glory.

But during the first half of the 20th century, denominations like the one to which we belonged were able to accumulate huge endowments, with real estate assets alone totaling hundreds of millions of dollars. And the interest received from that vast wealth enabled them to continue operating through the decades, even when income began to decline because devout members were fleeing their ranks. Even now, Bible-believing members are withdrawing their local churches from that mainline denomination, though they must fight for the right to keep the real estate they paid for.

Steve and I knew nothing of these events. For my part, I had no idea what I should do with my life. However, the idea of becoming a church pastor seemed like a noble and dignified ambition, which is a very poor reason for pursuing the ministry.

Steve and I survived freshman orientation and began the first week of classes. I think our very first class was Introduction to the Old Testament. It was taught by the bishop of our denomination for the west coast of Florida, so we were initially confident that we were going to learn from the best.

The very first words out of his mouth, however, shocked both of us, and to this day we can both quote him verbatim: "All of the stories in the Old Testament are merely myths used to present moral principles." Steve and I were sitting next to one another when he made that fatal statement, and we immediately exchanged looks of disbelief and disgust.

As ignorant as I was, I knew that the Bible dealt with God's involvement with the race through thousands of years of history. Indeed, it dealt with eternal issues. Multitudes still considered the Bible to be God's' divine Word, and I knew that more copies of that book was being printed every year than any other book. Equally important, our conservative Jewish friends also took "the stories" in what we call the Old Testament to be factual.

Both the Old and New Testaments are filled with accounts of miracles that God used to demonstrate His presence and power. So why should a so-called man of God open his class by denying their validity?

We immediately concluded that this man did not consider the Bible to be an adequate basis for his faith, and would therefore be making up his own religion as he went along. Worse, he was leading others into error, or driving them away, which, in retrospect, was the best thing he could do. In an instant of time, the stature of this "bishop," and the denomination for which he spoke, diminished in our eyes. We mentally walked away from our church and our calling, and immediately withdrew from his class.

Average Guy Meets Extraordinary God

Our instructor, the "bishop" had called those stories in the Old Testament "mere myths." As far as we were concerned, he was the "mythologist," a hypocrite and a false teacher, and we did not want to study under him, nor be involved in a religion in which he was a leader.

As a result, I began to neglect and even mock the Lord. But as I look back, I realize that it was actually God's way of protecting Steve and me. It kept us from following such men as this and from devoting our lives to error.

There is an incredible irony here. During the years I spent at that central Florida college, Steve and I occasionally drove past a tiny campus on the north side of town, and ignorantly repeated the mocking criticisms we'd heard from others. "That's a Christian Bible school, and the students are a bunch of religious fanatics and holy rollers."

Today that little school, obviously far more faithful to God's Word than the one we were attending, has grown to an enrollment of over 8,000 students. I wonder how my life might have been changed had I possessed the wisdom to listen to the still small voice that whispered to me to visit that little campus back in 1959.

My roommate, Stephen R. Wise, became a conservative Baptist and remained true to his faith through his evolving careers. He worked first in physical education, then as a college administrator, and finally as a Florida state legislator and state senator. As a senator, Steve chaired the committee responsible for allocating billions each year for public education.

The word "professor" means to profess or make a claim, and in the years that followed our mythologist's claim that "all the stories in the Old Testament are merely myths," I entered three different colleges, repeatedly dropping out to work on some special project of my father's, such as opening an upscale restaurant, or selling homes. I frequently traveled between New York and Florida, working in the various businesses he operated, from furniture manufacturing, and auto battery distribution, to food services, residential developments, motel operations, and home sales.

In 1966, I even made a run for the New York State Senate and was appointed Emergency Housing Officer for the Dutchess County Civil Defense department. During that tumultuous decade, Joy and I married and started a family. When my father passed away in 1968, I began searching for more meaning in life.

First, Joy and I attended a mainline church near our new home in

Highland, New York, but the pastor actually praised Communism from the pulpit. We then tried a couple of other churches, but they seemed more like social clubs than places of faith and worship. During the early '60s, I had resisted an invitation by my close friend, Bill Adams, Jr. to visit his church, but years later, after another friend, Al Salay, invited us, Joy and I finally visited.

Our impressions of the church were different. Joy had no use for a "shouting preacher," as she referred to the pastor, but the Holy Spirit somehow used his sermons to deeply convict me. Each week, when I left the church, I was determined not to return the following Sunday, but I felt compelled.

Years later, when our "shouting pastor" disgraced himself and was thrown out of the ministry, I realized that, despite his hypocrisy, he had preached the Truth. God had used that Truth to transform my life. As the Bible declares, "My word will not return to me void."[14]

I soon found myself attending Sunday School and Wednesday evening services. Joy and I became counselors to the teenagers, and we began tithing. My adult Sunday School teacher, Henry Flora, became a friend and supporter.

So it was, that some twenty years after I gave my heart to the Lord, and more than a decade after Steve Wise and I walked out of that "mythologist's" classroom, the Lord led me to a place of worship where his Word was honored. God made His presence real, and while I loved the variety and challenge of running a business, it wasn't a difficult decision to change the direction and style of my life.

In August of 1970, we enrolled at a conservative Bible College, in southern Pennsylvania, so I guess it can be said that I too had become one of those "religious fanatics" that Steve and I had ridiculed years earlier. We had come to believe that the Bible is the Word of God, and that It is our sole rule for faith and life. As a result, we were led to serve God, though I have never witnessed anyone doing any holy rolling.

I recently asked myself, "were those intervening decades wasted?" God forbid! For those years were filled with challenges and experiences that God used to better equip me for later pastoral work.

But I began to learn humility. When I entered Bible college, I went from being a respected businessman and the man called "boss," to a stu-

---

14   Isaiah 55:11

dent on probation and the least respected part-time employee in a local restaurant.

This was part of the process by which God shielded me from the errors of the "Christian mythologists." He changed me from being a self-proclaimed agnostic and blasphemer, and put me on the path to service. To me, at least, it was amazing! I'm reminded of this promise: *"He will not allow your foot to slip; He who keeps you will not slumber"* (Psalm 121:3).

Chapter 14

Freak Accidents and Illnesses

"Whether it is pleasing or displeasing, we will obey the voice of the LORD our God ... that it may be well with us ...."
Jeremiah 42:6

Why do we blame things on God that we should blame on ourselves, or on others, or even on the agents of darkness?

My childhood friends, Jimmy McCambridge and Brent Smith, both became ill and passed away while in junior high school. Other friends lost their lives in combat while fighting for our country. Some ask, "Why did God allow this?"

If someone is killed by a drunk driver, the law blames the drunk. But when a seemingly innocent young person is struck down by illness, someone inevitably asks, "How could God let a thing like that happen?"

Many years ago, a friend of mine rejected my attempts to speak to him about the love of God. He rebuffed me by asking, "How could a loving God allow my wife to wither away with muscular dystrophy?" At the time that he asked me that question, his wife was at home under the care of nurses, while he was having an affair with his secretary.

My friend's question implied that God is the bad guy. Yet, we should place the blame elsewhere. How about the devil and all his demons? How about the multitudes of selfish, greedy, ambitious, and even murderous people whose hateful words and careless or intentional acts have resulted in injury and death to countless millions? People like Hitler and Stalin? What about those who produced and sold tobacco products and alcoholic beverages that resulted in the deaths of so many. Or more recently, those who depressed our nation, closed our schools and stifled commerce, forced us to wear face masks, and infected us with dangerous vaccines whose deadly results are just beginning to manifest themselves in an epidemic of heart disease and cancer?

For that matter, how about you and me? I can recall a seemingly innocent question I once asked that may have inadvertently crushed the spirit of another person, and might even have precipitated her suicide. My responsibility as a human being is to offer love and life through Christ, not words, products, or fake remedies that harm and destroy!

It has become a far more dangerous world than the one I knew as a child. People today are being arbitrarily attacked and murdered in public places, suffering home invasions, having their autos and identities stolen, and even having the government force dangerous medications on them.

Bacterial and viral infections are blind to the character and the ages of their victims. Millions died from the Spanish Flu in the early 20th century. Millions more died from Covid. Apart from the risks that people pose to us, we also live in a world plagued with diseases. And man, not God, exacerbates the problems. For example, Covid was created in a laboratory, and the faulty vaccines that cost us trillions, were forced on us by government edict, while miracle drugs like Ivermectin were berated and outlawed.

All this points to the fact that not all pandemics are natural phenomenon. It is suggested that the Chinese Communists are responsible for the Covid pandemic, and it was exacerbated by people in our own government. My best friend Al, and my brother John, both succumbed to Covid. God is not the villain here!

We dislike accepting blame for our own failures. We hate even more the concept of "original sin"-- the idea that we were sinners at birth because of Adam's transgression. The idea that Adam could bring sin and corruption into the world, simply because he disobeyed God and took a bite of fruit, is unacceptable to most people—just another one of the "... myths used to present moral principles." Our society doesn't want to accept the idea that one man, the progenitor of the race, could bring disaster on all of us who followed him.

Yet, those same people would have no trouble accepting the idea that a U.S. President, with the consent of the Senate, has the power to make treaties with foreign nations that every one of us must abide by, even though we may disagree with them, and even though they might result in the collapse of our economy or a war that results in the deaths of ourselves and our loved ones. We even pay taxes to support those who make faulty and even criminal decisions.

Adam, like Jesus, was created innocent. Unlike Jesus, Adam was not perfect. If he had been perfect, we might not be in this mess. Adam and Eve lived in a climate-controlled garden, enjoyed perfect health, and dined on the finest organic foods. But God did not create them as robots. He permitted them free will, and though they lived the ideal life, they chose to sin. And when they decided to exercise their free will, weighing God's loving command against Satan's hateful lie, they succumbed to the temptation to do something that was forbidden, and disobeyed God.

And now we must earn our livings by the sweat of our brows, suffer pain in childbirth, weed our lawns and gardens, poison dangerous insects, wash our vegetables, dispose of our garbage, purify our water, process our sewage, store depleted uranium in subterranean chambers, wear surgical masks, and lock our doors.

You may be interested in the fact that DNA researchers in Basel, Switzerland recently determined that the human race all began with one man and one woman.[15] That leads me to comment that, the more things scientists discover, the more they confirm God's Word.

You're free to reject the idea of original sin. But you can't escape the result. The real point is that—whether you were born with the sin of Adam, or take perverse pride in sinning on your own—you and I have sinned and come short of the glory of God.

When you were two years old, if your mother caught you with your hand in the cookie jar with crumbs on your lips, nobody had to teach you to deny your theft. It came quite naturally. Whether you wish to call it original sin, or simply a propensity to err that none of us can avoid, we are all sinners. And, sooner or later, we will all have to deal with the consequences of our sin.

It's estimated that between fifty and a hundred million people perished during World War II. Only God knows the number! We can't even begin to comprehend the horror, but when we start directing our hatred toward others, we should begin to understand the reasons.

---

15   earth.com/news/humankind-originated-two-adults/

Average Guy Meets Extraordinary God

The Apostle Paul encapsulates our problem in one sentence: "*Wherefore, as by one man sin entered into the world, and death by sin; and so death passed upon all men, for that all have sinned*" (Romans 5:12). It may sound like an oversimplification, but my two friends, Brent and Jimmy, died because sin came into the world. That explanation may be difficult for us to swallow, but it all goes back to our beginnings.

Many are troubled as to why certain individuals live longer while so many "good" men and women die young. Yet the Hitlers and Stalins live long enough to set the world ablaze. Those wicked leaders received the power to rule from the people they later enslaved and murdered, and the people themselves often elevated them because they were selfish, short-sighted, irresponsible, or willfully ignorant. But those people were tainted because sin came into the world, and Hitler and Stalin were energized by the Devil.

At the age of three, I became seriously ill. I was one of 190,000 infants who contracted whooping cough in 1943, and I was one of those who survived, despite the fact that the newly developed antibiotics were only available on the battlefields. Why did God heal me when so many other infants were perishing from flu, pertussis, measles, tuberculosis, and polio?

Whooping cough is not the only disease with which I've been afflicted over the past 84 years. As I look back, I can't recall the many times my life has been in danger. Yet, I inexplicably survived while others perished. Should I feel guilty for being a repeat survivor of various dangers? I'm not qualified to judge. It is beyond my understanding and control. But I should certainly feel obligated to make the most of the life God has given me. What kind of dangers am I talking about? Here's one example.

After my father sold his first few house trailers in 1946, he began searching for additional locations. One evening, he sat me down on the bench seat in his 1948 pickup truck, and we drove across the beautiful Mid-Hudson Bridge to Route 9-W, in Highland, New York. I sat there with my little legs extended in front of me. I was in continual danger of sliding off the seat because seat belts and children's car seats wouldn't come into use for another twenty or thirty years.

We pulled into the parking lot of a closed gas station that was located on the west side of the big traffic circle in Highland. This building was far more substantial than the little frame structure with a single gas pump that my dad had owned years before. It was much larger, was constructed of concrete blocks, and had big picture windows on either side of the front door.

Dad obviously liked the location. There was enough space to display at least a dozen house trailers out front, which could be viewed daily by the hundreds of drivers who drove around the traffic circle. As he stood there, negotiating the rental, I stared out the window at the passing traffic. I watched in fascination as a tractor trailer rounded the circle, and saw one of its wheels came loose and begin rolling toward us.

"Daddy!" I shouted. He must have heard the concern in my voice because, instead of showing annoyance at the interruption, he looked where I was pointing and saw the wheel rolling toward the building. Then he grabbed me and ran toward the back of the building.

That wheel and tire was probably three feet high and weighed maybe a hundred pounds. When it broke loose from the truck's spinning lugs, it rolled toward us at twenty-five or thirty miles per hour. I had no concept of kinetic energy, nor the destructive power represented, but when that wheel struck the corner of the building, just to the left of the picture window, there was a tremendous crash.

My dad, and the man who owned the building, stood there in shock. When they examined the outside of the building, they discovered that the wheel had driven the entire bottom four courses of concrete blocks back about an inch off the foundation. Dad said that if it had hit under the window, rather than at the corner of the building, it would have broken through the wall, and we might have been killed. But it didn't, and no one was injured!

I guess I still thought it was a great location because I remember asking in my innocence whether the building could be repaired. But my father no longer wanted anything to do with that location.

Then, a week or so later, Dad returned to Highland. He had purchased an old run down storage shed, a little wood structure half the size of his first gas station. It had been abandoned on the opposite side of the traffic circle and sat in a forest of saplings that grew six or eight feet apart. He and several other men somehow loaded it on the back of Dad's truck, and he drove it back across the Mid-Hudson Bridge to Poughkeepsie.

Dad had used a carpenter's tape to measure from the ground to the top of the load, and was convinced that it would safely pass beneath any electrical cables. But he didn't take into account that the power company might not always maintain minimum legal clearances.

As my father drove through the crowded streets and tenements on the west side of town, and we passed Nick Beni's Italian Restaurant, our high load caught the electrical cables that crossed the street above us, breaking them. Dad, as a former student of electrical engineering, immediately warned Bobby and me to kneel on the seat, and not touch the door. When we started to lean forward in order to see better, he shouted that we must not touch the metal dashboard either. Then he told us to sit back and keep our hands in our laps.

But even from where we were kneeling, we could see out the windshield. We were both fascinated and frightened as we watched the broken electric cables dancing and skittering around the street. We watched as blue sparks flared when the end of a cable touched the pavement, and as the cables seemed to twist and leap around like writhing serpents.

The accident had shut off the power to all the businesses and homes along the street, and one very annoyed man came out of his door to yell at my father. Dad in turn shouted for him to stay inside and keep clear of the cables. The man took one look at those wires, sizzling and dancing in the street, and ducked back inside.

Repair crews from Central Hudson Gas and Electric soon arrived and shut down the power to the broken cables. The electric company conceded that the cables were hung too low, so Dad wasn't cited. But since it wasn't an act of nature, nor the result of my father's carelessness, some labeled it a freak accident. Whatever the cause, we could have been electrocuted that day.

Why weren't we killed the week before by the careening tractor-trailer wheel? Why weren't we electrocuted? The Bible indicates that the Lord takes interest in each of us from before our births. He does not dictate our every action, nor treat us as though we are marionettes or robots; but in His omniscience He foresees our future responses.

The big question is not whether we die before we feel it's our time. The big question is, "Will we be ready to face God when our time comes?"

Chapter 15

Rip Tides

"'Do you not fear Me?' says the LORD. 'Will you not trem-
ble at My presence, Who have placed the sand as the bound of
the sea, By a perpetual decree, that it cannot pass beyond it? And
though its waves toss to and fro, Yet they cannot prevail; Though
they roar, yet they cannot pass over it,"

Jeremiah 5:22

The headline read: "Vacation Tragedy: Florida Rip Current Kills Penn-sylvania Parents Of Six." When I read this sad news, it brought back the memory of a similar experience that almost cost Joy and me our lives. It occurred while we were vacationing in Florida, shortly after we were married.

We had purchased cheap plastic air mattresses, and were swimming at Madeira Beach, one of the long, narrow islands that are strung end-to-end, like pearls, down Florida's central west coast. The keys are bordered on the west by the Gulf of Mexico, and shield the narrow Inland Water-way that runs up and down the coast of mainland Florida. Madeira lies just west of the city of Saint Petersburg.

We had swum about a hundred feet offshore, and were now lying on our air mattresses, enjoying the clear skies, pleasant breeze, and rest-ful ups-and-downs of the waves When I looked toward the beach to see where we had left our belongings, I realized that we had somehow moved further offshore. We were now several hundred feet down the shore.

Average Guy Meets Extraordinary God

Fear gripped me as I realized that we were racing south on our fragile little yellow and white floats. Concerned that we might be swept out into the Gulf, we laid face down on the mattresses and used our arms to swim toward shore, but our efforts were futile. We were moving several miles an hour, far too fast to fight the rip tide.

Then it was as though we were turning a corner, and for a moment I felt relief because we were moving toward the island. But then I realized that we were being swept into a narrow opening between the south end of Madeira Beach and the north end of Treasure Island, the next key to the south. The current was much faster now, sucking us into that opening, and I shouted at Joy to try to make it to the safety of the rocks and slabs of concrete that had been heaped at the south end of Madeira to prevent erosion.

As we succeeded in moving closer to the rocks, the current grew less powerful. But we soon discovered that the tumbled mass of rocks offered its own peculiar perils, for the moment our flimsy rafts touched them, they were slashed open by the barnacles that covered their sloped surfaces. We suddenly found ourselves trying to stand or kneel on those razor-sharp crustaceans, our hands and feet already mildly lacerated. I saw blood lacing the water around Joy's feet, and fear again gripped me. Using our ruined air mattresses as slippery "rugs," we finally reached the high-water mark where there were no barnacles, and we were able to cross the remainder of the breakwater without fear of more lacerations.

When we finally reached the safety of the beach, we were met by people who had been watching our escape. One man said that we were lucky to have survived. He explained how, when the tide comes in, water piles up on the Gulf side of the islands, then races through the narrow openings between the islands to bring the water level in the Inland Waterway up to the level of the rising waters in the Gulf, and sometimes drowning unwitting swimmers.

Joy and I had just begun actively pursuing God. Immediately, we recognized that we owed our survival to His grace. We were learning not to spurn a God who should be respectfully feared.

And that's why I find the above headline so poignant. I was saddened to learn of the deaths of those two parents, and terribly sorry for the children they'd left behind. It reminded me of how blessed Joy and I were to escape a similar fate with only a few minor cuts, surviving to raise four wonderful children of our own.

THE COLLEGE YEARS:

THE ENCOURAGING HAND OF GOD

CHAPTER 16

Moving Day!

"And it shall come to pass, that before they call, I will answer; and while they are yet speaking, I will hear."

Isaiah 65:24

It was moving day! Months of prayerful preparations were finally completed, and we were at last ready to leave for Bible college. We had closed the business, said goodbye to our friends, and Joy and I, with our two little girls in hand, watched as a commercial hauler hooked his big truck to the front of our seventy-foot manufactured home, and prepared to haul it up our long driveway to the front of our three-acre home site. We would follow in our old Chevy station wagon, as he hauled our twelve-foot-wide home to Pennsylvania.

My immediate excitement at making this change was based on my belief that God was directing our path, but it blinded me to the enormity of the journey we were undertaking. I don't mean a journey in terms of the 150 miles from Highland, New York to our new home near Quakertown. I mean the kind of furious sea change that Ariel sang of in Shakespeare's "The Tempest," a spiritual hurricane that would sweep away everything familiar, and would challenge us to trust God as we rebuilt our lives using the Holy Bible as our sole rule for faith and conduct.

Joy, too, was excited, but as a young mother, her perspective was necessarily different from my own. What's more, she'd been raised in a

Christian home, and her outlook was undoubtedly more realistic and mature. She longed to take the Bible courses offered, but a lack of cash would limit opportunities.

Apart from classes, I would wind up working at least twenty hours each week at secular jobs during our entire time at college, and would have too little time for study, much less for my family. A financial windfall would permit Joy to attend a few classes, but only a few! When she did have the opportunity to attend, she shined.

On one occasion, we both signed up for the same course, a study of "Romans and Galatians." The instructor was a bit eccentric, and when he really liked a student's work, he would put the grade at the top of the page followed by several plus signs. When he returned Joy's first paper, it had an "A" at the top, followed by a couple of rows of plus marks—easily a dozen! "A + + + + + + + + + + + + +"

My paper, on the other hand, didn't have an A at the top, much less a single plus mark, and as the instructor handed it to me, he said with a chuckle, "Your wife got it all right, boy!" The other students laughed, and I bit my tongue in embarrassment. I thought my answers were reasonably good, but the instructor would have had no interest in hearing me try to excuse myself, much less argue that I worked every afternoon, thus limiting my study time. As a matter of fact, a lot of the older students, family men who were dedicated to the Lord, had to work to meet their needs.

I can now smile at what was then a painful jibe, and honestly admit that my wife had her own burdens. Joy was a wife and mother, so she too had plenty of demands on her time. And to this day, I take consolation in the fact that I was married to the brightest, kindest, and most beautiful woman anywhere.

But this was the day of our move, and that was yet future. We were voluntarily stepping off into the unknown, with huge challenges before us. And though we had far more experience in the world of business and politics than the men and women under whom we would study, I was a mere kindergartner in Christ. We hoped and believed that we were stepping out in faith, but our actions must have seemed laughable to those who had walked with the Lord for any length of time.

Our ignorance and our naivete left us all but blind to the trials we would face in the future. Though I'm now convinced that our ignorance was a matter of God's grace. If we had known what lay ahead, we might very well have left our mobile home parked right where it was and attempted to return to the life we had known.

Instead, we were determined to leave it all behind—home, business, church, relatives, and friends — and head into the unknown. We had just about enough cash to pay for the move, our first semester's tuition, plus a couple of months' rent at the mobile home park. I felt I should step out, and Joy enthusiastically joined me. It was time for an existential leap of faith into the unknown.

As I placed the last suitcase in the back of the station wagon, and made certain that our two little girls had their favorite stuffed toys, I saw the truck driver begin attaching signal lights to the back of our huge manufactured home. Then, to my annoyance, I saw a car coming up our tree-lined driveway, and stop right in front of our tow truck.

A moment later I was surprised to see a smiling face appear out of my past. It was John Francis McIlhenny, a former employee, a staunch Irish Catholic, a political supporter, and my friend. I guess I was on emotional overload because it took me a moment to understand what he was trying to tell me. He was now a real estate agent, and the man and woman he had brought with him were interested in buying our home site.

This was a bit of a shock for several reasons. First, we hadn't listed our land for sale. Yet John had somehow gotten wind of our decision to prepare for the ministry, and of our imminent departure. Second, I hadn't seen him in a couple of years, and, of course, I had no idea that he was now dealing in real estate. Third, he lived on the opposite side of the Hudson River, and about thirty miles north, which was a long distance for a real estate agent to travel.

But, apart from all that, I was surprised that John had found his way to our home at all. There were no other houses on our side of the highway for quite a distance in either direction. What's more, our driveway was unmarked, and our home lay over a hundred yards back from the road, hidden by thick woods. Not only that, but he arrived minutes before we were to move our home off the property, after which we would disappear to an unknown address, 150 miles south! Even today, his timing seems extraordinary.

John believed that his clients would be charmed by our three acre wooded parcel, with its stream down front, a pond in the back, and a long winding driveway through the woods that offered seclusion and privacy. Since the costly utilities were already in place, it might be the ideal place for them to build their dream home. But I was too caught up in our own activities to give further thought to his sales pitch. I had harbored a hope of keeping the land, but over the course of time, I would find that all but our most personal possessions would be stripped away to pay our way and test our commitment to Christ.

John and his clients wandered around the property for about twenty minutes, and just before they left, he stopped to wish us well. He asked for our new address in Quakertown, and asked if I would consider accepting ten thousand dollars for the property. John's last words were, "I'll be in touch," but I took those words with a grain of salt.

After they left, I parked our car at the front of the property and waited for the truck driver. At little more than a snail's pace, he pulled down the driveway that crossed the stream near the front of our property and started up our steep winding hill toward Route 9-W. Since our driveway met the highway at a sharp angle, his plan was to head north until he could find a place to safely turn the 90-foot rig around. Once pointed south, he would lead the way to our new home site in Quakertown, Pennsylvania.

But things didn't quite work out the way we had planned. He was pulling around the last curve at the top of the driveway when he came to an abrupt stop. The front end of our home was hitched to his truck, the rear end had dug into the driveway, and the wheels were suspended in air about an inch above a low spot in the road. He had bridged the trailer, and he could not move forward or back. Our not-so-mobile home was hung up at the top of our driveway, and we were stuck!

I called my oldest brother, John, and he drove south from his home in Saugerties, a drive of about twenty-five miles, to come to our rescue. John immediately told me that he wanted me to keep my clothes clean for the journey ahead. He forbade me to help, a far cry from the treatment he showed me as a youngster.

He located some heavy planks, set a hydraulic jack beneath the steel frame, got down on his knees, and raised one side of the home after the other, so that he could slide the planks under the wheels. When he released the jack, the tires settled on the planks, raising the back end of the trailer slightly above the driveway. The driver was then able to pull ahead a few feet before the rear end again hung up. John was forced to repeat the difficult process several times before the back of the trailer cleared the driveway and they finally got the rig onto the highway. I didn't even get to say goodbye or thank you, because John waved the driver on his way.

We had such a late start that we couldn't complete the trip that day, and instead had to pay for hotel rooms and meals, an expense which we had not budgeted. That was the beginning of sorrows. The home was again hung up turning a corner within a mile of the mobile home park in Quakertown, and it took hours to free it.

And when we were finally set up in in the residential development, and it was time to register for college, I realized that I had only enough money left to pay for the first semester. But I soon found a twenty-hour a week part-time job at a local restaurant. They paid me two dollars per hour, something of a come down from being the CEO of my own business, but we were committed to trusting the Lord and living one day at a time, not fuming over our financial prospects for the future.

I wouldn't characterize the Lord Jesus a "last minute Lord," but sometimes it seemed as though He was, for He often made us wait for answers to prayers until it appeared too late for His intervention. In this way, He began to teach us trust, obedience, and patience.

You've probably heard about the fellow who prayed, "Lord, make me patient, and do it right now!" Well, it doesn't work that way. Instead, we must learn to "*...glory in tribulations, knowing that tribulation produces perseverance; and perseverance, character; and character, hope*" (Romans 5:3-4).

I don't know how much I was trusting the Lord, but I tried to be obedient and I pressed on. I had not read our Lord's words about counting the cost before embarking on an enterprise, and I hadn't applied them to my own decision-making process until now. Some would say that I was an irresponsible and immature Christian.

I had taken that leap of faith into the unknown and was now facing the cold possibility of failure. But I was determined to stay the course, to know Him and the power of His resurrection. And we were on the way. I had made my decision to follow Jesus, and my beloved wife Joy never faltered. Like the Moabitess, Ruth, she has remained faithful for sixty years.

We were broke. I'd given up the position, prestige, and income I formerly enjoyed, and I would have to make the best of it. I would be hard pressed to add up the number of times I have felt crushed down by difficulties, with my prayers seemingly unheard and unanswered. In those early days of my Christian walk, I repeatedly concluded that I'd reached a crisis point, and my problems were beyond remedy.

But I began to learn that we grow through these experiences, going from faith to faith, like climbing a spiritual staircase. I'd hit bottom. Then,

God would do something so unexpected, so different from anything I could imagine; something so incredibly gracious and glorious, that I would struggle between my delight in Him and my shame at my own doubting.

Within a week of the time we arrived in Quakertown, I received a letter from my friend, John McIlhenny, the real estate salesman in New York, with a written offer to purchase our property in Highland. I immediately signed it and mailed it back, and within days, we had a cashier's check for $10,000. Since we owed nothing on the land, apart from income taxes, it was all ours to do with as we wished, and it provided the cash we needed to pay for my next semester. In fact, we wound up loaning a fellow student two thousand dollars to pay his expenses for the following year. Just now, I realized that Joy never said a word about my unilateral decision to help that student, even though the money I handed him would have paid her tuition for nearly two years.

And now, over fifty years later, it is difficult for me to comprehend God's timing in all this. My friend, John McIlhenny, had arrived at our home site with his prospective buyers mere minutes before our planned departure. And it came to pass, that before we called, God answered; and while we were yet speaking, He heard.

In fact, we experienced many such seemingly hopeless situations in the years that followed, but God never failed. He led us to our own Brook Cherith, and provided us with a barrel of meal that did not waste, and a cruse of oil that did not fail. Another miracle? Of course, but as the world will tell you, these events were just coincidences!

Chapter 17

"A good word..."

"Anxiety in the heart of man causes depression, but a good word makes it glad."

Proverbs 12:25

Like most students who enroll at a new school, my first morning was filled with anticipation and a little trepidation. But my situation quickly changed, and the testing of my faith began, before I even entered the first classroom. I pulled our old white Chevy station wagon into a parking space near the classroom building, slid out of the driver's seat, opened the tailgate, grabbed my briefcase, and proceeded to slam the tailgate down on my thumb. The pain was severe, and when I examined the nail, I discovered that blood had already begun pooling beneath it.

The pain spread from my hand to my head, and I was trying to decide what to do when another student stopped to wish me a good morning. When he saw the blood under my thumb nail, he suggested that I introduce myself to my new instructor and tell him my problem. But all I could think was that, after all the problems Joy and I had faced getting to Bible college, I wound up injuring myself minutes before my first class. Dispirited, I agreed. "I wonder if I even belong here," I told him, implying that I might not be in God's will. Then my new acquaintance said something that has remained with me. "Whenever you start to do God's will, the devil will try to stop you."

I would soon learn that he was far from the brightest mind on campus, but that didn't matter. God does not use the wise nor the mighty, but rather the foolish things of this world to confound the wise, and his words touched my heart. They were exactly what I needed to hear that morning. They heartened me, and I took his advice.

One look at my thumb, and my instructor in Personal Evangelism told me that I needed to see a doctor to have the nail "drilled" to relieve the pressure. And that's how I missed my very first class at Bible college.

It's not just what someone says to you, but the timing of their words that may constitute a mini-miracle. It was only the first day of classes. After all I'd been through, was I ready to throw in the towel? Certainly not. But at that moment, his words turned night into day. And that was just one of a number of experiences that helped prepare me for a grievous trial that lay just weeks away.

You might wonder what happened to the student who made that sage observation on the morning I smashed my thumb? I cannot recall his name, and I didn't see him again until he came looking for me on the last day of the school year. He somehow heard that we had sold our manufactured home, and he wondered whether I would loan him $2,000 so that he could return to school for another year.

Two thousand dollars? Adjusted for inflation, that would be over $15,000 in today's dollars. And I had planned to use some of it to get Joy into more classes, and perhaps visit the Holy Land that summer. But I loaned it to him. And Joy, who has always been incredibly generous, seemed fine with my rash gesture. I never did make it to the Holy Land, and she was ultimately limited to a few classes.

Since we didn't live on campus, and he was in different classes from me, I don't recall meeting that student again until a couple of years later. He sought me out on graduation day. By then, I was broke, and had no more money to lend, so I tried to find an excuse to avoid him. But he pursued me, and it's a good thing I stopped to listen.

He told me, "My future father-in-law does not want me to begin my ministry while owing anyone money, and he told me to give you this." Then he handed me a check for two-thousand dollars. That was another lesson for me: *"Cast your bread on the surface of the waters, for you will find it after many days"* (Ecclesiastes 11:1).

But the lesson I learned that first day at Bible college was better. God used the encouraging words of that student to build my faith and keep me going. His words were *like apples of gold in settings of silver"* for they were spoken at the proper time (Proverbs 25:11).

CHAPTER 18

"I guess we overreacted."

*"He said, '...the girl has not died, but is asleep.' And they began
laughing at Him."*

Matthew 9:24

Just a couple of weeks after I smashed my thumb, I returned home to learn that our five-year old daughter, Sandra, was ill. Her skin was dry and pale, her temperature was very high, and she was uncharacteristically docile.

That was unlike her, as she had always been a remarkably cheerful child. Even as a baby, I can recall finding Sandy standing quietly in her crib on a Saturday morning, a big smile on her face, with never a complaint. But now she was unresponsive, and we were frightened.

We had little money, but someone told us we could take her to a clinic in Quakertown. Upon our arrival, the nurse who checked her over seemed alarmed. She quickly moved Sandy into an examination room where a doctor immediately examined her. He told us that he was going to admit her to the local hospital. The facility was just a couple of blocks away, but he had Sandy taken there by ambulance so that she would be admitted and given a bed within minutes. We learned later that he didn't merely work at the clinic, but was also director of the hospital.

The next memory we have is of Sandra lying almost comatose in a hospital bed, her little legs straight out in front of her, swollen far out of proportion to their normal size. The doctor told us she was still running a high temperature and that they needed to take some tests. He said we should go home and return the next day when they would have the results.

He was clearly quite sobered by her condition, and this frightened us. On the way home, Joy and I were both crying. It was just a couple of years since my father lay dying of cancer, his legs also swollen, and I was troubled by thoughts of leukemia and Hodgkin's Disease.

The next morning, on the way to morning chapel, I met the professor who gave Joy the A++++++, and I quickly shared my concern. Then I told him with tear-filled eyes that I had determined that I must go on with my preparations for ministry, no matter what happened to Sandy. He was matter of fact and almost cold, but assured me that I had the right attitude and that he would pray. And Sandy's name was indeed brought before the entire student body during morning chapel service. In those days, chapel attendance was mandatory for all students.

That afternoon, we left our younger daughter, Cheryl, with a baby-sitter, and returned to the hospital. When we entered Sandy's private room, she was sitting up in bed, her legs crossed beneath her, and she was playing with a toy. She gave us one of her dazzling smiles and said, "Daddy, the doctor says that I can go home."

We were confused. Sandy did look great, but could she have misunderstood the doctor? How could she be released just like that? Just as she finished sharing her good news, the doctor came into the room. He affirmed her joyful statement, and I'll never forget his next words: "I guess we overreacted."

Overreacted? What about Sandy's elephantine legs and her sky-high temperature? I stood there amazed, thrilled with the doctor's news, and blessed by God's great love. I was ashamed that I had doubted Him, something that I must confess I have done on many other occasions through the years.

The doctor went on to say, "As a doctor, I have certain responsibilities, just as you will have certain responsibilities when you become a pastor." Therefore, he told us, "I won't be billing you for my services." It seems to me, in retrospect, that his generosity was an expression of his own loving obedience to Christ, and we remain grateful to the memory of this fine Christian physician. That afternoon we took two happy little girls home, amazed at the goodness of the Lord whom we had been serving for just a short time.

And what of "Professor A+++++++++++" whom I met on the way to chapel that morning? Through the years, Hobart Grazier would become a good friend, speaking on many occasions at our church, and taking meals with us. And he never hesitated to tell people that Sandy was his favorite girl, even into her teens. He gave her several books from his precious collection, including one autographed by L. Frank Baum, the author of *The Wizard of Oz.*

In the years that followed Sandy's abrupt illness and healing, we would hear other statements from doctors, like "I guess we overreacted." A favorite of mine came from my personal physician after I'd been locked in isolation in a Schenectady hospital for ten days: "You must be perplexed that all those specialists couldn't tell you what you almost died from." Another is from a surgeon who had scheduled an operation to remove cancerous tumors from my liver. When the follow up MRI did not show any lesions. He told me, "Surgery is not indicated."

And while I am not fit to untie his sandles, it brings to mind the words of the Apostle Paul:

> *...we were burdened beyond measure, above strength, so that we despaired even of life. Yes, we had the sentence of death in ourselves, that we should not trust in ourselves but in God who raises the dead, who delivered us from so great a death, and does deliver us; in whom we trust that He will still deliver us, you also helping together in prayer for us, that thanks may be given by many persons on our behalf for the gift granted to us through many* (2 Corinthians 1:8-11).

From time to time, my faith lapses. Then Jesus Christ, our Great Physician, finds it necessary to remind me of the numerous occasions when He intervened, and perhaps a doctor attempted to explain a miraculous healing with a statement like, "I guess we overreacted."

CHAPTER 19

"A Morning Prayer"

"About midnight Paul and Silas were praying and singing hymns to God, and the other prisoners were listening to them. Suddenly a strong earthquake shook the foundations of the prison. At once all the doors flew open and everyone's chains came loose."

Acts 16:25-26

Compared to 1959, today's college costs are astronomical. Tuition at the first college I attended was $500 per year for 32 credit hours. Adjusted for inflation, that $500 would be over $10,000 in today's dollars. But today, the annual tuition at that school is actually four times that amount, $42,000!

I experienced little financial stress during my college years because my parents paid all my bills. I always had a car to drive and a little spending money in my pocket. When I returned to college to prepare for the ministry a decade later, things were far different. My father had passed away. I was thirty years old, had a family of four, and could only look to the invisible God to help with my expenses.

Tuition at our little Bible school was dirt cheap, just $25 per credit-hour, or about $800 per year, just a fraction of that charged by other schools. But if you have struggled to work your way through college, you understand something of the challenges that Joy and I were facing. I was about to learn a little of what the Lord meant when he told Ananias what lay ahead for the Apostle Paul, *"For I will show him how many things he must suffer for My name's sake"* (Acts 9:16).

Since I had already accumulated almost three years in college credits, I assumed I would require only a year or so to finish. But the registrar rejected half my credits, forcing me to repeat similar courses. He told me that I would require three years to graduate. I made it in two-and-a-half.

I later learned that—apart from my gaining what they considered the absolute minimal knowledge required to effectively serve the Lord—they wanted me to remain at the college for several years because they were skeptical of my motives and were determined that I would prove my spiritual commitment. In retrospect, I'm glad they did.

I first thought that Joy and I would be able to get by without my having to work a job, but the reality of our situation soon dispelled that delusion. Instead, I wound up working twenty to twenty-five hours per week for my entire college career. Nevertheless, I was able to maintain course loads of 18 to 21 credit hours per term.

And though my brilliant and beautiful wife longed to attend classes on a regular basis, she was limited because of our lack of funds. So Joy, never one to waste time, immediately began a weekly Bible story time for the children in our neighborhood.

My time, by contrast, was divided between classes and work, with my few waking hours at home devoted largely to studies. One exception was our Friday nights. Friday was pay day, and our little girls were delighted when we splurged for "dinner" at a nearby hoagie shop, then browsed a local Christian bookstore, and finished up by doing our weekly grocery shopping. Another exception was a brief period in 1972 when I took time from my studies to sit with my family in the evening, our eyes glued to our tiny black and white TV set, as we watched little Olga Korbut win four gold medals in gymnastics at the Summer Olympics.

On rare occasions, I felt as though I was bound with chains. I was chafing, trying to serve two masters, God and mammon—Christian teachers and employment income. There was too little time to study for the former, and too little money from the latter.

In times of trial, God can provide heavenly solutions to earthly problems. We can look back 2,000 years at the Lord's deliverance of The Apostle Paul and Silas from prison (Acts 16) and dare to imagine that God might do something as remarkable for us. Such Bible-based supernatural occurrences are so rare and dramatic that, when they do occur, they evoke scorn from the skeptics and encourage faith in the saints. Some will be incredulous, while others may have their spiritual eyes opened.

To the Christian who experiences such a deliverance, it becomes a spiritual memorial. The people of ancient Israel, for example, were blessed with many miracles. In one case, an Old Testament prophet set up a monument of stones so that the miracle it represented would not be forgotten. The record states, *"Samuel took a stone, and set it between Mizpeh and Shen, and called the name of it Ebenezer, saying, Hitherto hath the LORD helped us"* (1 Samuel 7:12).

Individuals who witness such overt acts of God never forget them. And, ever after, the Holy Spirit uses their memory to encourage them in times of trial. When Joy and I left for Bible college, I hadn't given a lot of thought to what lay ahead, but I had seen others living sacrificial lives for God, so I believed that the Lord would provide for us as He had for them.

When Joy and I first drove onto the campus and viewed the facilities, we almost changed our minds about attending. We still measured our world through eyes of flesh, and while I never imagined that the campus would be particularly attractive, those facilities fell far below our expectations. Joy was dismayed, and even our little girls were disappointed. Little Sandra, who had visited other college campuses, turned to me and asked, "Is this it?"

It was a tiny campus. There was a large old brick building that housed the administrative offices, men's and women's dormitories, cafeteria, library, and chapel. Additionally, there were a couple of concrete block classroom buildings that had been laid up by staff and students. Married students lived in small, uninsulated cottages that had once belonged to the adjacent summer Bible camp.

And there was a huge old wooden tabernacle, formerly used for summer camp meetings. That crude but venerable structure had been a place of worship for many years, protecting countless saints from summer rains and burning sun. My graduating class of thirty-five seniors would one day celebrate our commencement in that vast open-air structure.

Those buildings were a long step down from other campuses where I had attended classes, such as The University of South Florida, Babson College, the State University of New York, and the magnificent Frank Lloyd Wright campus in Lakeland, Florida. Yet I knew that this was the sort of environment in which truly dedicated Christians frequently learned and labored. Christian campuses are different today. "Christian" Bible colleges and seminaries strive to build impressive campuses in order to attract greater numbers, generate more income, and impress the world, but those greater numbers necessarily include far more worldly students and teachers.

It was on this humble campus that I would learn that a great school cannot be measured by its history, architecture, the size and pedigree of its student body, or the caps and gowns, cords and stoles worn by its professors at graduation. A great school is characterized by its underlying beliefs and purposes, by the dedication of its students and staff, and by the positive impact its graduates ultimately make on our world. That's what comprises a great place of learning.

And using those measurements, I would come to realize that our little Bible school was extraordinary. Sadly, that great school is gone now, its buildings torn down and plowed under, its dedicated instructors passed on, and its name only a fading memory, a footnote in the catalog of a much larger liberal arts school that took its place.

But all that was in the future. Right now, our decision was made, and the die was cast. We would, by God's grace, enter that little Bible school in August of 1970, just a month or so away, and take consolation in the fact that it was at least accredited by the American Association of Bible Colleges.

I did not learn until after I enrolled that I had been accepted on probation. One instructor later told me that I scored higher on the entry IQ test than anyone in the history of the school, and I think that dubious record held until years later when our daughter Sandra scored higher. But that did not enhance my standing. In fact, it mitigated against me. They demanded a great deal more from me. But I wasn't one of the fresh-faced 18-year-old students that entered with me; kids who grew up in the church, many of them preacher's kids. They were enthusiastic young men and women who had absorbed the Scriptures with their milk.

The administration also feared that I had been tainted by the world and my motives in attending were at best unclear and almost certainly unsatisfactory. They had to be careful that I did not contaminate the other students, or disgrace the school, for "...a little leaven leaveneth the whole lump."[16]

Additionally, the instructors were skeptical. They expected me to be an egotistical wise guy, far too big for my britches; a very worldly man

---

16   Galatians 5:9

who would soon discover that the Christian walk was unappetizing, and would find me dropping out. They expected me to fail, and at least two instructors initially acted as though they wanted to accelerate that failure.

Those who reviewed my application took The Apostle Paul's words seriously, "*...that not many wise men after the flesh, not many mighty, not many noble, are called: But God hath chosen the foolish things of the world to confound the wise; and God hath chosen the weak things of the world to confound the things which are mighty*" (1 Corinthians 1:26-27).

They had no idea how foolish I felt. Sure, at one moment, I felt confident and even proud, but the next, weak and foolish. I confess to this: I was indeed green, and woefully ignorant of the journey I was beginning. I did not foresee the trials my family would face. But I imagined that I would be helped to grow, not treated with cynicism. And now, looking back, I was to learn that some of the greatest challenges and accomplishments in ministry are not in the classroom or in the pulpit, but in "walking the walk" day after day.

When we think of the twelve disciples who followed Jesus, our minds are generally focused on the miraculous healings they observed and the sublime words they heard. Can you imagine being one of the twelve who were privileged to spend their days and nights wandering the Holy Land with Jesus? What would it be like to be among them when they distributed the loaves and fishes, to see those elements multiplied to satisfy the hunger of thousands?

But the Holy Bible holds nothing back, recording both the the good and the bad. Yes, there were relatively rare moments of excitement and bliss in the lives of Christ's disciples. But, as with you and me, their lives undoubtedly consisted of long periods of relative tedium, interspersed with those brief interludes of glory or terror. And they were men of like passions as we are. Peter often seemed like an impulsive oaf. John and James wanted to be first in the kingdom. Judas was a thief and a betrayer. Such candid and unflattering portraits of the disciples demonstrate that the Bible pulls no punches in presenting Its truths.

Have you ever considered what the disciples experienced as they followed Jesus each day for three years? They sometimes walked twenty and even thirty miles in a single day, shuffling along in ill-fitting footwear on pathways strewn with filth. They were often hungry, parched, weary, and cold. And their lives were frequently in danger. Those three years represented their "Bible college," that period during which they were learning to put their growing knowledge and faith to work. And, although they sat at Jesus' feet for three years, they were far from perfect. I call it God's School of Affliction. And so it is for all of us; our training and testing continues as long as we walk this earth.

Perhaps none of the disciples would have graduated *Summa cum laude, "with the greatest praise."* After Christ's resurrection, the faithful entered their post-graduate work and after Pentecost, the Bible never again mentions the names of seven of the twelve. We only hear of them by tradition, myths, and apocryphal literature, tales which are unreliable.

In my second year of college, I worked in a lumber yard. One bitterly cold and overcast day I had to lift a heavy sheet of particle board by myself. I laid it on a table saw and ripped it into two pieces. I remember crying aloud to God:

"Why am I wasting my time here, doing this dirty and difficult work, while other students have time to study? I'm not learning anything!"

And I remember being shamed by the rebuke that I sensed at that moment:

"Oh, you're learning, Frank!"

And I was indeed learning. And I still am!

I am learning that, *"...in whatever state I am, therewith to be content"* (Philippians 4:11). I'm also learning that, though I do not see Him, yet believing, I *"... rejoice with joy inexpressible and full of glory"* (I Peter 1:8). And I am learning that *"...the peace of God, which surpasses all understanding, will guard your hearts and minds through Christ Jesus"* (Philippians 4:7).

But I ask myself, "Why aren't more men and women entering the ministry today? The fields are white unto harvest. Isn't God still calling people?" Is it a matter of ignorance? Do believers imagine they will face only hardship and sacrifice? Are they unwilling to pay what they imagine to be too great a price. Has the notoriety of the hypocrites and wolves among us blinded them to the wonder and glory of Christian service? Is it a matter of selfishness? Are those who are called daring to refuse God? Do they not understand that they must heed the will of God, wherever He leads and whatever it costs?

The alternative is too harsh to imagine! We are to live our lives His way, not ours. And we are to serve others, as we would like to be served. It's not always easy, but it's frequently glorious. A true Christian really has no choice. We are all to pick up our crosses daily and follow Him. And if we don't, we still won't be able to avoid trials. *"For man is born to trouble, as the sparks fly upward.*"[17] You will serve someone, and, as Peter warned, *"... it is better, if it is the will of God, to suffer for doing good than for doing evil"* (1 Peter 3:17).

I am still in the process of learning that Christ's yoke is easy, and His burden light.[18] I really wouldn't want to be harnessed with an ill-fitting yoke that chafed and bruised my spirit. But I certainly wouldn't want to *"... be unequally yoked together with unbelievers,"* which is the fate of so many who walk away from the blessings of Christ's calling. *"For what fellowship has righteousness with lawlessness? And what communion has light with darkness?"* (2 Corinthians 6:14).

No, I didn't yet realize that Joy and I were facing a life of trials. And it would be a long time before I truly understood that such trials are actually the privilege of our relationship with Jesus. Each test is an opportunity to exercise and expand the faith we have already received as a result of going through earlier trials. It's like an athlete building muscle, wind, and coordination. Running miles to strengthen myself for intercollegiate soccer was painful, but it prepared me physically and mentally to score goals. These are the experiences through which we grow as human beings and as children of God.

The Apostle Paul put it this way: *"For therein is the righteousness of God revealed from faith to faith: as it is written, The just shall live by faith"* (Romans 1:17, KJV). Going from faith to faith brings images of a baby growing to adulthood. As new Christians, we are like newborn babies, requiring the sincere milk of the Word. And like crawling babies, we are ambitious, eyeing challenges such as pulling ourselves to our feet, walking, or even climbing a staircase. We toddle over to that first step, drop to our knees, and try to pull ourselves up over that first riser.

Our Lord, like a loving parent, watches that we don't fall and hurt ourselves. As we grow, we begin climbing that staircase of faith, one difficult step at a time. Then, after years of spiritual growth, we are like teenagers, full of strength and confidence, maybe even dangerously proud, racing up that staircase two and three steps at a time. Yes, sometimes two steps up, and one back, but our faith will grow. And one day, we will meet Jesus, and faith will become sight!

I had foolishly concluded that, because Joy and I were entering God's service, we would be spared many of life's sorrows. I had a lot to

---

17   Job 5:7

18   Matthew 11:30

learn! I was that spiritual baby, crawling toward that first riser. I had a long way to go and I still do!

But I had also seen a lot of life from the world's side, so I had the opportunity to grow rapidly in some ways; to do some quick catching up. And I even found myself with some advantages over kids who grew up in the shelter of the church. No, I couldn't continue to live in the old world, to hold on to my "old man," or, God forbid, to practice sin; but I could purposely remember some of the "steps" that I had taken.

For example, I remembered clearly what it was like to be a child of darkness, and to understand the temptations I had to deal with as I was led to the Lord. And I realized that those memories would fade as I obeyed The Apostle Paul, *"...forgetting those things which are behind and reaching forward to those things which are ahead..."* (Philippians 3:13). So, I was determined not to slide back into sin, but to remember the wonder of my deliverance. I realized that it would be the memory of our own trials that would give Joy and me the understanding and empathy we would need to help others with the pains and sorrows they bore. I asked God that I might somehow remember what the unsaved might be thinking, and what they would therefore need to hear from me to win them.

One of my silliest illusions was that I mistakenly believed that my Bible college instructors and administrators would somehow be almost angelic. I soon discovered that they too had feet of clay, and that one or two of them were shockingly proud, ambitious, and even lazy and dishonest. Nevertheless, we were blessed by those who, despite their shortcomings, prayed for us as they struggled to train us.

It became clear that Joy and I were going to need the comfort and blessing of the Holy Spirit to endure. And God was faithful. Shortly after Joy and I enrolled, we had several extraordinary experiences. One occurred in late 1970.

I was successfully completing my first semester, and I should have been pleased with that accomplishment, but I was discouraged. I didn't know where we'd find the money to pay for the next semester. I was working twenty hours a week in a local restaurant, and receiving two dollars an hour, but it wasn't enough.

So, in addition to being a housewife and mother of two little girls, Joy began working from home, sitting up all night typing legal depositions, in the spirit of the ideal woman in Proverb 31. While I slept, she hammered away at a borrowed IBM Selectric typewriter, earning the extra money that kept us afloat. Our bedroom also served as her office, so both of us were losing sleep and becoming a little depressed.

The amount of work required to earn a Bachelor of Science in Biblical Studies was much greater than I had imagined. About then, I could have used a miracle! I had always thought of miracles in terms of brief dramatic events, such as Jesus instantly healing the blind, calming the sea, or making the lame to walk. But being called by God to ministry is a miracle. Ministry isn't just about standing in front of a group and preaching or teaching. The variety of possible tasks is endless, and for the true servant, unexpected experiences arise that can make each day a new adventure, or lead you into a commitment that may last a lifetime.

I'd never considered that God's anointing of Abinidab and Aholiab—with their diverse cunning skills as mechanics, sculptors, metal workers, carpenters, and artists—would require them to work long and hard to build the magnificent Tabernacle.

Maybe young David's perfection with the sling had been driven by sheer boredom that resulted in him practicing day after day while watching his flock, and communing with God by night. The days were evil, and he redeemed the time, so he was able to save that flock from the bear and the lion, and ultimately to save Israel from the giant Goliath, because he had calm assurance in his own preparation and God's presence.

When David unerringly cast that stone, he was clearly anointed. Of all the Israelites, it was only David that had the faith in God, the courage of his convictions, and the hard-won skills needed to challenge and overcome the enemy. So God guided that stone to the forehead of the blasphemer.

Consider the Psalms that David wrote, with phrases like, *"The Lord is my Shepherd; I shall not want...."*[19] Those words were born of David's experience as a shepherd, flowing through him from the heart of God as he meditated and prayed. He was faithful over a few sheep, and ultimately God made him ruler over a nation.

Whether you or I write a psalm or slay a Goliath, the fact is that, *"Every good gift and every perfect gift is from above, and cometh down from the Father of lights, with whom is no variableness, neither shadow of turning"* (James 1:17, KJV). By faithful labor, you will gain access to the gifts you require, and I have absolute conviction that, whoever you are, and whatever

---

19   Psalms 23:1

your strengths and limitations are, God can achieve remarkable things through you.

And that brings me to that very special event in our lives. One evening, when I was feeling particularly discouraged, I ignored my studies, and instead sat up reading a simple little book entitled *Prison to Praise*, by Merlin R. Carothers. I remember little about that book except the author's advice. Instead of ending my day by laying a litany of needs before the Lord, I went to bed singing His praises.

I slept soundly, but awoke abruptly at five a.m., a song going 'round and 'round in my head. It was unfamiliar, and I felt compelled to write down the words. So before I could forget them, I grabbed a piece of scrap paper, sat down in the chair that Joy used to type depositions, and transcribed the words that seemed to pour out of my soul.

Such a thing may not seem remarkable to you, but I am not a poet, and Joy and I were both startled that I wrote down an entire poem in less than five minutes. I later learned that the lyrics were "original," but the melody that went around in my head was not. Because the words were given me as I was awakening, I called it, "A Morning Prayer."

Nor would I label it "creative writing." I did not compose these words; I transcribed them. I was merely a penman. I had no doubt that they came from the Holy Spirit. The speed with which they flowed out of my heart and onto that scrap of paper, coupled with the progression of ideas and the glory they brought to God, were far beyond my mental and literary capacity, not to speak of my spiritual immaturity. This was as close to a "burning bush" experience as I have ever had.

Later that morning, while shopping in the college bookstore, I met the president's wife, and since I was excited about my experience, I shared it with her. She never doubted my sincerity and was so impressed with the testimony that she had me try to hum the tune. She thought she recognized it, and insisted that I follow her to the library to look for a hymnal that contained that melody.

We finally identified the great old hymn from which the melody came: The Church's One Foundation, and when she compared the lyrics with the words I had transcribed, she saw that they were entirely different. After we parted, she discussed the song with several staff members, and they decided to have it sung in chapel the following week.

There were numerous skeptics, including several instructors, who believed that the poem wasn't original, or that I had actually spent a long time composing it, and had therefore given false testimony about its source and origin. Why was it so difficult for those teachers to believe that God might give someone a poem that glorifies him? After all, they had lectured about the words of the prophet Joel, as quoted by Simon Peter, *"... your young men shall see visions, and your old men shall dream dreams ..."* (Acts 2:17).

Chester Roberson, who taught us theology and apologetics, wanted to know the truth, and followed the Apostle Paul's admonition: *"Test all things; hold fast what is good"* (I Thessalonians 5:22)

One Saturday morning, Brother Rob took me for a long drive to meet with another preacher, and after questioning me about my experience, told me he believed me.

The fact is that I had merely written down what came to me, and I felt uncomfortable changing a single word. And I declare to you that everything occurred exactly as I've written. Even today, over fifty years later, I would be unable to compose something like this, even if my life depended on it.

Then several remarkable events occurred that encouraged both faculty and students to accept my account, and I'll discuss them in subsequent chapters. But, for me, the song itself is a gift from God, an unexpected and amazing miracle. Its memory has encouraged me through many dark hours.

That's why this poem, this morning prayer, is a "Hitherto hath the Lord helped us," a monument erected in my heart on my journey with God. The song may remind you of a special event in your life as well. If nothing else, your salvation alone should be sufficient proof that you have been mightily blessed by God. Here are the words that flowed from the Lord to my heart, and from my heart to my hand, on that memorable morning.

> Oh, precious Lord our Savior,
> be with us through this day;
> and keep your hand upon us,
> each thing we do and say.
>
> For we are but your children
> and need your guiding hand,
> to keep us safely moving
> throughout this sin filled land.

> Your love is more than money,
> your trust is more than fame,
> your present help each morning
> more precious than acclaim.
>
> Our lives last but a moment,
> our dreams are for a day,
> we need you close beside us,
> our help along the way.
>
> This world is bent and broken,
> it needs the word, yes you!
> So help us Lord to start now
> to win a soul for you.
>
> To thy great list be added
> a former sinner's name,
> and thine shalt be the honor,
> the glory and the fame.

When times were tough, this song was used of the Lord to encourage Joy and me, and to remind us that the He will never leave us nor forsake us. And when our daughter Sandra recently traveled to Texas to visit us, she blessed our hearts by singing "A Morning Prayer" during a morning service at a nearby church.

The Book of the Acts describes how The Apostle Paul and Silas were beaten and imprisoned for preaching about Jesus, and goes on to tell how they sang praises to God at midnight. Unlike those heroes of the faith, I suffered no physical distress. Yet, I had been allowing myself to be imprisoned by mental depression and to wallow in self pity. However, after I read that book, God helped me, and I actually fell asleep praising the Lord.

Let me paraphrase Acts 16:26: I awoke because, "Suddenly there was a great (spiritual) earthquake, so that the foundations of (my self-imposed) prison were shaken; and immediately all the doors (of my mind) were opened and (my) chains (of depression) were loosed." There is a lesson here; a lesson that is written over and over in the pages of God's Word. Specifically, *"The Lord inhabits the praises of His people."*[20]

---

20   Psalms 22:3

If things seem dark to you today, you may find your shackles broken, as The Apostle Paul and Silas did, by making a joyful noise unto the Lord. If you feel spiritually exhausted, and bound with the chains of worldly cares, try singing a song of praise to Jesus Christ. You will be surprised how your praise touches God's heart, what chains He bursts asunder, and from what bondage He set you free.

CHAPTER 20

"No, you won't!"

"Do not be like the horse or like the mule, Which have no understanding, Which must be harnessed with bit and bridle..."
Psalm 32:9

One of our daughters recently reminded me of the following event, and perhaps it was indeed a miracle. Late one night, I was driving from New Jersey into New York, and had just entered the New York Thruway. It was a cloudy moonless night and my headlights seemed to be sucked up by the darkness. I was tired. I remember gripping the wheel tightly as I followed the curving highway around a steep rocky hillside.

I had been thinking about my best friend, and I recall saying aloud, "I'm going to tell Al that he should contribute time to the Teen Challenge Bible Institute."

I was instantly rebuked.

"No, you won't!"

It was startling! That voice was loud and authoritative. It seemed to come from just behind my left ear, from outside the closed window of the car. I was stunned. This was unique for me because it is the only time in all my 84 years that I sincerely believe I heard the voice of God or one of his angels.

It was not just my imagination. It was a voice of command, of authority, and of power. I was not about to question it. There was no question in my mind as to who would have forbidden me to take that authority unto myself, and I sheepishly responded, "Yes, Lord."

You may suggest that I was hallucinating, but the fact is that the rebuke I received was contrary to anything I might have imagined. I thought I had a great idea, and that I'd made an excellent decision. I was sure that my friend Al, and the people he would be helping, would be blessed by his involvement, and I had no question that the Lord would be glorified through his efforts. But I had given no thought to the possibility that I might be sticking my nose in where it was not wanted or needed, nor that I might be usurping God's, or even Al's, prerogatives.

Why do I believe I really heard a voice? Because the rebuke totally countered what I considered a positive and timely suggestion for a good friend. In fact, it didn't occur to me until I began writing this, that Al's wife, Helen, had just a short time before, similarly advised me of God's will for my own life. And, like Helen, I failed to see any reason why I shouldn't also be God's spokesman. I was to learn that making oneself a spokesman for God may be an exciting experience, but is also a very dangerous one.

A few months after my epiphany, I learned that Al had already begun contributing time to Teen Challenge. He had even built an office and a sound studio on campus where he worked at least once each week. I may have been right about the benefits of Al's working at Teen Challenge, but Al didn't need me to share God's will with him. Years later, when I told him of my experience, he waved it away.

I had begun to learn that guiding the lives of others is the Lord's business, and any involvement on my part was to be taken with great care. God has ways to restrain those who would impulsively, impudently, and egotistically seize his prerogatives. And if they will not listen, He has ways to correct them.

Yes, "iron sharpens iron,"[21] and godly believers will profit from bouncing ideas off one another, or having affirmed what they believe God has already told them. The operative words, of course, are godly and prayerful. Why would I know more about God's will for your life than you do?

I didn't need Balaam's mule[22] to rebuke me, or a fiery angel to bar my path, and stop me from advising Brother Al. The sharp rebuke I received

---

21   Proverbs 27:17

22   See Numbers 22

as I drove my car that night was sufficient. Perhaps it was because my motives were good. Unlike Balaam, I was intent on helping God's people, not harming them. So on that occasion, I was blessed to be rebuked and kept from overstepping my bounds. Regrettably, there have been many other occasions when I would have been wise to remain silent.

One final thought: This is the only time in my life when I believe the Lord spoke aloud to me, but He has used numerous other methods to curb me through the years. Being rebuked by the Lord is nothing to boast about. Sometimes I wish that, when I am about to err, God might again speak to me with more than a still small voice.

CHAPTER 21

"For Whom the Bell Tolls"

Therefore, send not to know for whom the bell tolls, It tolls for thee."
John Donne[23]

S hortly before we arrived at Bible college, we discovered that a young couple from our home church had also enrolled. They'd been very popular in the church, and on more than one occasion they'd been invited to sing duets during morning service. I was not surprised when they boasted that they were receiving complete financial support from the members.

Our situation was far different. At the age of 30—and having been active in both business and politics—it was no surprise that our decision to serve the Lord was met with skepticism, especially since we'd only been attending the church for about a year.

Our growing involvement had nevertheless been a very happy experience for us. Al Salay and I, along with a dozen others, had been baptized during a Sunday evening service. Then the pastor had enlisted Joy and me to serve as counselors to the youth group, and my growing interest had resulted in my purchasing about a dozen costly Bible study books from the pastor's bookstore. We had also begun tithing, a step of faith and a financial adjustment which I at first found difficult.

---

23   Accessed online July 1, 2025: https://hymnary.org/text/standing_by_a_purpose_true

But now we were, seemingly, on our own. As a result, tuition and living costs for our little family were rapidly exhausting the limited reserves from the sale of our property in New York. Additionally, I was enjoying precious little time with my family because of my exhausting schedule of classes and work. But Joy and I were determined to hang on.

As you might imagine, it was quite an adjustment. I went from serving as the president of a multi-outlet retail operation to working in a restaurant kitchen, checking orders. But the young couple from our church had ample money and a great deal of free time, and, as the old saying goes, "idle hands are the devil's workshop." They began exploring questionable doctrines, and following television preachers whose teaching was considered to be heretical. The upshot was that they began contending with, and even mocking, the instructors at our school.

They gave me a brochure prepared by one of their heroes that had no basis in Scripture. It described how various demons were driven out. For example, he wrote that the demon of smoking is manifested by coughing, and comes out as yellow sputum. Our friends were eager to experiment with their newfound spiritual power; eager to cast demons out of everyone in sight. They were also taught that they could have anything they wanted, forgetting James 4:3, which states: *"You ask and do not receive, because you ask amiss, that you may spend it on your pleasures."* They also overlooked the fact that their prayers needed to be in harmony with those of God. And they seemed totally oblivious to the fact that we should expect persecution in this world as we take up our crosses and follow Jesus.

Those self-aggrandizing and anti-biblical teachings—which appeal to those who demand a pain-free and prosperous walk with God—were sweeping across America, encouraging their followers to name it and claim it. The instructors at our college taught that we can only trust and act on what the Bible clearly teaches. But our friends were convinced that they knew more than their teachers, and they became openly rebellious. During our first semester, they quit college to follow those wolves in sheep's clothing.

When this young couple quit college, they lost the financial support of our home church. They now had to rely on the wife's income as a legal secretary, while he took up door-to-door sales. Although they were offended that we did not agree with them, much less join them, we tried, unsuccessfully, to remain on friendly terms. Perhaps I thought, we can help them find the way back.

The life of a door-to-door salesman is hard, and it wasn't long before our former friend showed up on our doorstep with his new product. Apart from our concern for their spiritual welfare, we felt an obligation to them. After all, his wife had helped my wife secure her nighttime job typing legal depositions. So, when he showed up selling fire alarms, I was an easy sell.

The "fire alarms" we purchased were nicely designed, but they were obsolete. They were essentially a shallow metal bowl, about two inches deep and six inches across, with a wind-up mechanism inside, sort of like an old-fashioned alarm clock. The fuse was inserted through a hole in the center of the bowl, and if there was a fire, it would melt at about 500 degrees Fahrenheit, releasing the spring mechanism, and causing a hammer to beat rapidly against the inside edge of the metal bowl, thus producing an extraordinarily loud clanging sound.

They were big, archaic, and of doubtful value. By the time the heat from any fire was great enough to melt the bismuth, anyone nearby would probably have succumbed to smoke inhalation poisoning. But I bought the alarms for an outrageous price because I wanted to help, and I dutifully promised I would hang them. The smaller alarms were to be hung near the ceiling in each room of our manufactured home, and the larger one near the furnace.

At a cost of several hundred dollars, it is little wonder that we were his only customers. Feeling a bit sick that I'd spent the equivalent of a couple of month's income from my restaurant job, I felt an odd sense of obligation to hang the alarms immediately. It was simply a matter of putting a screw into the wall paneling, and hanging the alarm, as though it were a picture. I gave the alarms no more thought as we went to bed that night.

Sometime during that very first night, however, I was brought partly awake by an incredibly loud ringing. I was very hot and groggy, my eyes were heavy, and I wanted to go back to sleep, but that unbelievably loud and annoying racket prevented me. I realized that I was soaked with sweat, and I almost dozed off again, but the persistent ringing finally brought me to consciousness.

In spite of the intense heat, a chill of terror went through me as I realized that I was hearing one of the alarms, and concluded that our home must be on fire. I nearly panicked when I remembered that our bedroom was at the rear of our manufactured home, while our two little girls were sleeping several rooms away.

I turned on the light and had to yell at Joy several times before she was able to shake off the stupor that enveloped her. Looking down the hall, I saw no smoke, so I shouted above the noise that she should wake the girls, put on their winter coats and shoes, and get them outdoors. Then I led the way down the hall, trying to figure out where the ringing was coming from and praying that we could reach the girl's room before any flames broke out.

I passed the bathroom and came abreast the wooden door that hid the front of our oil burning furnace. I realized the ringing was coming from the largest of the alarms, which I had hung inside that cabinet. I was still shaking off the throes of sleep and was driven more by terror than reason.

I reached out to open the door to investigate, but when I touched it, I almost burned my hand. The wood was ready to burst into flame, and beneath the sound of the alarm, I could hear the furnace roaring. It made a continuous thunderous sound, like a run-away chimney fire above a wood stove.

It took me a moment to realize that I had to somehow shut the furnace off. I ran to the electrical box in the dining room closet and not taking time to isolate the circuit breaker that supplied the furnace, I shut off the main breaker. When I ran back down the hall, I no longer heard the furnace roaring, but the alarm continued its deafening clanging. Unable to see anything, I found a flashlight, returned to the circuit box, shut off the furnace, and turned back on the main breaker.

Then, while Joy took the girls outside, I returned to the cabinet. Using a potholder, I opened the door. In retrospect, that was a very foolish thing to do, for the introduction of fresh air might have caused a blow back. Thank God, it didn't! Joy had taken our children to a neighbor's home to keep warm, and they called the fire department. If you've ever seen the remains of a mobile home after its aluminum siding has melted at intense temperatures, you'll understand my gratitude that we didn't all perish that night.

It was about three in the morning when we finally got back to bed, and it took hours for the furnace and surrounding walls to cool down. But, thank God, the danger of fire was averted. The furnace was under warranty, and the next day a technician made the repair. He told us that the upper limit switch had failed, which explained why the thermostat didn't shut the furnace off when the house reached the desired temperature. No matter where the wall thermostat was set, the furnace would have kept running until it grew so hot that it finally set the house afire.

Without the racket produced by that big and archaic fire alarm, we would likely have died in our sleep. The alarm, which I had installed hours before, had saved our lives!

Did my installing the alarm cause the furnace to malfunction? Absolutely not. The oil-fired burner was almost brand new and state-of-the-art, like millions of others in conventional homes across America. It had its own sheet metal door, and I had installed the alarm about a foot away, at the front of the closet.

I can only say that I'm glad that the upper limit switch hadn't failed the previous night, and that I hadn't waited to install the alarms, for I would probably not be writing these words today. Come to think of it, I'm glad that I'd taken pity on my former fellow student, and paid him an exorbitant price for the not-so-silly devices.

What happened to my friend? From all I can determine, he and his wife divorced, and at some point he may have committed a crime that cost him jail time. But I'm glad that we knew him, and I pray that they finally found their way back to Jesus.

And while all of these things may seem coincidental, I am glad that there aren't any "coincidences" with God. For this event helped me to understand that Christians need not be "...*afraid of sudden terror, Nor of trouble from the wicked when it comes; For the LORD will be your confidence, And will keep your foot from being caught.*"[24]

Way back when John Donne wrote, *"Ask not for whom the bell tolls,"* he was referring to the church bells that were rung at someone's death. But the night our fire alarm rang, it was God's gracious warning that saved our lives.

---

24   Proverbs 3:25-26

CHAPTER 22

Brother Al's Fleece

"Gideon said to God, 'If You will save Israel by my hand as You have said—look, I shall put a fleece of wool on the threshing floor; if there is dew on the fleece only, and it is dry on all the ground, then I shall know that You will save Israel by my hand, as You have said.'"

Judges 6:36-38

After I received *A Morning Prayer*, I was sort of on a spiritual high, but our lives soon returned to normal. I went on attending classes and working my afternoon job, while Joy spent her nights typing legal depositions and her days caring for our two little girls. Both of us tried to forget that soon we would not have sufficient income to continue.

Then one afternoon I received a small package in the mail. It contained a cassette tape, an audio letter from my best friend, Al Salay. He opened in that soft melodic voice of his by saying that he'd originally been a little doubtful about whether God had really called me to Bible college, much less to ministry. Then he said that my persistence in the face of numerous obstacles, and especially the fact that the Lord had done wondrous things for us, persuaded him that I was in God's will.

Once he was convinced of God's call on our lives, and of our sincere response, he looked for means to assist us. Both he and his wife Helen wanted to help us financially, but they needed every dime of income to support their large family. They too had recently begun tithing, and every cent of their income was committed. The most they could send was the ten dollars monthly that Helen had offered nearly two years earlier when she had prophesied that I would enter the ministry.

What's more, Al had little hope of a raise because his employer, IBM, had initiated a freeze on both hiring and pay raises. Worse, even if IBM had been offering pay raises, it was unlikely that Al would receive one. And it was my fault! I had done something that angered management and resulted in Al's being formally reprimanded.

It occurred while I was running for the New York State Senate. Al was my campaign manager, and when Dr. Paul Adams, the Conservative Party's gubernatorial candidate, called me to say he was making a campaign swing through Dutchess County, I invited him to meet me at Al's office at IBM.

But I didn't check with Al first, and I did not know that IBM had a firm policy against employees expressing their political views at work, much less bringing a major candidate of any political party to the IBM offices. Because of my actions, Al was called on the carpet, and while that incident didn't result in his being fired, it certainly didn't improve the likelihood of his receiving a raise in the midst of a depressed economy.

As the audiotape played on, Al told me how he began praying for a raise in pay. He said that he had laid a "fleece" before the Lord, as Gideon had done in Judges 6:37. Of course, Al didn't lay down a literal sheep's fleece, nor was he asking for confirmation that the Lord would be with him in battle.

Instead, Al told the Lord, "If you provide me with a raise in pay, I will send Frank the entire amount of the raise—except for the tithe and taxes that I will owe on the money." Then he waited. And waited.

And nothing happened.

After some time had passed, it occurred to Al that perhaps the Lord might want him to give any raise to someone else. So, he revised his fleece. He told the Lord that, if the raise was received before a certain day and hour, he would send me the entire increase, again excepting tithe and taxes. But if it arrived after that day and hour, he would give it to another ministry. At no time did he ask for the money for himself.

Hope faded, and on the final day of his fleece, a Friday, as the clock wound down to the end of the workday and his self-imposed 5 pm deadline approached, he packed up his briefcase, put on his coat and hat, and left his desk. As he neared the exit, his manager shouted his name. He said he had been looking for Al to tell him that he had just received a raise in pay. God answered Al's prayer just a moment before quitting time on the very last workday of his fleece.

The first question that comes to most people's minds is, "How much was the raise?" It was the next thing that Al discussed on the tape, and the amount seemed incredible. After he deducted his tithe of 10% of the entire raise, and paid his state and federal taxes, he planned to send us one hundred and fifty dollars every month. And continued doing so until a month after we finished college.

That may not sound like much, but it was 1970, and adjusted for inflation, it was equivalent to more than $975 per month in today's dollars. But since he received his pay every two weeks, Al was faithful to send a check in the amount of seventy-five dollars every two weeks.

Al did not tell me about his fleece until after God had honored it, so I would never have known if he went back on his commitment to God. The devil may have tempted him, but if so, Al never mentioned it, which makes my respect for this Christian brother even greater. I can only imagine the comfort that extra money would have meant to his family.

To illustrate how far Al's and Helen's generosity went, after we sold our manufactured home, God provided us with a two-story, three bedroom house on 10 acres overlooking the beautiful Green Lane Reservoir. We rented that house for only seventy-five dollars per month, leaving us with another seventy-five each month to apply toward other expenses. With Al's and Helen's gift added to the income I earned working twenty hours each week, God met our needs.

It should not be a surprise that Joy and I look back on Brother Al's fleece, and God's amazing answer, as another example of, "Hitherto hath the Lord helped us."

Chapter 23

"He leads me beside still waters"

"The Lord is my shepherd; I shall not want. He makes me to lie down in green pastures; He leads me beside the still waters. He restores my soul."

Psalm 23:2

Brother Al began sending us money during my second semester, but in spite of that, Joy and I realized we could no longer make the payments on our manufactured home. The twenty-mile round trip between the Quakertown mobile home park and the college was costly in both time and money. It became obvious that we should sell the home, find a more economical home, and use the equity toward college tuition.

When the manager of the mobile home park somehow learned that we were interested in selling our home, she called me to tell me that she probably had a buyer. But she warned me that regardless of who bought our home, we would have to pay her a finder's fee of several hundred dollars or the buyer would be required to move the home out of her park. It was extortion, but such practices had not yet been outlawed.

The manager sent her prospective customer to see our home, but I was doubtful that he could raise the money because he was merely an enlisted man in the navy. He and I did agree, however, that if he could finance the purchase, we would keep our furniture. I was therefore shocked the next day when he presented me with a cashier's check for our entire asking price and told us he was eager to close the deal. The transaction was completed at the park manager's office, where she made certain she received her "finder's fee." Nevertheless, Joy and I were elated.

Classes were out for the summer and I was between jobs. The buyers had agreed to wait a month to move in, and we were about to leave for Maine to serve as counselors at a Christian youth camp. We were confident that, upon our return, we would be able to rent one of the cottages on campus and complete our move before the deadline.

On our journey north, we stopped at our former bank in Poughkeepsie to pay off the loan on our manufactured home. Joy expressed her concern that we were now without a place to live, and I tried to ease her concerns by repeating that we now had money in the bank and I expected to rent one of the cottages on campus when we returned. She had seen those tiny cottages, and my assurances did not encourage her.

We drove to Maine and enjoyed our volunteer work as children's counselors at a lakeside campground. But the two weeks we committed to that trip left little time to arrange and complete our move. Upon our return we immediately drove over to the college to see about renting a cottage.

Those cabins had been built decades earlier for families who attended the denomination's summer camp programs, but the camp had long since been relocated. Now the cabins were occupied by the families of students. We had been led to believe that we would be able to rent one of those tiny cottages.

Since the cabins had been built to shelter summer campers, and not for year-round use, they had no insulation. They had exposed studs, and cold air leaked through the cracks in the clapboard siding, so in bitter weather, they were impossible to adequately heat. Several students had warned us about their lack of insulation, primitive plumbing, inadequate wiring, and tiny rooms. One student's wife showed us how difficult it was to make their bed because the bedroom was so small that, with the bed shoved against the outside wall, there was only about a foot of space to move along the opposite edge.

The cabins were cold in winter and hot in summer, and there would not be space for most of our furniture. But somehow, I convinced myself that we could make do. Their charm lay in the fact that a "two-bedroom" cabin rented for only $35 per month, plus electric.

But the electric was a problem. The students used excessive amounts in winter to operate illegal portable heaters, thus running up their bills.

Worse, the heaters frequently overloaded the ancient circuits, thus blowing fuses and were therefore fire hazards.

Even so, we had no choice. We had to move as soon as possible. Then crisis loomed. Despite their undesirability, there was not a single vacancy.

Yes, the college was small, but because the staff consisted of highly dedicated people who were willing to work for meager wages, it attracted mature and committed ministry students. Among the student body were quite a few married couples, most with children, and they were occupying all available cabins.

So, upon our return from our working vacation, with the deadline to move staring us in the face, we learned that there was, in a manner of speaking, no room at the inn. We were perplexed. Green Lane was a rural community. There was an apartment complex nearby, but the rent was more than we had been paying for the beautiful home we had just sold.

School was out for the summer, the staff was gone, and after receiving the bad news, I stopped our car in front of the administration building while we pondered our next step. We had no idea what to do. The two girls sat quietly in the back seat while Joy and I discussed the situation. Then we all bowed our heads in prayer.

There had been no one in sight when I parked the car, but while we were praying, someone knocked on my window, startling us. I looked out to see an unshaven man in worn and soiled clothing standing expectantly by my door. When I rolled the window down, he asked if I was Frank Becker, and introduced himself as the campus maintenance man.

Unshaven or not, I knew that he had a servant's heart, because he sure wasn't being paid a living wage. During our first semester, tuition was only twenty-one dollars per credit hour, so there wasn't much money to pay staff. In fact, some of our instructors only received thirty-five dollars a week. These people were dedicated servants!

After it was confirmed that I was "Brother Becker," the man asked whether we had found a place to live. He went on to say that an elderly lady, who owned a home overlooking the Green Lane Reservoir, had fallen and broken her hip and wasn't expected to return home. He thought that her children might consider renting us her house. He made no promises beyond committing himself to talk to the family.

We'd never been to the Montgomery County Park, so it was a real eye opener. Following his instructions, we drove down some winding country roads, passed beneath the base of the high dam that impounded the reservoir that ended just behind our campus. We then found ourselves driving through a breathtakingly beautiful valley. Hundreds of acres of lawn lay on our left, surrounding two lakes, the upper lake impounded by a low dam before flowing into the lower. Forests surrounded the vast lawns on all sides. We could see a public beach and picnic area on the far side of the upper lake. Everywhere we looked, flocks of Canadian geese browsed on the rolling lawns.

As we drove along the edge of the park, between the wooded hills on our right, and the rolling lawns and lakes on our left, there were no houses. This was priceless real estate. But because of the reservoirs, the only houses around the lake had been built before the park was established and therefore were very valuable.

As we neared the far northwest corner of the park, we saw a little stuccoed house with green trim, setting on a knoll behind three big maple trees. We decided to pull in and ask for directions, but when we stopped, we learned that this was the house for rent. The college maintenance man had already spoken with the owners. They asked us a few questions and then showed us through the house.

After they left us, key in hand, we gazed out across our new front lawn. It sloped down for over a hundred feet to where it bordered the town road. Across the road, the lawns of the park itself spread for nearly a half mile south and a mile east, but the west end of the lake lay little more than a hundred yards from our new front door.

Wesley Newell, a fine classmate, and for fifty years the pastor of a church in Cape May, gathered a group of students to help us load and unload our moving van. That house on the knoll was to become our home for the next year-and-a-half. The landlord

Our $75 a month home overlooking the Green Lane Reservoir

mowed the lawns as well as the eight-acre field behind our house. We built a little tree house for our two girls in the large tree that stood near our front porch and set up floodlights on the front lawn so that we could play badminton at night.

When the Salays, came to visit from New York, Helen stepped down from their Econoline Van, stared out across the park, then turned to me and said, "Jesus really loves you, Frank." The truth is that Jesus loves all his children, but we felt especially favored at that moment because he provided us a little taste of paradise for just seventy-five dollars a month. And he even provided the seventy-five dollars a month! We had been weary, but the Lord had made us to lie down in green pastures and had led us beside the still waters.

CHAPTER 24

Childlike Faith

*"Verily I say unto you, except ye be converted, and become
as little children, ye shall not enter into the kingdom of heaven."*
Matthew 18:3, KJV

———————

It was springtime, and we were living in the little house overlooking the Green Lane Reservoir. My recently widowed mother had come from Florida to visit us and was sitting with my wife and our two little girls at the breakfast table. I was rushing out the door to make my morning class when Joy asked if I had any money for groceries.

When I replied, "No," my mother was clearly upset. But our two little girls, aged four and six, were not. Together, they said "Why don't we pray!" So, we joined hands, bowed our heads, and they prayed one of their simple, never-doubting, prayers.

That afternoon, when I returned home from work, the girls laughingly told me about the three letters in the mail that contained checks totaling hundreds of dollars. It was wonderful having money to buy groceries, but it was more wonderful watching my mother try to deal with her granddaughter's childlike faith, and the magnitude of God's faithful reply.

CHAPTER 25

An Old Stick in the Mud

"He will not allow your foot to be moved; He who keeps you will not slumber."

Psalm 121:3

———————

Toward the end of World War II, Dad took our family on a rare day trip in our old Chrysler sedan. We traveled to his sister's farm in Stone Ridge, New York. There we played with our cousins, swam in their creek, and feasted on fresh sweet corn and fried chicken.

To offer us a thrill, Dad took a shortcut to the farm. When we turned off Route 32, it looked more like a cow path than a public road. We wouldn't even have been sure the narrow unpaved trail was a county road if someone hadn't nailed a shingle to a tree with the name, "Old Tongore Road," crudely painted on it.

The first quarter mile downhill was impossibly steep and winding, and we found ourselves skidding around curves and raising a cloud of dust that hung in the air behind us. Dad called it a cow path, because that's exactly what it had been. In the 1920s and 30s, it was not unusual for a rural roadway to follow an old cow path because cows tend to take the easiest route, even if it means almost turning in circles. That's just what this road did.

It wound back and forth down an extremely steep hill, then made a hairpin turn around the trunk of a huge old oak and finally leveled off just before passing a pretty little pond. Dad would only risk driving down that steep trail on a clear dry day, and he never attempted to drive back up. Years later, the authorities closed that road because there had been so many accidents along its short length.

I recently tried to locate Old Tongore Road on a modern map. I couldn't find it. I even wrote my cousin, who has lived her entire life within a few miles of that spot, but I could learn nothing about Old Tongore Road.

I found one road in that area that might once have been Old Tongore, but if so, some of its kinks have been removed, it has been dead ended, and it was renamed Old Duck Pond Road. It seems likely that it was the same road, because Old Duck Pond Road comes to a dead end just a short distance beyond the only pond revealed on the map. I remember the pond well, for the road wound around it and, as I recall, there was a tiny chapel nearby. To my aunts and uncles, the lovely area around that little pond was known as "The Vail."

Twenty-five years after my Dad drove us down Old Tongore Road, while Joy and I were on Christmas vacation, we drove from Pennsylvania to visit my widowed aunt. It was snowing lightly, with about an inch on the ground. I decided to show our two little girls where my dad used to give us a thrill ride.

After I turned off Route 32 onto Old Tongore Road, I saw a large sign that warned that it was a dangerous road that should be avoided in rain or snow. It further warned that horns should be sounded when approaching each curve to alert oncoming drivers. By the time I saw the sign, we were already going downhill and it was impossible to stop and back up. The dirt surface of that narrow road had long since received a layer of blacktop, but it was still impossibly steep and winding.

It was soon obvious that it would be dangerous in wet or snowy weather, even if there had not been an unseen layer of ice hidden beneath the snow. As we started down the hill, I thought I was being prudent when I put the car in second gear and began tapping the brakes to slow our speed. But by the time we passed the sharp curve around the old tree, our horn blaring, I could sense that I was losing control.

We slid to the left side of the crowned road as we came out of a wide curve near the bottom of the hill. Although I pumped the brake pedal, the tires broke loose. We found ourselves sliding out across a frozen cornfield, the stubble of its cut-off stalks in neat rows, like tiny soldiers on parade, standing just inches above the frozen brown earth.

It was a strange sensation when we first began sliding over the frozen ground, almost as though we were accelerating. We bumped up and down as we passed over each plowed row, and everything suddenly seemed to move in slow motion. But when I looked ahead, my heart sank because I realized we were heading for a drainage ditch that crossed the field.

I had been pumping the brakes, but now I pressed the pedal to the floor as we slid inexorably toward that trench. We weren't moving very fast now, but it was obvious that we were going to slide over the edge into the ditch. I could see its far side and realized that someone had laid up vertical walls of field stone, and that our front wheels would drop straight down to the bottom.

I had a pretty good idea as to what might happen to us. Just a couple of years before, we'd been following our best friend's car when it went off the road, crashed into a tree, and their son was fatally injured. Our 1960s station wagon had no seat belts, and I could picture the front bumper smashing into the bottom of the moat-like ditch, with the car standing on end, and our two little girls dropping from the big back seat to crash through the windshield.

We were just a few yards away from the trench, moving at a walking pace, when I prayed, "Lord, help us!" Just as our front wheels were about to drop over the edge of the gully, the car abruptly stopped and we were thrown forward. I sat there for a moment, stunned by the turn of events. Then realizing that we might still be in danger, I told my wife and daughters to quickly and carefully get out of the car.

When I exited the driver's door, I saw that our front bumper was mere inches from the edge of the ditch. The top of that wall was flush with the surface of the field. It had not impeded us. I looked down into the ditch, and my heart was in my mouth. The ditch was deep and wide, and the stonework served to retain the earth where the stream bed passed through a culvert under Old Tongore Road. If the car had plunged over the edge, it would have been a wonder if any of us had survived.

I then walked around the car, trying to understand why we had stopped so abruptly. The car sat at an angle to the ditch, so the front tire on the passenger side was closer to its edge. And when I looked, I discovered that the tire was pressing against something protruding up out of the frozen mud.

Someone had discarded a piece of firewood, about a foot long and perhaps four inches in diameter. It was buried almost completely in the frozen mud. But sticking up out of the mud, from the side of that hunk of firewood, was the stub of a sawn branch. That sawn off branch was only about an inch-and-a-quarter in diameter and rose only a few inches above the surface. Our tire had slid into it, and it had been just enough to keep our car from sliding over the edge.

I looked across that vast field and could only marvel that we just happened to strike that one discarded piece of firewood. If we'd slid just a few inches to either side, we would have gone over the edge of the trench. We gathered there and gave thanks to God. Then, with no apparent damage to our car, we backed slowly across the field and got back on the road. Driving very slowly, we made it the remainder of the way to my aunt's house.

When we left her home a few hours later, my aunt Charlotte advised us to avoid returning the way we had come We headed north on the Hurley Mountain Road. It runs along the left edge of a rich agricultural flood plain. Much of the road is bordered on the left by steep shale banks and tall cliffs. On the right, it drops off several feet to a zigzagging stream bed that runs between the road and the fields that laid fallow under the winter sky.

The snow had continued to fall and was now several inches deep, so I was driving slowly. But as we made our way around a curve, the car again broke loose from the pavement and spun around. This time I felt even more helpless because I dared not even tap the brakes until I knew we were headed in the right direction.

If I misjudged, we'd slide off the right side of the road, over the steep embankment, and either crash onto the stream's rocky shore or into the roaring water itself. On the other side of the road, we would crash into the mountainside that had been sheered away to make room for the road, and perhaps bounce across the road where there were no guard rails. That's not to speak of the possibility that we might run into another car coming from the opposite direction.

Normally it would be impossible to make a U-turn on that narrow road, but when our car finally came to a stop, we found ourselves parked undamaged in its center. The car was pointing back the way we had come. We had done a 180 degree turn and wound up in the middle of the road. After again humbly giving thanks, we drove very slowly back down the road for nearly a mile, until we found a crossroad where we could turn around and resume our journey north.

Some might scoff at what they'd judge to be poor driving, but that's only a stronger argument for divine intervention. Perhaps someone could rationalize one of our escapes, but Joy and I will never forget how God saved us from disaster twice in the same day. He did so without so much as leaving a scratch on the car, or on one of us, and not even knocking the wheels out of line.

After I wrote the above account, our son, Matthew, reminded me of a similar event that took place twenty-five years later, one that clearly was my own fault. Matt was about ten years old at the time. We set out from our new home to attend church, but the road in front of our house was coated with a thin layer of black ice. It too was a narrow, winding, up and down road, surfaced with blacktop.

I drove at walking speed, and we had only gone about one hundred yards when we realized that we needed to return home. But when I came to a complete stop in the middle of the road, the car suddenly began sliding sideways toward the edge of the crowned road. Joy and our four children got out of the station wagon, pushed on opposite corners, and turned the 3,500 pound car around until it was pointing back toward our home. As I drove slowly back toward our driveway, I sensed the tires were occasionally gripping, and that the rising sun had caused the ice to melt a bit.

That's where I really erred. I decided to go down the road to the North Park Store to buy the Sunday newspaper. Joy argued that, since we couldn't safely drive to church, we certainly shouldn't drive anywhere else. I was driving, so I won my point, but ultimately lost the debate.

The road was fairly level, so I safely passed our driveway and continued on. We began going downhill as we started around the last curve before reaching the intersection with the state highway. Our station wagon began sliding to the right, toward a row of large trees on the outside of the curve. It seemed to correct itself as the right-hand wheels scraped on gravel that lay beneath the snow on the edge of the road, then veered toward a tree that was over a foot in diameter. Just before we would have struck that tree head on, the entire car slid to the left, and seemed to race forward as it slipped between that tree and another. In the midst of our prayers and screams of fear, we side-swiped one tree, then bounced sideways against the other, and finally slipped through the narrow opening.

We continued sliding across the snow-covered lawn for about fifty feet, until the car finally came to a stop. Jamie jumped out first, and the rest of us quickly followed. After I learned that no one was hurt, I checked the damage to the car. The driver-side mirror was snapped off, the rear window on the driver's side was smashed, and the rear bumper had broken off. Oddly, there was no damage to the car's body.

The car started easily enough, and I was able to turn it around on the lawn. Then after praying, we made our way back through the trees to the road. During the time we'd been assessing the damage, the rising sun had melted the thin layer of ice on the road, and we were able to make it safely home.

I didn't repeat my suggestion that we should go to the store for the Sunday papers. But, for some reason, I did recall a couple of Bible verses, "Thou shalt not tempt the Lord thy God,"[25] and, "... He shall give His angels charge over you, to keep you in all your ways."[26]

So, God disciplined me, but he also preserved our family, for which I am eternally grateful.

---

25   Deuteronomy 6:16
26   Psalms 91:11

THE PASTORAL YEARS:

THE ANOINTING HAND OF GOD

CHAPTER 26

The Surprised Superintendent

"To me, who am less than the least of all the saints, this grace was given, that I should preach among the Gentiles the unsearchable riches of Christ."

Ephesians 3:8

As I was entering my final semester in Bible college, Joy asked me, "What's next?" One of my professors wanted me to pursue a master's degree, or even a doctorate. He told me I'd make a good college professor. But I'd have none of that. I had concluded that the world was in desperate need of pastors, and that's where I felt my call.

I was doing well in school, while still holding down a part-time job, and I was busy. The students honored me by electing me president of the Student Judiciary and Vice-President of the Student Body. Since we rarely had disciplinary problems, the two offices required little of my time.

The faculty, on the other hand, was pleased that I edited the school newspaper and encouraged me to press on, although I was unable to motivate any of them to write an article for the paper and that was discouraging. Then, when a faculty member was terminated and pleaded with me, a mere student, to publish a special issue of the paper to argue for his reinstatement, I halted publication. Staff members who learned of this were happy with my response.

Average Guy Meets Extraordinary God

Without these other responsibilities, I still had plenty to keep me busy. Apart from regular course work, I was preparing my senior sermon on God's calling of Jeremiah. This was to be delivered before the entire faculty and student body during a morning chapel service. I was also preparing an hour-long lecture for my apologetics class on an alternate view to Einstein's theory of relativity.

Since I was a babe in the woods in terms of pastoral work, and I was about to return to a world of new challenges, I was taking courses in pastoral procedures and church administration. But I had to agree with the complaints of other seniors that these courses were shallow and poorly taught. I had one thing going for me. Although the school administrators had initially been skeptical of my motives for entering the school, the Lord had given me substantial real-world experience, and those memories would serve me well.

I was ten years older than many of the graduates and was no longer so starry-eyed that I imagined all God's men were above personal politics. I had seen leaders lie and manipulate others in order to gain personal advantage, and I was determined not to follow down that slippery slope. I knew that I was naive, but I had no idea how bad things would get in years to come. What I did know was that I needed to be as wise as a serpent and harmless as a dove as I served God.

It was late 1972, I was just a few months from graduation and far too busy to give much thought to what might lie ahead. I would be finishing at Christmas time, while the remainder of the seniors would graduate in May. Most would take rolls in churches as pastoral assistants. We would learn the ropes while serving as youth or education pastors, music directors, or worship leaders. Few churches would call a wet-behind-the-ears college graduate to serve as lead pastor.

Most graduates who want to start right out as pastors become "pioneers," or church-planting missionaries. They work at secular jobs to support their families, while struggling to plant new churches. They typically have just a few parishioners, limited income, meet in rented or donated space, and feel like small fish in tiny ponds.

But Joy's question was valid. I had closed the door on graduate studies, so what, indeed, was next for us? I wanted to pastor. Would I too start as a home missions pastor?

My name had been forwarded to the administrator of the fellowship in New York, and one evening, while at my desk, I was surprised to receive a personal phone call from him. Already in his sixties, and highly respected, he was destined for a larger role.

He was all business, and after the brief social graces had been attended to, he asked whether I was still interested in serving in New York. When I told him,

Frank at his desk in Green Lane, 1972

"Yes," he asked whether I'd be interested in candidating a church.

When I again replied in the affirmative, he went on to explain that I would be the first of three pastoral candidates to visit a small church in the Finger Lakes region. We would each spend a weekend at the church, preaching, teaching, meeting the members, and being interviewed by the board. After all three of us had visited, the congregation would vote for one of us. It was a competition in which it was hoped the Holy Spirit would guide the decision of the local quasi-sovereign fellowship.

The administrator went on to explain that I should consider it an opportunity to be exposed to the process. He said that I shouldn't be discouraged by the outcome. After all, the two other men were seasoned preachers and pastors.

I eagerly seized the opportunity, and on the appointed day Joy and I loaded our two excited little girls in our old station wagon and drove the 275 miles to north central New York. It was a dizzying experience. We were put up in the small local motel, ate meals with a couple of parishioners, were put under a magnifying glass by the members, and I preached the Sunday morning service.

After I delivered the evening message, we were asked to wait in our car while the church held a business meeting. As we sat in the car, the motor running to keep us warm, the church treasurer came out. He waved for me to roll down my window and asked whether I'd consider accepting the pastorate.

One of my college professors had warned me that I should never take a church on less than a 90% favorable vote, reasoning that a new pastor soon loses popularity, and with declining support, might not survive the first crisis. So that's what I told the treasurer. He was a fine man, and I was grateful for his understanding.

A few minutes later, he returned to ask whether I'd reconsider and accept the pastoral role on a vote of 85%. After a moment's thought, I told him, "Yes." He then told me that we were free to go back to our motel, and could start for home in the morning, promising that I would receive a call soon.

Since they weren't to vote until the third candidate had visited them, we had no idea when that would be. But upon returning home, I immediately got hold of a stack of empty cartons and began packing my books. When Joy asked why I was packing, I told her that the church was going to call me, and I wanted to be ready to move as soon as I finished my final exams.

"But they haven't called you!" she exclaimed. "How do you know?"

"I don't know how I know," I replied. "I just know."

I had packed half a dozen cartons of books when, a day or two later, I received a call from the church treasurer. He asked whether I was still willing to accept the pastorate, and I again said, "Yes." Then he confirmed that they had voted to call me as their pastor the night we sat in our car outside the church. They offered me a generous salary, health insurance, the use of their parsonage, and a paid vacation. And they wanted us as soon as possible, preferably in time for Christmas.

So, I called the administrator in New York to let him know what had occurred. When he asked who was calling, I gave him my name and had to remind him that he'd called me about candidating the church. Since the candidating process for three men should have required at least a month, he asked me why I was calling him.

I told him, "The church has called me to be their pastor."

"What?" he exclaimed, clearly surprised.

I repeated myself.

He was silent for a moment, obviously convinced that I was confused, or that something had been lost in the translation. He asked me a few more questions in an attempt to clarify the situation. Before he hung up, he said, "I'll give them a call." Any word of congratulations was noticeably absent.

It took me a while to realize that the administrator had made me the first of the three candidates because I was a novice, a mere college student, whereas the other two were experienced men. Ostensibly, when their preaching was compared with my initial appearance, and what was assumed would be my stumbling presentation, I would serve to make the two men who followed me look better. As a fledgling Bible school graduate, I wasn't considered either sufficiently knowledgeable, experienced, or mature for the task.

One of my instructors warned me that I was sent there as "cannon fodder," to provide the required third candidate. I was expected to fail, but I should understand that there was no animosity intended. It was to have been a good growth experience for me, and if I also learned a little humility from their rejection, it would benefit my character.

What was strange was the growing certainty that I would be called by the church. It was a matter of imputed faith, not something that I somehow cranked up or generated out of my own mind. My confidence was a gift from God.

I might otherwise have been double-minded, uncertain of God's calling, and wondering whether I would be adequate to the challenge. After all, Joy and I really were novices. We had been at the college for two-and-a-half years, and it had become home to us. Accepting this challenge presaged another huge change in our lives. But for some reason, I was unable to entertain any possibility of rejection.

How do I explain my confidence that the church would call me? Where did the faith come from that caused me to pack those six cartons of textbooks? The phone call from the church affirmed my faith, but it also increased it, adding encouragement that I could fulfill my future responsibilities.

Oh, yes, the surprised superintendent did call back to confirm my call. And this time he did say, "Congratulations."

CHAPTER 27

"Pride Goeth Before Destruction"

"Pride goeth before destruction, and a haughty spirit before a fall."
Proverbs 16:18, KJV

I was 33 years old, married to a bright and beautiful woman, father of our two bright and beautiful little girls, and was settling into my first pastorate. I thought I knew something of the world because, as I've already mentioned too many times, I had managed several businesses and had muddied my hands in politics. But I had not grown up in the church. In many ways, I had not grown much at all.

I was fresh out of Bible school, with barely sufficient knowledge of the Bible. I had little familiarity with the life of a church, and virtually no experience as a pastor. Worse, I had only a little understanding of the widely diverse beliefs and prejudices held by the members. So, when the district administrator learned that the church had called me in preference to two far more experienced men, it was understandable that he seemed dumbstruck.

In spite of that, I believed that God had called me to pastor that church, and it was that conviction that enabled me to proceed in faith and confidence. Most people equate the word "church" with a building, but a church is really a group of people of like-minded precious faith who happen to occupy a building. Hopefully, their like-mindedness is based on the belief that Christ died for their sins, but if that's all they have, then their relationship is still tenuous.

To achieve unity, each believer must continually grow spiritually through personal application of the Word of God to their own lives. The Apostle Paul explained, *"...till we all come to the unity of the faith and of the knowledge of the Son of God, to a perfect man, to the measure of the stature of the fullness of Christ"* (Ephesians 4:13). In any fellowship, it is often the younger and more enthusiastic members who obey the Apostle Peter's metaphorical command. That is, as newborn babies desire milk, they desire the sincere nourishment of God's word that they may grow thereby.[27] Too often, however, we are not unified, and most of us fail in the important goal of becoming of one mind and one spirit.

There were a number of retired pastors and missionaries at that first church, and I could sometimes sense a spirit of restraint and judgment. The pressure was on me to avoid offending anyone, while somehow conforming to everyone's diverse tastes and opinions. In other words, I had to somehow walk between the raindrops, or risk becoming a spiritual chameleon—a hypocrite.

I did not initially understand my peril, so as a young soldier of the Cross, I was constantly in danger of blundering into one of many social, political, and theological mine fields. Any success I enjoyed was probably because I gave the concerns of others little thought, determined to do things God's way, and help my flock grow in the Lord. If someone had dare suggest that I needed a pulpit committee, I would have insisted that I already had one, the Father, the Son, and the Holy Spirit.

People who speak of a bed of roses have never laid down in one. I have too often experienced the prick of the thorns and the smell of the manure. It was clearly the Holy Spirit, and not my own pride, that helped me overcome the barbs.

But whatever the case, the congregation had voted me in and I was not about to compromise God's Word, even if they voted me back out. And that was a real possibility! Perhaps my pride put me in danger of destruction, but I suspect that while God was dealing with my immaturity, He was also using my rough ignorance to smooth some of the abrasive edges on others. In retrospect, I would not recommend my behavior to other pastors.

One of the minefields a pastor can stumble into involves the church building itself. If you so much as change the color of the paint on a closet

---

27   See 1 Peter 2:2.

wall, you are in danger of being declared anathema. There are always older saints who will boast that they were "...dedicated, saved, baptized, and married there." Some act as though they had already been buried there.

Our church auditorium had an old inoperable pipe organ off to one side, its tall gold pipes rising behind the choir loft. The pulpit or lectern, stood in the center of the platform, signifying that the preaching of the Word is central to worship. A piano stood on one side of the platform, an electric organ on the other.

The organist was married to a retired pastor, while the pianist was married to the church treasurer—both fine men. One Saturday night, while visiting the pianist's home, her teenage daughter told me that the congregation wanted to hear their new pastor sing a solo. I didn't like that idea, but they insisted, and stood me by their upright piano while they began rehearsing me.

And the next morning, I did indeed sing an old hymn, accompanied only by the pianist. While I was singing, the organist left her bench in a huff, walked down into the congregation, and plunked herself down beside her husband. I think that the entire congregation was as surprised as I by her behavior, and that afternoon I learned that she felt slighted because she had not also been invited to accompany me.

She and her husband were influential members, and I found myself standing on a powder keg with the fuse lit. What to do? As far as I was concerned, she had acted out her frustrations publicly, and I impulsively responded in like manner. During the Sunday evening service, I explained how I had come to sing with just the pianist accompanying me. Then I assured the congregation that no insult had been intended, but I stated that if the organist was not back at her instrument at the next service then I would find someone else to play that instrument.

On Wednesday evening, she was back at the organ, and nothing was ever spoken again about the matter, although I did hear a rumor that even her husband told her she had been wrong. I have never heard of another pastor taking such a stand in public, and I'm now a little ashamed at my own audacity. She was a fine woman, perhaps embarrassed by our seeming neglect and she acted impulsively. And while she erred publicly, I wonder whether I might have done better to speak to her quietly.

Jesus taught that, if your brother sins against you, it is your responsibility to go to them. (Matthew 18:15-17). But she had committed the act before the congregation, and I dealt with it in like manner. Thank God that He extinguished that fuse before the powder keg exploded. Was my action prudent or a matter of pride?

Upon my arrival, I immediately began making changes to the building and rarely consulted anyone. I installed bookcases in my study, built a little Noah's ark in the corner of the nursery where toddlers played, gave permission to a gifted teen to paint a beautiful mural on the wall of the young adult's room, and installed floodlights out front to illuminate the beautiful building. In fact, the congregation seemed delighted with my enthusiasm and my determination to get things done, and they were happy with the results.

As far as I was concerned, a pastor was called by God to lead a flock, and whether the church had a board of trustees, elders, or deacons, they were there to support the pastor's vision. I argued that the Book of Acts revealed that pattern. For example, at Antioch, there were certain prophets and teachers, and... *"As they ministered to the Lord and fasted, the Holy Spirit said, 'Now separate to Me Barnabas and Saul for the work to which I have called them'"* (Acts 13:2).

Then they sent them off with a prayer and left them alone to do their work. The only check on their work was done at the end of their missionary journey when the Apostles in Jerusalem dealt with the dispute over whether Gentile converts must be circumcised. There they confirmed The Apostle Paul's judgment (Acts 15:19-20).

I didn't think that the pastor had absolute power or wisdom. After all, the congregation could vote him out anytime. But my early actions produced positive results, bringing enthusiasm to the congregation and increasing attendance. I did consult the board before proceeding with plans to paint and carpet the auditorium, and they were enthused. But there was a time or two when I would have been prudent to take the congregation's pulse before acting. And today I might just amend my position to suggest that it's good for a pastor to surround himself with wise individuals, because "iron sharpens iron,"[28] and in the multitude of council is wisdom ordained.

But in those early days, I frequently undertook projects without bothering to consult the members of the church board, thus denying them an opportunity to veto my activities. Perhaps I considered it easier to seek forgiveness for a fait-accompli than to risk being refused permission to undertake a project. Or perhaps I thought of myself as the "boss" in my

---

28   Proverbs 27:17

old business, not requiring anyone's permission. I'm sure I thought that the success I achieved would stifle any criticisms.

I was a take charge guy, and sometimes my zeal outpaced my wisdom. Despite that, the people were very pleased with the outcome of my earlier projects, as well as with our numerical growth. Even before I completed my first year, they offered to substantially increase my salary and add a week of vacation time.

My mother once commented, *"Give a fool enough rope, and he'll hang himself."* Proverbs 16:18 warns, *"Pride goes before destruction, and a haughty spirit before a fall."* Because of what I'm about to describe, it's a bit surprising that the church didn't fire me. I stepped out in pride, and if I had fallen to my destruction, the church wouldn't have had to fire me; a funeral would have sufficed.

Our building was originally a Methodist Church, but it has served various groups over the previous century. At the time I was called to pastor, it needed a face lift, but its small and increasingly enthusiastic congregation included a number of godly men who were willing to sign personally for a bank loan to make needed improvements. Five thousand dollars was a lot of money for a small congregation to raise in the early 1970s, easily equivalent to $30,000 in today's money.

We were having the auditorium painted and carpeted, the cedar shingles on the steeple replaced, and the brick cleaned. In retrospect, I can scarcely believe that I made most of those decisions myself. There were no committees and no interminable discussions. I chose the carpet and the colors of the paints, and I negotiated with and hired the people who did the work.

Then I identified another improvement I wanted to make, and I didn't recognize any potential downside. I was confident that my idea would beautify the auditorium, and I decided that I could accomplish the work by myself. And I probably harbored a suspicion that if I brought it to the attention of others, I might meet opposition. I wanted to surprise everyone, and, oh boy, did I!

Though nearly 50 years have passed and my memory of the building may be flawed, my recollection of the events, being intensely personal, remain clear. The day this event occurred, I was the only person in the building. The sanctuary or auditorium was essentially a square room with rounded corners, as was typical of many Methodist church buildings erected during the 19th century. A raised platform was built across one corner, and the floor of the auditorium sloped downward toward that platform so that everyone could see and hear the speaker.

The pulpit was in the center of the platform, typical of denominations that considered the preaching of God's Word to be central to worship. There was a piano to one side and an electric organ on the other. The gilded pipes of an antique, non-functional pipe organ, partially paid for by steel magnate, Andrew Carnegie, occupied the wall to the left of the pulpit.

If memory serves, the sixteen-foot walls met a tray ceiling. A short distance in from the walls, the ceiling rose upward in a curve toward the center of the room, like a wide, shallow bowl. The flat top of the bowl was about twenty feet above the floor of the auditorium, and a second bowl rose above it, this one a dome made of beautiful multi-colored stained glass. This glass dome was about twelve feet in diameter, and perhaps four feet high.

Fiberglass insulation had been laid above the ceiling, including the glass dome. It was tucked between the joists, but simply laid atop the leaded glass dome. The insulation was covered with a thick layer of dust, so it must have been installed decades before.

I had made it my mission to remove those batts from above the stained glass dome, and thus uncover the beauty of the glass for the edification of those who worshiped below. Looking up from the auditorium floor, there were three circular wooden frames in the plaster ceiling, evenly placed around the stained glass dome, just a foot or two from its outside edge. Each of those frames was about four feet in diameter. I later learned that they were functional. They were actually ventilators.

Nested across each of those circular wooden frames were two wide curved boards, like half moons. One of them was fixed permanently in place. The other was hinged and could be tipped up to allow ventilation on hot summer days. When the windows below were opened, the open vents in the ceiling permitted the heated air to rise, creating a draft that cooled the auditorium. The ventilators had not been in use in many years and had also been covered with insulation. On the floor, far below the glass dome and its surrounding ventilators, stood row on row of beautiful solid oak pews.

So one morning, when I was sure I would be alone in the building, I took my tool box in one hand, hung a six foot step ladder over my shoulder, and made my way into the attic. It was dark, but enough light seeped in from the soffits, and I carried a flashlight to find my way in the murky darkness. My goal, of course, was to reach the stained-glass dome in the center of the sanctuary ceiling and remove the insulation.

At the attic door, I discovered a light switch. When I flipped it, a lone bulb near the center illuminated the area around the dome. I made my way carefully along a crude wooden walkway. It was made of scrap boards laid crosswise atop parallel ceiling joists. This walkway led to a makeshift ladder that enabled me to climb to the top of the trey ceiling and reach the edge of the glass dome. The ladder was constructed of scrap boards nailed to the edges of the studs.

Climbing that curved surface above the trey ceiling was something like climbing up a hill between batts of dusty fiberglass, with cobwebs hanging here and there. This was, after all, a place where only skilled workmen very rarely climbed.

Then I found myself on another narrow walkway across which I made my way to the base of the stained-glass dome. When I reached the dome, I took mincing steps until I discovered that a narrow walkway ran around its perimeter.

It was my plan to remove the fiberglass, clean the stained glass surface, and mount a floodlight above it, thus dazzling the congregation below with its beauty. I used a garden rake to carefully drag the fiberglass off the dome, and let the batts lay where they fell. It all appeared to be going very well. It took longer than I had anticipated and was a dirty job.

My first disappointment came when I realized that the leaded glass was coated with a century of thick dust. It was obvious that I needed to wash it off, and I was very concerned that I might damage the glass or even drip dirty water on the new carpeting below. But I made my way back out of the attic and down the stairs to the kitchen, where I found a mop and pail. Filling the pail with hot water, I struggled back up the stairs and through the attic. It was a challenge to get the bucket to the edge of the glass dome without slopping water over the edge, and by the time I had accomplished that feat, I was tired.

My work with the sponge mop and bucket proved futile. Within just a minute or so, the water in the pail was black with what looked like coal soot, and all I had achieved was to smear the dirt over a few square feet of the dome. And I couldn't imagine my carrying bucket after bucket of water up and down the stairs, from first floor to attic, exhausting myself and spilling a lot of water along the way. I began questioning the wisdom of my plans and gave up the idea of cleaning the glass. I hoped that sufficient light would pass through the dust to illuminate the dome, and that others would soon be inspired to help me clean its surface, once they recognized its potential beauty.

It was soon clear that I'd given too little thought to the reason why the dome had been covered in the first place. It had obviously been insulated to stop the drafts that passed through the numberless cracks between the pieces of stained glass and the lead that held them in place.

And then my situation suddenly improved. I noticed that the electric light was about eight feet above one edge of the dome. The fixture was screwed to a flimsy post that ran vertically from joist beneath my feet to a rafter near the peak of the roof, and it was adjustable. It could be aimed at the center of the dome.

That light fixture couldn't have been better placed. All I needed to do was lean my step ladder against that vertical board, climb the ladder, change the standard bulb for a flood lamp, and focus it on the center of the dome. But I would need to take care about where I positioned the base of my step ladder.

The ceiling of the sanctuary was about a century old, and the heavy ceiling joists beneath my feet were about eighteen inches apart. Thin wooden lathe strips had been fastened to the bottom edges of the joists, and a couple of layers of plaster had been troweled over the lathe strips from below in order to produce the smooth finished ceiling.

I had been very careful to keep to the walkways the workmen had laid atop those joists. If I were to step off those crude pathways and put my foot down between those heavy wooden joists, my weight would tear through the thin wooden lath strips. I, along with some of the plaster ceiling, would crash to the floor below.

In order to support the legs of my ladder, I was prepared to lay some boards across those ceiling joists, but even there, my way seemed to have been prepared for me. I pulled up the insulation where I wanted to place my ladder, and discovered a large flat wooden surface just a foot or two out from the base of the post. I assumed that was where someone had once placed his ladder. So I positioned the legs of my ladder on those boards, leaned its top against the light pole, and started up the ladder. I moved slowly, afraid that the ladder might slip off the side of the narrow flexing board against which I'd leaned it, and I would find myself falling face first through the glass dome.

But my danger lay elsewhere. Little did I know that I was about to illustrate Alexander Pope's observation that, "Fools rush in where angels fear to tread;"[29] and Newton's First Law of Motion, "An object at rest remains at rest, and an object in motion remains in motion at constant speed and in a straight line unless acted on by an unbalanced force." Above all, I was about to demonstrate that pride goes before a fall.

When I reached the third rung, I realized that I still couldn't stretch high enough to reach the light fixture, so I climbed to the fourth step. My knees were now touching the top of the six-foot step ladder, and I still had to stretch in order to unscrew the old bulb and replace it with the flood lamp. Relieved that I had accomplished this without incident, I lowered my right foot to the third rung of the ladder, and with that slight movement, my world changed so suddenly that, by the time I grasped what was happening, it was almost over!

I found myself staring at my forearms. It took me a moment to realize that my elbows were leveled on either side of me, and were resting on the tops of the joists which had, a moment before, supported the wooden platform on which my step ladder had been resting. Then I realized that I was hanging by those elbows, with the rest of my body dangling down through a hole in the ceiling of the sanctuary.

I won't say I was shocked. Maybe bemused. I realized that I must not move, or I would fall through the wide hole. It had not yet occurred to me how much it would hurt if I fell through that hole and landed on the back edges of the pews that were about twenty feet below. Then it came to me that my arms and elbows didn't hurt.

Later I would do the math. When the ladder dropped away from beneath me, I had been standing on its fourth rung, four feet above the platform on which the ladder stood. Since my shoulders had been over four feet above my feet, my arms dropped over eight feet before striking the perimeter of the new opening in the ceiling. And yet they had stopped my fall. I had fallen eight feet, and I felt absolutely no shock or pain! Nor was I upset or frightened.

I was surprised that my arms had somehow caught the edge of the large opening, and that I hadn't simply slipped on through. It didn't seem difficult or painful to remain hanging there. How could that be? When I turned my head slightly from side to side, I saw that the hole was at least four feet across. Why hadn't I just plunged on through?

I was very calm. I am not sure that I was even infused with adrenaline, which would have explained any temporary absence of pain. Instead,

---

29   See https://hymnary.org/text/standing_by_a_purpose_true

I felt strangely secure. And, neither then, nor in the days that followed, did I show any signs of bruising, nor did I ever suffer pain.

The initial thought was, how did my elbows happen to catch the edge of this opening and why hadn't I fallen through? But that was followed by a far more important question: Why don't my arms hurt, and why am I not falling through? And finally, have I the strength to pull myself back up out of this hole to safety?

Then I became conscious of pressure on my right foot, and I realized that the step ladder was hanging from the toe of my shoe by its fourth or fifth step. I couldn't look down to see it, but this seemed somehow funny to me. I concluded that, since the Lord hadn't let the ladder fall to the floor below, and since I didn't want to drop the step ladder and cause additional damage, I should try to save it.

So, still hanging there by my elbows, I reached one hand across to the base of the post that supported the light fixture and grabbed hold of it. Thus braced, I raised my right foot to bring the ladder closer, reached down with my right hand to grab the top step, and awkwardly worked the ladder back up out the hole, finally sliding it onto the joists beside my head. Then, grabbing the base of the light post with both hands, I pulled myself up through the hole. I lay there for a moment before slowly and very carefully getting to my feet.

I still wasn't shaking or feeling pain. Just a sense of amazement. Physical strength did not account for my survival. I was not a body builder. I was five foot, eight inches tall, I weighed maybe 140 pounds, and because I had played intercollegiate soccer, most of my musculature was in my lower body. From that moment, I had no doubt that something supernatural had occurred.

It took two trips, but I carried everything back downstairs, and finally made my way to the sanctuary to get a close look at the damage I had caused. Looking up, I saw that one of the three ventilators had broken free of the ceiling, leaving a hole so wide that I realized I could not possibly have held on to the edge by myself, nor prevented myself from falling through to the floor on which I now stood.

Then I looked at the remains of the wooden circular vent assembly that I had dislodged. It was now strewn across the carpet around me. I actually counted the pieces. There were thirty seven of them, from a tiny piece of quarter-round molding about an inch and a half long, to an entire section that was several feet across.

Then I gave my attention to the pew upon which the ventilator had crashed. The pew had been manufactured of smoothly sawn strips of oak, laminated together to form the curved seat and back of the pew. Those strips were about an inch wide by over an inch deep. They were glued together and planed and sanded until smooth, and they ran the length of the pew.

When the circular wooden ventilator fell, it turned on its edge, and smashed into a couple of strips of the oak pew, driving them down to the floor, and leaving a long narrow gap about two inches wide that ran the length of the pew. I stared at the back of those pews and wondered how many bones I would have broken if I fell across them. If the wooden step ladder fell through to the floor below, I have no doubt that its splintered remains would have been strewn over the floor as well.

And now I was faced with the challenge of somehow reassembling the shattered pieces of the vent. I would need to glue and nail it back together. Then I would have to repaint it. And finally I would have to somehow lift the heavy device back up into place, twenty feet above my head, wiggle it into the hole, and hold it while I nailed it back in place. That observation caused me to look for the nails that originally held it. They were small finishing nails, now bent, leaving no question in my mind as to why my weight broke it loose.

At that moment, a passage from Scripture came to mind, a verse that applied to our Lord. But then I thought, perhaps it applies to those of us who love him. It certainly seems to have applied to me.

"For he shall give his angels charge over thee, to keep thee in all thy ways. They shall bear thee up in their hands, lest thou dash thy foot against a stone" (Psalm 91:11-12). A stone? How about a pew? Later in the day, I mentioned my debacle to a faithful friend in the church, a godly person, and he told me not to worry.

I returned with my tools the next day to reassemble the ventilator, and discovered that someone had already done the repairs. They'd even repainted it, and somehow remounted it in the ceiling. They had also exchanged the broken pew with one from the choir loft. One of the ladies told me that a couple of men in the church had done it for me, but wouldn't tell me their names.

When I described the incident during the next service, the responses of the members of the congregation were not, to say the least, entirely favorable. One or two were clearly upset that I'd damaged their precious church and broken a pew, even though most of those pews had remained vacant for years. Others stared at that damaged pew, and at the ceiling above, and shook their heads in wonder. And I suspect a number were glad I wasn't killed. Several actually quoted Psalm 91, and applied it directly to my situation.

To this day, I marvel at how many of our people did not give the Lord credit for my survival. Certainly, there was nothing about me to deserve a life-saving miracle. But isn't that the point? Perhaps the Lord looked upon me as a careless young preacher struggling to serve him—just a rash and outspoken advocate for Christ, an impetuous Son of Thunder—but evidently worth saving.

Perhaps it was understandable that some questioned my testimony, even whether I had actually fallen through the ceiling. That was ironic, because they were believers who claimed that miracles are for today. Looking back, it reminds me of the question that the Lord Jesus asked, *"... when the Son of Man comes, will he find faith on earth?"* (Luke 18:8).

For my own part, I again saw that the Lord loves and cares for even the simplest, most undeserving of his creatures. Think about that verse: *"For he shall give his angels charge over thee, to keep thee in all thy ways. They shall bear thee up in their hands, lest thou dash thy foot against a stone"* (Psalm 91:11-12). That prophecy concerning the Lord was uttered long before his birth, but it contains comfort for all of us.

Nor should we forget this truth: *"Pride goeth before destruction, and a haughty spirit before a fall"* (Proverbs 16:18, KJV). Every time I read those words, I am both sobered and cheered, because many years ago the Lord vividly demonstrated to me that He is full of love and mercy, and can bear us up when we fall.

CHAPTER 28

"It's gone! It's gone!"

"One thing I know: that though I was blind, now I see."
John 9:25

My mother was born in 1914, and grew up on a hard scrabble farm on Grafton Mountain. During the Great Depression, her father served as a uniformed fire warden at the now historic Dickinson Hill Fire Tower. My mother had three brothers, two of whom served in World War II. She attended a one-room schoolhouse and was faithful to the Baptist Church in Grafton, New York. For nearly fifty years, her cousin, Bill O'Dell, pastored that church, and I was privileged to speak to its members on one occasion.

She met my father when he was attending Rensselaer Polytechnic Institute, in nearby Troy. Mom was always known as a real lady, not stuffy or self-righteous, but gracious and correct. She never spoke of personal issues, particularly nothing related to her health.

When Mom was about sixty years old, and had been a widow for five years, she came to visit us. As I was concluding an evening service, many came forward for prayer. I was surprised to find my mother among them.

I was moving from person to person, hearing their needs and praying quietly with them. When I reached my mother, I assumed she would be making a request for a friend or relative. Instead, she expressed concern for a very personal issue.

"I have a growth on my breast," she told me, and went on to say that a surgeon was scheduled to remove it when she returned to Florida. It was a surprise to hear my mother share such personal information, and it took me a moment to realize that she was looking at me as God's representative and not as her little boy.

As the third of four sons, I had continually competed for my parent's attention and respect. But until now, my becoming a preacher hadn't seemed to make any difference. Remember Jesus' words? *"A prophet is not without honor except in his own country, among his own relatives, and in his own house"* (Mark 6:4).

I was so surprised by my mother's prayer request that I suspect I merely went through the motions. I had no sense that there was any faith underlying my words. Then, as the service ended, I began conversing with others, and the entire matter slipped my mind.

The next morning, I had a busy schedule at the church and was occupied with my own thoughts as I walked home for lunch. As I went through the front door, my mother came rushing to meet me.

"It's gone!" she shouted. "It's gone!"

I looked around in confusion, wondering what might have been stolen or misplaced.

"What's gone?" I finally asked.

"The growth," she said. "It's gone!"

It took me a moment to recall our previous night's conversation. What could I say? I hadn't prayed in faith, at least not as I understood faith. To my shame I'd forgotten about her life-threatening lesion. But my failure, at least in this case, had not hindered God.

My mother would never have brought such an intimate need before strangers, and for that reason, I had been shocked that she shared it with me. But she did, and the Lord healed her. Mom never required the scheduled surgery, and she lived another thirty-three years. Like the blind man whom Jesus healed, my mother didn't need a theological explanation. She had experienced a miracle and she gave Jesus the glory.

CHAPTER 29

"Thank God we'll never pastor in this town!"

"Now the word of the LORD came unto Jonah the son of Amittai, saying, 'Arise, go to Nineveh, that great city, and cry against it; for their wickedness has come up before me.' But Jonah rose up to flee."

Jonah 1:1-3a

It was August of 1973. I had been a pastor for just eight months, and our little family had enjoyed our first vacation camping on the shore of New Hampshire's Ossipee Lake. On our way home, we found ourselves driving through the rust-belt city of Troy, New York.

I was somewhat familiar with the city because my mother was born in Rensselaer County. During the Great Depression she and her mother worked in Troy as seamstresses at Cluett-Peabody, home of the world-famous Arrow Shirts. And that's where she met my father. My future mother and grandmother were sitting together on the doorstep in front of their apartment house on a warm summer evening in 1933 when my future father, an electrical engineering major at Rensselaer Polytechnic Institute, drove past. The rest is history.

Twenty years later, my brother John also attended RPI, earning his degree in Petroleum Geology, and qualifying as a naval officer through their ROTC program. It was during our occasional visits to RPI that I became vaguely familiar with the city.

Troy's halcyon days began around the War of 1812, and it became one of America's great industrial cities. Troy was home to many thriving industries, including steel foundries, instrument makers, meat packing plants, and clothing factories. Items as diverse as church bells, military uniforms, artillery cannons, canned beans, and precision instruments were manufactured in Troy. Troy even boasted America's first Bessemer steel mill.

I have a five-by-five foot map of Troy and Rensselaer County, printed in 1863. It has engraved pictures of major structures, plus maps of nearby villages. It was printed when Troy was producing or packaging much of the food, clothing and armament used by the Union armies during the Civil War.

The city claims to be the home of the legendary "Uncle Sam," a meat packer who passed away in 1854. His iconic caricature, dressed in red, white, and blue top hat and tails, has graced millions of posters that challenged Americans to join the military or buy war bonds. But Troy's glory faded during the early 20th century. During Prohibition, the flow of goods through the city was replaced by a flood of illegal alcohol, with bootleggers like Legs Diamond bringing notoriety.

My brother and most RPI students held Troy and its politicians in contempt. They didn't hesitate to point out published accounts of graft and corruption, and the resulting physical and moral decay of the city.

Now as Joy and I bounced along the brick-paved streets that had seen little improvement since they were laid down more than a century earlier, we glimpsed Troy's shuttered factories and run down neighborhoods. I found myself saying aloud, *"Thank God we'll never pastor in this town."*

Someone once said, "Be careful what you wish for." I might add, "Be careful what you don't wish for." Certainly, our Lord has an amazing sense of humor. Even now, the irony of my words continues to bring a smile to my face because, four months after I uttered them, I was called to pastor in Troy.

I wonder how different things might have been for the prophet Jonah had he joyfully obeyed God's command. There was one difference between that ancient evangelist and me. I was eager to reach my Nineveh. In retrospect, it seems that Jonah had a better idea of what he was facing, and that might explain why his flesh resisted the will of God. I was happily ignorant of the trials I would face, and went willingly to my Nineveh, like an ox to slaughter. The Lord might well have said of me, "I will show him what great things he must suffer for my name's sake."

Fifty years have passed, and as I weigh the pros and cons, I cannot imagine a sane man making such a decision. I'm trying to recall what must have filled me with such discontent that I chose to leave a seemingly idyllic pastorate to face what was obviously a disaster? I may not yet understand everything, but I do know Who led me to make that decision.

A year earlier, when I accepted my first pastoral position in that pretty little village north of the Finger Lakes, the church had about twenty-five in attendance. Five of such attendees were former missionaries or pastors. They represented a healthy percentage of the congregation, proud and experienced professionals who quietly but critically reviewed my every effort. Perhaps I wanted to move on because I sensed that one or two wanted to keep a tighter rein on me, to micro-manage my time and efforts. It might seem like a small thing, but having enjoyed one of the few perks of business ownership—the freedom to make decisions—I was not prepared to let anyone but God take control of my life. And maybe not even Him!

But consider what I was relinquishing. During the year I served that little church, we grew significantly, and there was a great deal of excitement and enthusiasm. Our Sunday school workers were deeply committed and we had a new young adult group. We had given the exterior of the church a face lift, and we had the auditorium painted and carpeted.

My family enjoyed living in a large and comfortable parsonage, and we suffered no want. The church board members had shown their support by raising my salary by nearly twenty percent and by doubling my vacation time. It was a beautiful little rural community, and the typical pastor would consider it a plum.

But I felt a compulsion to move on, so I visited the state headquarters in November of 1973 to request a different church. I finally met the administrator who had originally called me to candidate, and he made it clear that he felt I should remain where I was for at least another year. When I persisted, he said, "I have only one church open." I later learned that he was not being completely candid. What he meant was that he had only one church open for which he would consider letting me candidate and ironically, it was in Troy.

I told him I would pray about it, and returned home. A few days later, our church hosted a visiting missionary. Over dinner, she told us that one of her relatives had pastored in Troy, and she warned me that the work was "burned over" and should be abandoned. The church had a bad reputation because the last pastor had been thrown out of the ministry. She went on to say that the people of the city were difficult to reach with the gospel because Troy was over ninety percent Roman Catholic. She added that the fellowship was down to four people, there was no money, and the church building itself was in shambles.

She told me that I'd be better off starting a new church from scratch, so that I wouldn't inherit the disgrace or the financial burdens associated with the existing church or have the denomination trying to control me. But I didn't want to go off on my own, so I ignored her sage advice, and called the administrator to tell him I would accept the challenge. He was surprised, and still tried to talk me out of it, but finally arranged for another official, who had once lived in Troy, to drive there with me to appraise the situation.

When we arrived at the church, I joked that the building looked like it had been designed by one of the non-Christian cults. We entered through a square clapboard tower that had a crenelated top, like some ancient castle. I wondered whether the gaps in the roof line were designed for their members to shoot arrows down at attacking heretics.

The snow on the roof of the steeple was melting, and when we entered the vestibule, there was a stream of water pouring down to splash at our feet. It flowed under the doors into the auditorium, ran across the sloping floor, and disappeared under the edge of the speaker's platform. When we went down the cellar stairs, we discovered that the water was pouring down from the auditorium above, and soaking into the cellar's dirt floor.

Two tiny restrooms sat on concrete slabs near the base of the crude staircase, and were dimly illuminated by light bulbs that hung from cords. It seemed obvious that no one would ever visit them except in emergency. I don't recall ever doing so, but my wife, who was expecting our third child, recently told me that they were like a port in a storm, and she didn't mind too much. The pastor's apartment was on the second floor, and had peeling paint, cabinet doors hanging from broken hinges, broken plumbing, exposed wiring, floor covering that was cracked and peeling, and trash everywhere.

The church itself had just four members, and they comprised the board of directors. Two of them were over seventy, and were so infirm that they never attended a single service. The other two, the Berggrens, were a wonderful young couple who drove fifteen miles from their home in Schenectady to keep the Troy church alive until it was on its feet again. If and when that miracle occurred, they planned to join a vibrant church near their home.

The Berggrens tithed what was a substantial amount in the 1970s, and that sum was ultimately used as our sole support. Yet it was far less than half what we had been receiving in salary and benefits, and we would also have to raise money to pay for rental housing. Fortunately, the churches of the fellowship were temporarily paying the utility bills for the church building itself.

Today I have the benefit of hindsight to explain my decision to move to Troy, but others concluded that I was actually putting my family's welfare at risk. Christmas was just around the corner, we were expecting our third child in March, and since we had completed college a little more than a year earlier. We had only a few hundred dollars in savings, which was scarcely enough to rent a truck to move our furniture. But I stubbornly clung to the idea that God would provide, and I was determined to make the change.

In retrospect, I know that Jesus was leading, but I continued to ignore his cautionary words: *"For which of you, intending to build a tower, does not sit down first and count the cost, whether he has enough to finish it?"* (Luke 14:28). Yet, in spite of the difficulties, I felt very uncomfortable in my very comfortable pastorate. Once again, the Lord was leading with the carrot and the stick, and I felt compelled to make the move.

What was the upshot? We moved to Troy just before Christmas in 1974. On Sunday, December 29th, we conducted our first service. I was encouraged because we had about fourteen people in church. There wasn't a lot of enthusiasm among the few occasional attendees, but they were glad the church once again had a pastor. At one of our early services, when I suggested that we would have fifty people in Sunday School within a year, there was audible laughter.

As it turned out, they were wrong. But there was rough sledding ahead, and within days it became obvious that I would have to take a job to support our family. *"I would have lost heart, unless I had believed that I would see the goodness of the LORD in the land of the living"* (Psalm 27:3).

Joy and I never regretted moving to Troy. We came to love the people of the city, many of whom were open to the gospel. But on more than one occasion I wound up in open warfare with some of the city fathers. I even received phone calls threatening my life when I opposed a city ordinance specifically dignifying homosexual relations, while they ignored the needs and rights of every other minority.

Nonetheless, our ten years in Troy would be the most challenging, yet joyously productive period of our lives. Within our first sixteen months, we sold the old church building, purchased a far nicer one, bought a house to serve as a parsonage, and we were averaging nearly 300 in Sunday School. I'm very glad that the Lord ignored me when I said, "Thank God we'll never pastor in this town."

CHAPTER 30

"One thousand dollars!"

"Now to Him who is able to do exceedingly abundantly above all that we ask or think..."

Ephesians 3:20

It was a two-hundred mile drive from our first pastorate to Troy. We were exhausted after unloading the big U-Haul and carrying our possessions upstairs to our rental apartment. It was three days before Christmas, and over the next two weeks, I would find myself working long hours to settle into our new home and church.

Joy had entered her final trimester of pregnancy, but would risk her health rather than leave a single unopened carton setting around, or a single task undone. I wanted to help lift her burdens, but I also had to minister to our small but needy congregation. I also needed to earn the money to pay the rent and feed the four of us, so I felt pulled in several directions.

I was broke. If a large church in Schenectady hadn't donated a used refrigerator for our apartment, I wouldn't have been able to buy one. The realization of our financial predicament didn't immediately impress itself upon me because I was simply too busy. I was like a punch-drunk boxer who was simply trying to stay on his feet until the bell rang at the end of the round. But there seemed to be no end to the round!

Within a few days, I was able to supplement our income by driving a school bus. I made both the morning and afternoon run, but it didn't bring in enough money. The future looked bleak.

The denomination's supervisor had not made me aware of the fact that, as pastor of a church with only four members, I was considered a "church planting missionary." This designation would soon present legal and financial repercussions. But at that moment, it was beneficial because a few of the area churches were sympathetic to our plight. One of them invited our family to their annual Christmas party.

I was unprepared when the pastor asked me to share my vision for the future of our little church, and I felt I made a poor presentation. But the folks liked Joy and our two daughters, and gave us a love gift of twenty-five dollars. It might not sound like much, but that would buy enough groceries to feed our family for two weeks.

A few nights later, I was sitting at my cluttered desk, tallying our bills. It was then that reality came crashing down on me. "What have I done?" I asked myself. "We were worry-free at our last church, and now we are insolvent."

Our third child was due in about two months. The bills were piling up, and even if I could find a lucrative full-time job, and neglect the church, it appeared impossible to catch up. Yet I knew that I just couldn't give up the work to which God has called me.

I was in the middle of my pity party when the phone rang. It was the pastor of the church that hosted us at their Christmas party. I was in such a foul mood, and so far from being an overcoming Christian, that I didn't even want to talk to him.

He opened the conversation by telling me that the people of his congregation really appreciated my determination, and they were praying for us. Then he said that one of the men in his congregation had given him a check for us, and he asked, *"Are you sitting down?"*

I interpreted his question to mean that the check was for an unusually large amount, perhaps as much as a hundred dollars, and that I should be prepared to sound surprised. A hundred dollars was indeed a considerable gift in those days. But ol' man unbelief had a grip on me, and I thought to myself, "What's a hundred dollars in our situation?"

The pastor wasn't to be denied his little surprise, and he persisted, repeating his question. *"Are you sitting down?"*

And with a sense of guilt at my thankless spirit, I lowered myself onto my desk chair, and replied in the most cheerful voice I could muster, *"Yes, I'm sitting down."*

He almost shouted, *"One thousand dollars!"*

I was speechless.

According to the Bureau of Labor Statistics, a thousand dollars at that time was equivalent to over $6,600 in today's dollars. As incredible as his news was, I just sat there, like Jonah in the heat of the day, brooding under his withering vine.

I hadn't been exercising faith and thanking God in the midst of my tiny tribulation. I hadn't even been asking God to provide the money we needed to pay our bills. And now, instead of rejoicing in Christ for this glorious gift, I found myself wondering how we would get the rest of the money we needed to catch up. Once I identified my lack of thankfulness, I was swept with guilt and shame in the light of God's incredible grace.

While the pastor was hanging on the other end of the phone line, I began condemning myself. How could I act this way? I had seen the Lord perform many marvelous works. He saved my little family from drowning. In freezing weather, He started an air compressor that had a broken spark plug. As we were about to leave for Bible college, He sent a buyer for our land. He answered Brother Al's fleece, enabling him to send us $1,500 per month for nearly two years. He miraculously healed our daughter and sold our home in Quakertown for far more than I anticipated, not to speak of the spectacular little house he provided on the Green Lane Reservoir. And so much more! And just now, I had been thinking about quitting.

Talk about unbelief! I might as well have joined the Israelites who had crossed the Red Sea and then rebelled against God. I was doubting our Lord while in the middle of a telephone call that assured me of deliverance.

I was suddenly so ashamed. Think of it! In 1973, millions of families would have to work two to three months to earn a thousand dollars. It's a testimony to the love and mercy of God that He didn't destroy me right on the spot.

The remainder of the phone call was brief. I offered sincere thanks for the gift. The pastor told me that he'd bring the check up to me the following morning.

My humiliation was well deserved. I asked myself how I would be able to inspire others if I couldn't endure a little hardship myself. And then the Lord reminded me that we all slip and fall. *"For a just man falleth seven times, and riseth up again"* (Proverbs 24:16).

Sometimes we forget that our journey to spiritual perfection is long, progressive, and fraught with temptations. I was far from perfect, but thank God, I wasn't what I had been. Sometimes I felt as though I was taking two steps forward and one step back. Then I recalled the words of the Apostle Paul to the church at Philippi:

> *"Not that I have already attained, or am already perfected; but I press on, that I may lay hold of that for which Christ Jesus has also laid hold of me. Brethren, I do not count myself to have apprehended; but one thing I do, forgetting those things which are behind and reaching forward to those things which are ahead, I press toward the goal for the prize of the upward call of God in Christ Jesus"* (Philippians 3:12-14).

That incredibly generous thousand-dollar gift did indeed see my family through our immediate difficulties. But it did far more than that. Some members of our church considered it evidence that I had been truly called to Troy by God. But for me, the gift demonstrated once again that I am absolutely dependent on our Lord for everything, and Jesus never fails!

Above all, it stood as a miracle of deliverance. And after that day, I determined that I'd be part of a greater miracle. I prayed that, in the future, and no matter what the trial, I would keep the faith, hope against hope, knowing that He would deliver me. I haven't always been true to that commitment, but God has always done abundantly above that which I could ask or even imagine!

CHAPTER 31

"Have you given any thought...?"

"Now to Him who is able to do exceedingly abundantly above all that we ask or think, according to the power that works in us, to Him be glory in the church by Christ Jesus to all generations, forever and ever. Amen."

Ephesians 3:20-21

We arrived in Troy a couple of days before Christmas in 1974, and conducted our first service the following Sunday. The building was in rough shape. The roof leaked, the paint was cracked and peeling, and the floors sagged. But the worst were the two restrooms.

To visit them, people had to go down a narrow stairway beneath naked light bulbs, into a dirt-floored cellar, then make their way a short distance along a concrete walk. It was dismal, it frightened little children, and it was hardly the sort of place to attract visitors. One thing could be said for the building. Anyone who remained at that church was serious about their relationship with God!

A few weeks after we arrived, I decided to brighten up the large Sunday school room. We had few children to occupy it, but hope springs eternal. So, I opened a gallon of sky blue paint I found in a corner of the room, climbed to the top of a swaying ten-foot step ladder, and started painting the high ceiling. I could only paint about a square yard of the ceiling before I had to climb down and move the big ladder, so I couldn't accomplish much before I had to clean my tools and rush off to drive a school bus. The worst part was that I had no one to help me. In fact, one member, who never lifted a hand to help, criticized me for not accomplishing more. Working alone can be discouraging, for as the Bible observes, "One is good, but two are better."[30] In fact, there were so many demands on me that I never returned to my painting.

On April 3, 1974, a violent tornado with winds up to 300 miles per hour, struck Xenia, Ohio. It did incredible damage, and the next day, my brother John and I drove straight through to Xenia to see if there was anything my tiny church might do to assist in their recovery. Upon our return to Troy, the local TV station featured our story, and I began a "Xenia, Ohio Tornado Relief Program."

I checked with the Red Cross, and discovered that items like kitchenware, dishes, and towels, would not be provided by relief agencies. So, I encouraged the people of Troy to bring such items to our church. And while many did so, I was pretty much alone in sorting and packing them for shipment.

General Electric executives in Schenectady learned of my need for transportation, and generously arranged for a tractor trailer to carry our donations to a church in Xenia. From there, the items were distributed to those suffering loss. With that mission accomplished, I returned to my regular duties as a pastor and school bus driver.

Our church was joined on either side by residences, and there was only enough room between the structures for sidewalks or narrow lawns, so we did not have a parking lot. The lack of parking spaces would have made little difference back in the days when most people walked to their neighborhood churches. But in 1974, most drove to church, and they needed spaces to park their cars.

One Sunday morning, as I stood on the front porch of our church, I looked up and down 4th Street, and I realized that there were cars parked end to end for as far as I could see. It was obvious that any visitors to our church would have difficulty finding places to park and would have to walk long distances. Once they reached the church, the elderly and infirm would have to climb the steep old staircase to the front door because we had no ramp.

Worse, I hadn't yet learned that the City of Troy considered the parking spaces in front of each residence to be reserved for the use of

---

30 Ecclesiastes 4:9

the homeowners. The police would issue tickets to violators. That lack of parking spaces would inhibit growth for years to come.

Our attendance had risen to about two dozen people, and it was clear to me that with limited parking, it would be a continual struggle to attract people to our run-down building. I realized that we would ultimately need to relocate. Since we had few adherents and no money, it was a problem that we would not be able to deal with in the immediate future. As a result, I gave no thought to where we would find another facility, much less how we'd find the means to buy or rent it. In any case, any solution to our problem would have to come from God. I scarcely knew what to ask for, so my prayers were non-specific and sought some nebulous solution.

In a clumsy effort to attract visitors to our ugly building, I decided to imply that we were planning to relocate. It wasn't dishonest, as that was my heartfelt desire and long-term plan. So, I painted a big sign on yellow oil cloth and hung it beneath the stained glass window on the front of the building. It simply read, "Temporary Home." I didn't intend to deceive anyone. It was a statement of intent and an expression of faith. Although, admittedly, my faith was a bit anemic. I didn't infer how long it might continue to be our "temporary home," and several of our people laughed at me for my delusions. They considered our situation to be hopeless. As things turned out, God made it an extremely temporary home.

I'm pretty sure the sign didn't contribute to our growth. I think I put it up on a Saturday, and the following Monday I received a call from the manager of the Lansingburg branch of Marine Midland Bank. He didn't waste any time. As soon as he identified himself, and confirmed that I was the pastor, he asked, "Is your building for sale?"

I was completely surprised by this unexpected question, and replied tentatively, "I don't know. I guess so."

"When can we see it?"

I needed time to digest the possibility of actually selling the church, and to discuss it with the members of the church board, so I replied, "How about a week from Thursday?"

"How about tonight?" he countered.

So I called one of our board members, Bob Berggren, our only financial supporter, and he became very excited. He promised to call the elderly lady who was our other board member, to advise her of events. Then he asked, "How much are you planning to ask?"

I admitted that I had no idea how much we should ask.

He said, "Try to get at least five-thousand dollars so that we can pay off the mortgage." That was the first I'd heard that the building was mortgaged.

I told him that I'd ask $5,500, which was about the average price for a house on that street at that time, and he responded, "Sounds good, but try not to lose the deal."

Then he went on to tell me that the deed for the property was in the hands of the denominational leaders. Up to that point, I had no idea that we weren't totally independent.

I was at the church at the appointed hour, and was surprised when a large group of men arrived. They were involved with a local youth program, the Lansingburg Independent Baseball League. They'd been tax exempt since 1970, just three years earlier. The group included the most powerful political figures in Troy, including Mayor William O'Neil and the city manager, plus several leading businessmen.

Someone asked me how I happened to come to Troy. I gave a brief testimony of how God had called me from my business to enter the ministry at the age of thirty and how I had recently resigned the church in central New York to come to Troy. Several of them seemed very interested, and kept asking me questions, but the more businesslike among them brought the discussion back to the purpose for their visit. They were interested in our building as a meeting place and clubhouse for the league, a charitable program for kids in the area.

As they talked among themselves, a realization grew in me. "They are going to ask how much we want for the building!" I had already told Bob Berggren that I would ask fifty-five hundred, but as they continued speaking with one another, my mind starting ratcheting numbers.

I clearly remember my flow of thoughts. It's crazy, but I think I'll ask seventy-five hundred. But as they continued whispering among themselves, I experienced a burst of faith or foolhardiness. No, I thought, I'm going to ask ten thousand dollars!

Bob's repeated warning to be careful not to lose the deal gnawed at me, and I vacillated. It could have only been a minute or two, but as they continued talking among themselves, I was reminded that a seller can always lower his asking price, but he can never raise it. I suddenly decided, I am going to ask twelve thousand, five hundred dollars.

Then someone casually asked, "Have you given any thought to how much you want for the property?"

And the reply seemed to burst from my lips. "Yes, the board would like seventeen thousand, five hundred dollars." And I didn't lie. I knew that the board would be delighted to get seventeen thousand, five hundred dollars for the old building.

I held my breath, but no one seemed troubled by my figure. They simply said they'd discuss it and get back to me.

An hour later, I called Bob Berggren, and he expressed concern that I might have driven them away by the amount I asked.

The next day, however, I received a call from the manager of the local Marine Midland branch, informing me that they agreed to my asking price. I in turn gave him the phone number for the denomination's office. Then I called the administrators to inform them of the situation, and was flatly told that their attorney would take over negotiations, and I was to consider myself out of the loop.

And I was. Without my knowledge, the attorney inexplicably dropped the price three thousand dollars. And, without consulting me, the lawyers agreed that the buyers could take possession in just thirty days.

"Thirty days! What just happened here?" I wondered. And I wasn't the only one. Members of the congregation were asking me, "Pastor, what are we going to do? Where are we going to go?"

God had sent a buyer for our property, and I had negotiated the sale, but now we had no place to hang our hats. What's more, the denomination took possession of the proceeds—fourteen thousand, five hundred dollars, less the mortgage payout and legal fees—leaving us with neither church nor cash, but with the burden of locating a place to worship within a month.

We went to prayer.

Then someone told me of a vacant Lutheran church building a few blocks away. We contacted the pastor of a nearby Lutheran church for guidance, and he put us in touch with the Albany Synod. The outcome was that we were able to rent the entire building for two-hundred dollars per month.

The building was in excellent condition, the sanctuary equipped with carpeting, pews, a lectern, and an electric organ. The large meeting room downstairs was furnished with folding tables and chairs; while the kitchen was equipped with commercial appliances, pots and pans, dishes, and flatware. What's more, everything was in good working condition.

After a few months, we decided to try to buy the building, so I called an all-night prayer meeting. Virtually every member joined us, as well as some folks from other churches, and many stayed to pray all night. A few days later, we successfully negotiated the purchase of the building for just twenty-thousand dollars, with no money down, and interest free payments.

And we soon exceeded the 50 in Sunday School that I had projected a year earlier. In fact, within months, we reached 160. Even today, I'm amazed by the speed with which the Lord moved. I had put up a sign on the front of our old building that read, "Temporary Home," and less than a month later we were in a far superior building.

While I was fumbling through each day, the Lord was way out in front of us, guiding us through what the world would call an incredible series of coincidences. It brings to mind the verse: *"It shall come to pass that before they call, I will answer; And while they are still speaking, I will hear"* (Isaiah 65:24).

The question that those city fathers asked that night still brings a smile to my lips: *"Have you given any thought as to how much you would like for the property?"* I thought I had. Then I opened my mouth, and it appears that the Lord filled it!

CHAPTER 32

"A Shelter from Storm"

"And there will be a tabernacle for shade in the daytime from the heat, for a place of refuge, and for a shelter from storm and rain."
Isaiah 4:6

From the moment the representative of the Lansingburg Independent Baseball League asked me whether our church was for sale, to the moment they agreed to buy the building, less than forty-eight hours transpired. Then I learned that our denomination's leaders had agreed to our vacating the building in less than thirty days.

The need to immediately locate a new meeting place threatened the existence of our frail fellowship, and events were moving so rapidly that I scarcely had time to ponder where we might relocate. In the Book of Acts, the word *"immediately"* is used a dozen times to reveal how quickly God acted to build his Church. Now we needed God to act in a similar miraculous way to solve our dilemma.

We were barely receiving sufficient offerings to meet our obligations, and since the denomination now held the proceeds from the sale of our building, we would be hard put to pay a single month's rent on any kind of meeting place, much less establish credit and make a down payment to buy another building. Like the ancient Israelites who had followed Moses into the wilderness, and then complained that they missed their leeks, onions, and garlic; the decrepit old building we had just sold suddenly began looking pretty good to some of us.

It soon became obvious that the denomination's failure to help us find a new home necessitated God's involvement. In retrospect, it opened the door for the Lord to clearly demonstrate His purpose and His power by delivering our tiny fellowship from a desperate situation. The scope of our dilemma helped us better appreciate the magnitude of the deliverance that followed.

Joy and I were expecting our third child in less than a month, and I was driving a school bus mornings and afternoons to supplement my fifty dollar a week salary. And, of course, I had my pastoral responsibilities, including teaching adult Sunday school, preaching Sundays, both morning and evening, and teaching again on Wednesday night. I had little knowledge of our community, and even less time and energy to search for a building.

But God is faithful, and after we miraculously sold that old building for nearly three times its estimated value, the Lord showed us the way through the wilderness. He directed us to the vacant Lutheran Church building that I described in the last chapter. It was also in north Troy, and when I spoke with a representative of the Lutheran Synod, they were willing to rent us that building for only two-hundred dollars per month, without so much as a credit check.

We were to share the building with an organization that used the basement to teach young girls handicrafts, and the woman in charge was annoyed that she had to share any part of the structure with a church. We, in turn, disliked finding the building filled with her cigarette smoke whenever we entered. But she resolved that matter herself. She carelessly dumped an ash tray containing a burning cigarette into a waste basket just before leaving the building, and if a neighbor had not seen the smoke streaming out a basement window, and called the fire department, the church would have been destroyed.

The Lutherans evicted her and decided that they were no longer willing to bear the liability for a building they would never again occupy. They offered us the church for twenty-thousand dollars—including the pulpit, pews, and an electric organ, plus a fully equipped kitchen, even folding tables and chairs. And they agreed to a twenty-year interest-free mortgage, with no money down, and payments of just two hundred dollars per month.

We had been hard-pressed on every side, perplexed, persecuted, and struck down. But we discovered that we didn't need the denomination's money or assistance. Once again, Jesus fulfilled his words, *"I will build My church, and the gates of Hades shall not prevail against it"* (Matthew 16:18).

As Isaiah pointed out, God is faithful! *"And there will be a tabernacle for shade in the daytime from the heat, for a place of refuge, and for a shelter from storm and rain"* (Isaiah 4:6).

Chapter 33

Back to the Basics

"Now Jesus and His disciples went out to the towns of Caesarea Philippi; and on the road He asked His disciples, saying to them, 'Who do men say that I am?' So they answered, 'John the Baptist; but some say, Elijah; and others, one of the prophets.' He said to them, 'But who do you say that I am?' Peter answered and said to Him, 'You are the Christ.'"

Mark 8:27-29

During the Civil War, Troy was an industrial powerhouse. It was now rife with the problems common to the rust-belt cities that had flourished during the 19th Century. The city was troubled with spiritual malaise, and the resulting poverty, crime, drugs, and political corruption.

Shortly after Joy and I arrived in Troy, we were told by a few older and more mature Christians that our church was destined to fail. They pointed out that an overwhelming majority of residents claimed to be Roman Catholics. Someone challenged me: "What chance does a Protestant pastor like you have starting a church in a city that's overwhelmingly Catholic?"

"Well," I replied, *"First, I don't consider myself a 'Protestant.' I'm not protesting anything. I'm promoting the Lord Jesus Christ!"*

And I meant it!

To them, our situation was hopeless, but we shook off their negativism and began praying for God's wisdom. If the Lord wasn't supporting our efforts, we would fail, no matter what methods we might apply. Of course, any effort to interest a life-long Catholic in a personal relationship with Jesus Christ promised to be difficult, and would be actively resisted by powerful individuals in the community. Yet, if we ignored the Catholics, who was left? Most people assumed the only way to build a congregation was by enticing people away from existing "Protestant" churches.

Which led to someone else asking, *"What right do you have to proselytize people from their Bible-believing churches?"* But that was exactly the point. Few churches in Troy were "Bible-believing." Most were Roman Catholic. Then there were the historic main line churches that had turned to liberal theology and rejected the authority of the Bible, the virgin birth, Christ's divinity and resurrection from the dead. By contrast, our teaching was based on the holy Scriptures, not vain traditions or current social values. We had the scriptural mandate from Jesus Christ, *"Go ye therefore, and teach all nations..."* (Matthew 28:19, KJV).

On the other hand, we did not wish to attract shallow souls who would swap churches every time they felt an impulse, as though they were involved in a game of musical chairs. We had no desire to draw people who left a church at the drop of a hat, simply because they didn't like the color the walls were painted, or were miffed because someone dared to sit on a pew that they considered their special property.

A healthy church should be a growing church. Our effectiveness would not be measured by the number of people in the pews, by the size of the weekly offerings, or by the beauty of the building in which we met. It'd be measured by the love that our members displayed toward others and by the fruit they produced.

Neither Jesus nor his disciples placed much importance on buildings. His sermons were not delivered in the Temple in Jerusalem, but on mountainsides and lake shores. For more than two hundred and fifty years following Christ's ascension into Heaven, believers gathered almost exclusively in homes, not in the purpose-built structures that we today call "churches." Jesus commanded his disciples to go to the Jews first, but they had little success in the synagogues. So they were sent to the non-Jews, and their experiences were as unique and varied as the personalities they met.

Philip was led to the Gaza Road where he met the influential Ethiopian Eunuch, the man who served as Queen Candice's treasurer. The Apostle Paul and Silas were in prison, glorifying God, when an earthquake opened the doors to salvation for the jailer and his household. Peter correctly interpreted a vision, and ultimately led Cornelius, the Gentile centurion, to the Lord. Peter lost his claim to be the Apostle to the Gentiles because he curried favor with the Jews, so God called Saul of Tarsus. And Saul, later called The Apostle Paul, met Lydia on the side of a river, not in a "church."

We in Troy were not among those giants of the faith, but we soon learned that individuals and churches grow fastest by prayerfully attempting what seems impossible. Just as you should be baptized by immersion, and not merely sprinkled, so you must immerse yourself in God's work. A little dab just won't do ya'. It's through intense individual involvement that every Christian matures most rapidly and becomes most effective.

Some say "bigger is better," but smaller is often smarter. Smaller churches are the best incubators. The house churches and the small and growing conventional churches are always short of resources—human and material—and frequently provide greater opportunities for service, encouraging and even demanding participation. And when that church inevitably outgrows its meeting place, perhaps the thing to do is split the fellowship, sending one group off to another location, and watching as more people grow in faith through intense individual involvement.

A church should delegate responsibility and commensurate authority to those willing to undertake a task of any nature, from teaching a class to singing a solo. These spiritual conscripts often feel unprepared because they are unprepared. Yet they soon begin to learn that they can do all things through Christ who strengthens them. The burdens they bear necessitate prayer, then God instills His Word, and He is faithful to grow their faith. Thus, the small church becomes a place where individuals pray, labor together, and discover their greatest joy in life. This concept is discussed at length in *The Depression Proof Church; God's Answer to the Church in Crisis.*[31]

Back then, however, when I was asked how I would approach church growth, it came to me that most of us had the wrong idea. Just as farmers spread seed over fertile soil, so we are to spread the Word of truth, and not just within the walls of a "church" building. Jesus told his disciples, *"The field is the world"* (Matthew 13:38). "Church" is a place where we go to be

---

31   Becker, Frank. The Depression Proof Church: The Biblical Answer to the Church in Crisis. (Greenbush, 2012).

edified; to learn and grow spiritually. But we need to go out in the world to evangelize.

Human nature hasn't changed. America is largely a secular society, and the shallow values that most people embrace are not very different from those held by the people of the ancient world. As the Apostle Paul observed in Romans 3:23, "... *for all have sinned and fall short of the glory of God....*"

It would have been a mistake to limit our outreach based on some set of human values or standards, whether socioeconomic, racial, ethnic, or even religious. The fact was that the majority of Troy's population was unsaved. They existed in spiritual darkness, and they desperately needed to hear the good news of Jesus Christ! How they responded would be up to them.

We are not to limit our appeal to the religious and self-righteous. As Jesus taught,

> *"Those who are well have no need of a physician, but those who are sick. But go and learn what this means: 'I desire mercy and not sacrifice.' For I did not come to call the righteous, but sinners, to repentance"* (Matthew 9:12-13).

While instructing His own disciples in soul-winning, Jesus told a parable about a man who was giving a feast, and how he became angry because those he invited failed to attend. He told his servants,

> *"'Go out quickly into the streets and alleys of the city, and bring in the poor, the crippled, the blind, and the lame.' 'Sir,' the servant replied, 'what you ordered has been done, and there is still room.' So the master told his servant, 'Go out to the highways and hedges and compel them to come in, so that my house will be full'"* (Luke 14, 21-23).

So our little group of believers began doing precisely that. We went out into the streets of Troy and talked about the love of Jesus to anyone who would listen, including the poor and despised and neglected. And if people from other churches happened to be attracted to our teaching—teaching based exclusively on God's word—they were welcome to join us.

We joked that we would not rustle another denomination's sheep, but if they jumped the fence to get where the grass was greener, we would not turn them away. The truth is that we do not belong to any church or denomination, but to the Great Shepherd, Jesus Christ.

I realized that some of the things I had been taught, and some practices that I had witnessed, were not scriptural. Unlike Jesus and his disciples, very few pastors were leading their people out into the highways and hedges to appeal to the lost. They wanted to appeal to the rich and influential members of the community, and seemed to be counting on the sermons they delivered inside the walls of their buildings to attract people. So they continually harangued their members to bring in friends, associates, and relatives. But do you remember the warning in the book of James?

> *"Listen, my beloved brethren, Has God not chosen the poor of this world to be rich in faith and heirs of the kingdom which He promised to those who love Him? But you have dishonored the poor man. Do not the rich oppress you and drag you into the courts? Do they not blaspheme that noble name by which you are called?"* (James 2: 5-7).

Then I wondered, "How are we to build a church by serving people who have no money to support it?" It took me a while to grasp the essence of the assurances Jesus had given us. He declared, *"I will build my Church,"*[32] and Paul assured us, *"my God will provide all of your needs."*[33] Jesus did not tell us to concentrate on witnessing to the popular, the powerful, and the wealthy. Quite the contrary!

But we are to be involved in a local fellowship. We are to: *"... consider one another in order to stir up love and good works, not forsaking the assembling of ourselves together, as is the manner of some, but exhorting one another, and so much the more as you see the Day approaching"* (Hebrews 10:24-25). I suddenly realized that we had begun doing precisely what our Lord had commanded.

Our members began to greet strangers we met, showing sincere interest in their lives, and real concern for their problems. And when we spoke to them of Jesus, it was to introduce Him as our best friend. And if we were permitted, and most people were willing, we prayed with them.

---

32   Matthew 16:18

33   Philippians 4:19

And while most people guard their personal thoughts, we soon learned that most are also spiritually hungry.

Yes, other pastors were succeeding in building huge congregations with fine music, flowery words, and a multitude of programs. But the crowds they attracted did not seem to feel very sinful and they didn't seem to have a sense of deliverance. They weren't inspired to win souls, nor to grow much beyond entertaining one another.

Our people expressed their gratitude to God through their actions. Yes, our ministries operated on a financial shoestring, but somehow we carried on. We sowed the Word of God to all and attracted many who had nothing material to give in return. Yet they often shared what they did possess in gratitude, love, and service.

And a strange and wonderful thing happened. Word started getting around about how we were reaching out to those no one else wanted, especially the children. And a few people, who had been attending glamorous churches with elegant programs and well-dressed congregations, began to visit us to see whether we were the real deal. They had a hunger to participate in such a mission.

But, oh, it was difficult! In the years that followed, we would deal with bubble gum on the pews, coffee on the carpets, lust in the locker room, and drugs in the cellar. But we persevered.

And God moved! He moved so dramatically that our small congregation secured over a thousand confessions of faith in one year. We wanted to bring the good news to everyone, but of course not everyone was willing to listen.

But it all began with our getting back to the basics; telling people who Jesus really is. Peter confessed, *"Thou are the Christ!"* And Jesus told him, *"Upon this rock* (your confession of faith), *I will build my Church."*[34]

---

34   Matthew 16:18

CHAPTER 34

The Candy Stripe Express

"Then the master said to the servant, 'Go out into the highways and hedges, and compel them to come in, that my house may be filled.'"

Luke 14:23

By focusing on those who wanted to hear, including children, it wasn't long before a number of dedicated and loving individuals were attracted to our ministry, and joined us in God's service. And what vehicle did God initially use to convey our message? Advertisements in the local newspaper? Radio? TV? No! It was a vehicle that I had earlier spurned.

Just weeks before we moved to Troy, one of the men in our village church told me of a newly emerging ministry where churches were using school buses to bring people—particularly children—to Sunday School. He actually offered to buy a bus and take responsibility for the ministry, even becoming licensed to drive it. Such an effort might have electrified that little church, but I wonder. A lot of those folks were already upset by a relatively few "noisy" kids every Sunday morning. And it would require finding volunteers and training them to work with those crowds of unruly children.

It could only have been the Holy Spirit that inspired this fine brother to offer to make such an incredibly generous investment in cash, labor, and time. But I had secretly committed myself to leave the church and ignored his wonderful offer. I can only hope that I didn't stumble that fine man, and that today he has an honored place in glory.

Even after we arrived in Troy, and I was growing frustrated with my own failure to satisfactorily motivate our small group, I was occasionally hearing tales of other churches using school buses to reach the lost. Yet I remained indifferent. At some point, I attended a meeting where a visiting evangelist regaled pastors about the potential of the bus ministry, providing us with both scriptural motivation and practical methods, but I wasn't ready to budge.

Then one night, while several members of our church were sitting in our living room discussing our disappointing growth, I received a phone call from the pastor of my home church. Under his ministry, I had been baptized, and made the commitment to close my business and return to college to prepare for ministry. So when he called me out of the blue, I was happy to hear his voice.

"Frank," he demanded, "have you thought about getting into the bus ministry?" When I replied, "I've thought about it," he told me, "We are bringing in over two-hundred kids each week on our fleet of buses, and I've got two old Reo's that run fine, and I'll sell them to you for two hundred dollars each."

Well, there it was. At least the third time that someone wanted to "help" me start a bus ministry, and I was still dubious. But after I hung up the phone and related the conversation to the others in our living room, they weren't. They were excited by the idea. But it didn't matter. We didn't have four-hundred dollars.

The following Sunday, I announced the availability of the buses, and two elderly ladies, who suffered from severe arthritis, heard about it. They had saved two-hundred dollars to pay for acupuncture treatments, but they instead donated the money to purchase the first of the two buses. Another woman, who lived in public housing, had just received a small inheritance upon the death of her husband, and she donated it to buy the second bus. When I think of those three women, I'm reminded of Jesus' praise for the poor widow who gave her all.

"And he looked up, and saw the rich men casting their gifts into the treasury. And he saw also a certain poor widow casting in thither two mites. And he said, "Of a truth I say unto you, that

this poor widow hath cast in more than they all: For all these have of their abundance cast in unto the offerings of God: but she of her penury hath cast in all the living that she had" (Luke 21:1-4).

I was the only one in the church who was licensed to drive a school bus, so a friend drove me the 75 miles to pick up the first of those two old Reo buses. And they were old; over twenty years old. But they were work horses.

At that time, I was employed by the bus company that transported students for the local school district, and I was driving a school bus every weekday morning and afternoon. The manager gave me permission to use their garage and equipment to repaint the first bus. We covered the National School Bus Yellow with white, then added red and blue stripes from end to end.

I lettered the words, "Troy's Largest Sunday School" above the windows, and "The Candy Stripe Express" below. We focused on Jesus' words: *"Suffer little children, and forbid them not to come unto me: for of such is the kingdom of heaven"* (Matthew 19:14, KJV). Within weeks we had both buses on the road and were bringing in fifty or sixty kids and a few adults to attend what we called "Junior Church."

Many parents loved the idea that we were picking up their children on Sunday morning. To them, we were babysitting their children at no charge, and they had the morning to themselves. But we didn't care. It was a great trade off.

Proverbs 22:6 states, *"Train up a child in the way he should go, and when he is old he will not depart from it."* We had the parent's approval to do what they were failing to do, to teach their children the Word of God. We were happy to help them meet their responsibilities.

During the 1970s, bus ministries flourished, and countless unchurched children across America were introduced to Jesus Christ. Most church drivers were conscientious and competent, and there were very few accidents. But the enemies of Christ's Church noted the impact that bus ministries were having and began to speak out against them.

They lobbied state legislators to pass more restrictive motor vehicle laws and pushed for frequent inspections of church facilities by fire marshals and building inspectors. They attempted to tax church buildings, church schools, and even parking lots. As a result, there are few bus ministries today. Keep in mind, this was the ministry of the moment, a program anointed by the Lord. And like most meaningful ministries, it required hard work, personal sacrifice, and faithfulness.

We started our ministry a year or two before the harassment began, and we were blessed to have a popular state legislator on our side, threatening those who threatened us, so we enjoyed amazing success. But it soon became obvious that we did not have the resources to handle the growing crowds. We had too little money, too few people, and too little space to minister to the numbers our bus workers were bringing in.

It was then that my new friend and fellow worker, Paul Morrissette, somehow arranged to rent the Catholic Central High School for use on Sunday mornings. The principal was a fine man, more concerned with the best interests of Troy's children than with denominational rivalry. We were thrilled to accept his generous offer to rent the school every Sunday for a mere $35 per month. Apart from all his other responsibilities, Paul somehow maintained order while we occupied the school, and was faithful to have it cleaned up after the children departed. But when the local newspaper brought attention to our program by publishing articles and photos showing hundreds of bus children entering the school, the principal found himself pressured by his associates to terminate our use.

During that period, however, we added more buses, even renting a couple, and paying unsaved drivers to drive for us on Sunday mornings. Paying drivers was a bitter pill, as we didn't want unsaved people involved in our ministry. We wanted our own faithful members to step up and get driver's licenses. Two fine brothers soon answered the call, Tom Muckle and Ara Shahinian.

Paul had become our new bus director and somehow kept the ministry going. He prayed, and scratched and scraped to gather the funds needed for gas, upkeep, to garage the vehicles, pay the drivers, and buy treats for the kids. Paul enlisted and trained bus workers and Junior church teachers, and the Lord anointed him to keep it going. So many wonderful people became involved that I can't begin to list them all, but they were amazingly faithful. One month they brought in an average of 299 adults and children.

Early on, we experienced some very comical situations. One morning, for example, as I opened my Bible to preach to the seven people in my tiny congregation, our pianist, Heather Flora, left her bench and started to jog up the aisle to the front door. Surprised by her behavior, I asked from the pulpit where she was going, and she shouted back, "I have to get up to the high school to teach."

Her departure left a half dozen people in the auditorium, including two visitors. I later learned they had been attending a prosperous church in upscale Loudonville. As I stood at the pulpit, and looked out across a sea of empty pews, I tried to explain that most of our people were up at the high school ministering to hundreds of bus kids.

After the closing prayer, I hurried from the pulpit to shake our visitors' hands, but before I could reach them, they hurried out of the building. I thought my message had been reasonably good and was disappointed that they evidently wanted to evade me. Later, however, I learned that they had rushed up the street to the high school to see for themselves whether I had told the truth. They arrived just in time to watch over two-hundred children board the buses.

That middle-aged couple was hungry to be part of a work that was enthusiastically reaching out to the lost, rather than merely being part of a "church" to "meet, eat, and retreat." As a result, Jeanette and Norm Hoogkamp immediately threw themselves into the work.

A fast-growing ministry is unwieldy, and often difficult to manage. In a sense, the bus program had become the tail wagging the dog, and its rapid growth presented many challenges. Our church was like a teenage boy who grows so fast that he is always outgrowing his clothes. A fast-growing church can never seem to provide the space, equipment, workers, or money that is needed.

We had one wonderful and brilliant young newlywed couple, Richard and Shirley Sexton. Rich worked for General Motors (GM) and had been sent east to do post-grad work at RPI. After returning to the West Coast, Rich became a pastor, while continuing to work at GM to support his family.

Shirley, a brilliant young woman, was one of our Sunday School teachers. She taught a class of fifty preschoolers by herself. Her tongue-in-cheek cry best illustrated our challenge. "Can't we get seat belts to keep them in their chairs?" But, like her husband, Shirley labored on, touching little lives for Jesus' sake.

Because of God's working through faithful servants like Rich and Shirley, we truly became "Troy's Largest Sunday School." Yes, we were criticized for bringing in more children than we could handle. But if you can comprehend how difficult it was to induce them to come, their parents to allow it, to arrange bus transportation, to maintain space to teach them, to have qualified teachers, and the money needed, you might understand that getting them there was a miracle of God. Anything we might teach them about Jesus was far better than the nothing they would have received at home.

A few people, who might have helped lighten our load, actually excused their walking away with the argument that there were too many children. But when Jesus preached his "Sermon on the Mount," he didn't limit the crowd. He preached to perhaps twenty thousand and never turned a soul away.

Only God knows who will respond spiritually. The fields are white unto harvest, and his command, is "Go ye therefore and teach...."[35]

The math is simple. As an old salesman once told me, "The more you show, the more you sell!" And we figured that the more kids who heard the gospel, the more would be saved. So what if we weren't the greatest teachers in the world? To their shame, few others were stepping up. We did our best, and because we did, there are many men and women today who ascribe their salvation to the work we began in their hearts fifty years ago. We did our part, but the glory goes to Christ. *So then neither he who plants is anything, nor he who waters, but God who gives the increase* (1 Corinthians 3:7).

The bus ministry attracted a disparate group of Christians who found unity in Christ as we reached out to win our city. Were we as effective as we might have been? As compared to who and what? We did our best, and the intensive work of that ministry caused most of our workers to grow spiritually and at a phenomenal rate. It doesn't make much difference what "vehicle" is used to bring in the lost. What matters is the message, and our message was clear: *"For God so loved the world that He gave His only begotten Son, that whoever believes in Him should not perish but have everlasting life"* (John 3:16).

In order to attract kids on the bus routes, I sculpted the head of a mouse by pasting papier-mâché over a wire frame. One Saturday morning our daughter, Cheryl, lowered that painted mask over her head, donned a black raincoat, and went out with one of our bus workers, attracting crowds of children. Some began calling us "The Mickey Mouse Church," but we had to be careful of being sued for trademark infringement, so we never called him Mickey.

Our initial church attendance grew from about twelve to an average of one hundred and sixty within sixteen months. While some stayed

---

35   Matthew 28:19-20

away because they thought we lacked dignity, many others joined us. And our workers soldiered on. We faced frequent problems, like a devastating outbreak of head lice that had a number of mothers, including my wife, figuratively tearing out their hair.

Folks were always coming up with new ideas. With little more than my acknowledgment, they secured a permit to use a city park, and on a Sunday morning we had our own "Feeding of the Five Thousand." The members decorated the edges of a platform with cardboard that was cut and painted to look like the waves of the sea. They got hold of a rowboat to simulate a fishing boat on the Sea of Galilee and set it on the deck. They dressed in costumes and used a sound system to share the Bible story. And then they fed the 5,000, praying over and distributing hundreds of hamburgers and orange drinks contributed by the north Troy McDonald's.

And because we knew that we never had enough workers, equipment, or money, all of us learned a far more important lesson. For one brief shining moment in our lives, the members of our little church learned to truly rely on the Holy Spirit. Our incredible workers showed themselves to be faithful disciples of Christ. They united their hearts and hands to give every little child "a cup of cold water" in Jesus' name.

Until we reach Heaven, we will not know the fruit of their labors. We do know this: a number of those adults and kids went on to become ministers, missionaries, and youth workers. And that's really the point here, isn't it? That God somehow gathered a group of individuals who became so dedicated to His cause that they continually thought about little else than to win a city to Christ.

Night and day, they figuratively ate, drank, and dreamed about the challenges they faced, and they discovered their solutions in the Holy Spirit. And when a worker became ill, or appeared burned out or overwhelmed, they prayed together, and discovered one wonderful truth, *"I can do all things through Christ who strengthens me"* (Philippians 4:13).

They trusted God because they realized they could achieve success in no other way. Occasionally, someone quit, but the work went on. Their success wasn't rooted in a papier-mâché mouse named "Mickey," nor in a bus called the "Candy Stripe Express." Those faithful disciples shared biblical motives and the love of Jesus, and the Holy Spirit anointed their labors.

CHAPTER 35

"Troy's Largest Sunday School"

"I know your deeds. See, I have placed before you an open door, which no one can shut. For you have only a little strength, yet you have kept My word and have not denied My name."
Revelation 3:8

It was shortly after we relocated to the church building on 7th Avenue that Paul Morrissette became involved, and was determined to help me with anything I undertook. He was incredible! He insisted on coming in every morning to labor at my side and would prove himself to be one of the finest Christian men I have ever known!

Paul had a family of four at the time. He was a skilled sheet metal worker, but his heart was intent on serving God. He soon became the director of our fledgling bus ministry. This faithful man worked wonders. Almost overnight, we found ourselves with a noisy crowd of kids gathering for children's church in the basement, while we adults met upstairs in the auditorium.

One day we decided to bring the kids up to the main auditorium to join the regular morning service for a few minutes, so that the adults could see evidence of the work we were carrying out in obedience to Christ. But the bus kids didn't want to join us, and they became loud and disrespectful. Before we moved them back downstairs, one man in the congregation began shouting at them and calling them names.

He grabbed one little boy by the arm, and the child reportedly called him a "fat old man" and kicked him in the chin. From that day forward, that man was adamantly opposed to our outreach to children, both the bus ministry and the children's church. He didn't seem to care if every one of them perished. "Church" was to be run his way. That man became increasingly divisive, ultimately inciting a church split.

The debacle that occurred that morning, coupled with our rapid growth, made us realize that the basement of the church was no longer adequate to meet the needs of our growing bus ministry. But it was Brother Paul who investigated possible alternative sites, and negotiated the rental of the high school mentioned in the previous chapter.

Before long, we were running five school buses across the city every Sunday morning, carrying hundreds of children to the high school. And Paul somehow recruited volunteers to serve in the roles of bus drivers, bus captains, and Sunday school teachers. I know, because if he was short a driver, Paul called on me to fill in. I no longer had the luxury of a few minutes of prayer before the morning service, or to consult with others involved. Instead, it was out the bus door and up to the pulpit.

All of our church programs were launched on a wing and a prayer, and we were often criticized for a perception that we failed to properly plan and prepare. It's true that we were rarely able to fund a program at its inception, but we were happy if we were initially able to raise seed money. And we quickly learned whether the Lord supported a program, because we relied on him. He had promised to supply all of our needs, not our greeds (Matthew 6:33).

Things rarely went smoothly. That winter, one of our buses broke down, and Paul arranged for the two of us to repair the engine in a North Troy truck repair shop. I remember putting on my old work clothes, dragging out my battered tool box, and kneeling in prayer beside Paul on that greasy floor before starting to replace the rings and valves in an 8-cylinder bus engine. But Paul wound up doing most of the work.

I also remember midweek services when people laughed because Paul and I had grease under our fingernails, paint on our clothes, or sawdust in our hair. But Paul wasn't my only hero. Figuratively speaking, our entire congregation got on their knees to seek God's blessings and then rolled up their sleeves to accomplish whatever He required.

On America's two-hundredth anniversary, in keeping with the Apostle Paul's admonition to pray for and honor those in authority, I asked Neil Kelleher, our New York State Assemblyman and Senator Joe Bruno, to join me at the pulpit. They were to receive engraved plaques that expressed our appreciation for their efforts. Assemblyman Kelleher told the congregation, "When I met your pastor, he had a Bible in one hand and a hammer in the other." People laughed, but the truth was that many of our members had responsibilities for several different jobs.

What was it that drove so many of us to labor so hard? We were already saved and destined for Heaven. But we had received a command from Jesus Christ to make a difference in this world. His last recorded words served to commission and empower us:

> *All power is given unto me in heaven and in earth. Go ye therefore, and teach all nations, baptizing them in the name of the Father, and of the Son, and of the Holy Ghost: Teaching them to observe all things whatsoever I have commanded you: and, lo, I am with you always, even unto the end of the world.* (Matthew 28:18-20, KJV)

Although most Christians ignore his command, Christ did not make it an option. It's our mandate, yours and mine! It's not a matter of, "All those in favor, say 'Aye.'" It is a royal command. You will ignore it at your own peril. Your options may seem limited in how you approach His work, and your abilities limited, but approach it you must.

Were we fanatics? Hardly. Ask a believer from Nigeria, India, or China, where they often shed their blood to exercise their faith. God's work is a serious and sometimes dangerous business, and we need to firmly establish our convictions. The increasing attacks on Christians and Jews reveal that we are involved in a struggle with the forces of evil. *"For we do not wrestle against flesh and blood, but against principalities, against powers, against the rulers of the darkness of this age, against spiritual hosts of wickedness in the heavenly places"* (Ephesians 6:12).

As far as raising money is concerned, God obligated Himself to provide whatever we need. Jesus assured us, *"But seek ye first the kingdom of God, and his righteousness; and all these things shall be added unto you"* (Matthew 6:33).

The members of our church didn't have months to waste, setting up committees to do exploratory research and conduct endless meetings. Such enervating meetings are often non-productive and divisive, grating on nerves and encouraging party spirit. Our process was simple. If someone suggested an idea that might help us reach the lost, or to streamline an existing program, and if it did not violate Scripture, I'd gather the leaders of the ministries that might be affected, and we would pray about it. If we found ourselves in agreement, we'd try to recruit the workers and train them, while trusting the Lord for the resources.

Often the person with the new idea was also the person who wound up leading the project. This was not a flawless process, and from time to time some carnal soul would get in the way, and we would fail to carry out God's will, such as opening a daycare. Other times, we would acknowledge that we had erred, and we might backtrack. But we were determined to know and do God's will.

Most of our training was done on-the-job. We were blessed with a cross-section of society, from well-educated engineers and business people, to those in the trades who might lack formal education. But it was those who had the strongest commitments to the Lord Jesus who enjoyed the greatest success.

People frequently shared what they had learned from their own experience or research. We would try to codify it for future workers, and prayerfully make changes as conditions dictated, and—by the grace of God—the work grew. It wasn't so much like throwing people into icy water to learn whether they could swim, as it was helping them learn that they could do all things through Christ who strengthened them. The challenges tended to make them fall on their knees in surrender, and it was there that they discovered what the Lord could do through them. And I learned something else. Ordinary people aren't "ordinary." Sparks of creative genius can flow from the Holy Spirit to the simplest soul whose heart is stayed on Him.

The Lord always seemed to provide sufficient resources to keep us fired up, but never enough to let us become spiritually proud, lazy, or complacent. We were almost continually under a little strain, and that kept us in prayer. It's amazing how living in the trenches and under the enemy's fire tends to keep God's servants humble, generous, loving, and prayerful.

We continually shared our successes and failures, in an effort to learn from them. As the Apostle Paul wrote, *I also was with you in weakness and fear, and in great trembling*" (1 Corinthians 2:3). But we were frequently thrilled to hear the testimony of someone who had tasted the power of God in his ministry. And we did a lot of laughing and weeping together.

During that period, the Lord was adding dedicated people to our numbers. Other Christians in the Capital region began to learn that we were successfully reaching people of every age. We preached the simple message of salvation through faith in Christ. Some mocked, but others became interested, and a few joined us, clamoring to be involved.

Children loved the mouse costume when we took to the streets on Saturdays, so someone labeled us the "Mickey Mouse Church." The pejorative stuck, but we took it as a compliment. Those who would never soil their hands reaching out to the poor might mock us for being unsophisticated and crude, but our "mouse" attracted children. As the Bible teaches, Jesus loves the little children!

The rumor got around that people wouldn't want to attend our church unless they were ready and willing to become seriously involved. A few even called us fanatics. It saddened me that those who were shallow in heart were thus dissuaded from attending our church and hearing the message of salvation. At least their negativism rarely impacted our workers. God often saved us from those who lacked spiritual backbone, as well as the nay-sayers and Pharisees. I don't know that any of us were fanatics, like many of those who follow professional sports. However, we did consider a decision for Christ to be a matter of life and death. As a result, we were challenged to become soul winners.

If you have never had anyone tell you that they consider you their best friend, you should go soul winning. Some use a sword to decapitate their enemies, but Christians instead offer their enemies abundant life! We take the sword of the Lord, which is the Word of God—the Bible—to teach others about the freedom and joy they will discover when they receive Christ as personal Savior. Soul-winners risk rejection, verbal abuse, and much worse. But they bring the message of peace and life and love. That is why they are "more than conquerors,"[36] because instead of murdering their enemies, they offer help for today and bright hope for tomorrow.

As the prophet Daniel wrote: *"Those who are wise shall shine like the brightness of the firmament, and those who turn many to righteousness like the stars forever and ever"* (Daniel 12:3). Soul winners are the shock troops of Christianity. When someone is delivered from an eternity in Hell, they often consider the person who helped them find new life to be very special; a mentor and trusted friend. When someone understands that he or she is

---

36   Romans 8:37

going to spend eternity in Heaven because you intervened in their life, and when they recognize that you helped them gain the highest prize, they will look upon you as one of the most important persons they will ever know.

Just as we love Christ because He first loved us, those whom you lead to the Lord will appreciate you because you helped bring them from death unto life. Their friendship is an unexpected residual benefit of soul winning, and their appreciation is far more valuable than a paycheck or a pat on the back from your boss. It's perhaps the most important thing you'll ever accomplish that has eternal value. Proverbs 11:30 states that *"The fruit of the righteous is a tree of life; and he that winneth souls is wise."*

The members of our church never let me forget that I was to be a leader who led by example. The bus ministry was not our only outreach. The stalwart of heart went out on the streets and started conversations with strangers with the purpose of leading them to the Lord.

Paul Morrissette began scolding me because he felt I wasn't getting out on the streets at least once a week to win souls. And while I might excuse myself because of the demands on my time, his concern was valid. I'd been neglecting my soul winning responsibility. He seemed harsh, but his was an honest concern. The truth is, like most people, I have always been uncomfortable about buttonholing strangers, whether to sell them something or even help them find Christ. Paul seemed determined to test me, to see whether I was in the faith. So we made an appointment to go soul winning together.

He took me to a small, mom and pop store across the Hudson River, in Watervliet. There was an old-fashioned soda fountain behind a mahogany counter, with stools bolted to the floor, and a mirror stretching along the wall above the back bar. But I didn't have time to appreciate its charm because Paul had blind-sided me. As we were entering the place, he told me that the owner was a mean, middle-aged, unshaved, foul-mouthed brute who hated anyone who tried to talk to him about God. Paul was challenging me to try to win him to the Lord.

But I had been praying all morning for God's grace, acknowledging that I couldn't accomplish anything meaningful without consciously seeking the Lord's assistance. I don't remember what I said to that man that day, but I do remember praying silently that I wouldn't fail God. Nor did He fail me.

Before we left the store that day, that man, with tears in his eyes, prayed with me to receive Jesus as his personal Savior. Then the storekeeper took Paul and me upstairs to meet his elderly mother and asked me to pray with her too. And then that mean, middle-aged, unshaved, foul-mouthed brute insisted on giving me his treasured old gold pocket watch, a time piece that had belonged to his father and grandfather. That watch, made during the Civil War, is quite valuable today, but it won't be sold because it remains among my most treasured possessions. It's another monument to God's presence and power in my life.

Don't sell Paul short. He always put his money where his mouth was, and he was faithful. It was he who was led of the Holy Spirit to challenge me to visit that man. Just as Andrew introduced Peter to Jesus, so Paul introduced me to that unsaved man. But it was the Holy Spirit who won the man to Christ, so we might call it a team effort. We are, after all, ambassadors for Christ (2 Corinthians 5:20).

Not all of my soul-winning efforts ended so well. I remember going to Troy Plaza and speaking to a thirty-something woman about the Lord. I noticed that she had marks up and down her arms, like cigarette burns. Despite the crowds passing by, she was eager to speak with me, and agreed that she wanted to receive Jesus Christ as her Savior. She agreed to pray with me, so I began leading her through a prayer of salvation, line by line. When I suggested she pray, "I won't continue abusing myself with sex or drugs," she stopped me and said, "No, no! I can't do that. I'm sorry...." Then she turned and ran away.

Soul winning, like every other aspect of the Christian walk, must be anointed by God. We are to do our best, but trust in Him. If we fail, perhaps someone else will succeed later. But, again, we are dealing with eternal souls, so let us also have a caring spirit of fear and trembling.

As I remarked earlier, the ministry had become too large for our little building, and Paul had reached an agreement with the principal of the Catholic Central High School, just a few blocks north, to use their facilities on Sunday mornings. That Catholic priest supported God's work, even though it was being accomplished by us dreaded "Protestants." But some of his fellow clergy showed great resentment because we were busing their children to our dreaded protestant Sunday School. Several told their congregations that they should not let their children ride our buses. But we continued visiting the poor and despised of the city and filled our buses with whoever would come.

One clergyman tried to embarrass me. The woman who sold us the house that served as our new parsonage was one of his parishioners. He asked her to call me to say that he might be willing to rent us his vacant school building. Paul and I stood on the sidewalk outside his church as she introduced us to him. He actually began insulting us for stealing children from his church. It soon became obvious that he had no intention of assisting us in any way. While he began attacking us verbally, the woman surprised me by hugging me—an act clearly designed to put our relationship, and my character, in question. It wasn't the first time I was blind-sided by clergy, media, or politicians of Troy. It wouldn't be the last.

Early every Saturday morning our entire staff met in the basement of our new church to hash out problems, to encourage and pray for one another, and to feast on the spectacular breakfasts that the ladies of the church prepared as a labor of love. It's been fifty years, but I especially remember that Jeanette Hoogkamp was joined by Gem Garabedian and Guy Vozzy's mom, as they prepared those fabulous Bus Breakfasts.

Our bus captains were busy people. Each one had his or her own bus route, and most of those routes wound through the depressed areas and public housing projects in south, east and north Troy. They actually walked their routes every Saturday morning, knocking on doors and inviting folks they met along the way to ride their bus to church.

God is interested in numbers. In fact, there's a book entitled "Numbers." And the Bible is quite specific about Jesus feeding 5,000 men, plus women and children, and the fact that 3,000 accepted Jesus as Lord on the day of Pentecost. So, we had an unofficial contest among bus captains to see who had the most riders each week.

The youngest bus captain was our eleven-year-old daughter, Sandra. Our daughter Cheryl, two-and-a-half years younger, was bitterly disappointed that she too couldn't be a bus captain. But soon enough she was hailed by the children along the routes as "Mickey Mouse." We avoided calling our "mouse" Mickey for fear of being sued for copyright infringement, but the kids on the streets expressed their own opinions.

Cheryl, of course, was accompanied by the bus captain on that route. But since Sandra was an actual Bus Captain, Paul Morrissette insisted that she be accompanied on her route by one of our men. As it turned out, Sandy never needed her bodyguard to protect her from predators. She boldly knocked on doors to invite unsaved parents to bring their children to junior church, while her "bodyguard" was too shy to do so. By incorporating teenagers and small children into ministry at the earliest possible point in their maturity, we provided opportunities for them to gain a sense of divine purpose and value.

Sunday mornings brought the culmination of each week's labors. The bus captains would ride their assigned buses—pointing out to their respective drivers where they were to stop, helping riders safely cross the street, conducting their own Sunday school session on the bus, leading riders in songs, telling Bible stories, listening to children share testimonies of triumph, and praying with everyone. We lived by the adage, "If you don't have a program for the kids on the bus, the kids on the bus will have a program for you!"

We never seemed to have sufficient funds for the bus ministry. It was through prayer and hard work that brother Paul somehow kept those old buses rolling. He often took money from his own meager fifty-dollar a week paycheck to buy candy for his "bus kids." Please keep in mind the fact that Paul wasn't one of our relatively carefree college students. He had to provide for his talented and deeply committed wife, Pauline, and their two beautiful daughters, Michelle and Chrissy.

Largely because of Paul's efforts, thousands were exposed to the gospel, with hundreds saved. He was joined by a score of others who made enormous personal sacrifices because they recognized that the Lord had placed before them an open door, which no one could close.

CHAPTER 36

A Christmas Miracle

                    - Lyrics by Clare Herbert Woolston (1864)

I was broke! My role model was the Apostle Paul, who attempted to support himself, rather than become a financial burden on his fledgling churches, and who sought to avoid any criticism for exploiting his ministry for filthy lucre. I rarely had enough money, and I wanted to plow most of the offerings back into the ministry, but I wasn't the only one!

I think that, for a while, Paul Morrissette and I each received fifty dollars per week. When income wasn't sufficient, Paul returned to his sheet metal work but somehow faithfully maintained his ministry. Over the following months, others joined the staff, and received little more than a pittance for their unstinting labor. If memory serves, a number of the faithful, including Lee and Peggy Hach, Judie Muscatello, Stanley Birnbaum and Kevin Nicholas, each received only thirty-five dollars per week during the late '70s. The most I ever received was one-hundred dollars a week, the amount I was receiving when I left the church north of the Finger Lakes. As a result, each of my co-workers, along with own my family of six, generally lived hand to mouth. They were, and are, true giants of the faith!

Several members, including I think, Guy and Lucy Vozzy, and Paul and Pauline Morrissette, sold the land on which they planned to build their homes and gave the proceeds to the church. I still believe that a leader shouldn't ask his followers to do something that he isn't willing to do, so at one point—just months before I resigned the denomination to found an independent church—I borrowed five thousand dollars from a bank and gave it to the church. I wonder if the bank would have approved that personal loan if the manager had not been attending our church.

My family has experienced many financial trials through the years, sometimes because of my poor money management, but often because Joy and I were happy to sacrifice financially to serve the Lord. Church planters and missionaries are often underpaid, and pastor's wives and children frequently suffer. My wife, "the queen of the manse," was, with her children, apt to find herself wearing hand-me-downs and cast-off clothing.

That may account for why some preacher's kids (PKs), later walk away from the Lord, though I think it has more to do with parenting and implanting the Word of God than any perceived poverty. The Bible assures us, *"Train up a child in the way that he should go, and when he is old, he will not depart from it."*[37] Joy and I praise God that our four children and their mates have remained true and have trained up their own children in the way they should go.

Nonetheless, children are in danger of becoming embittered when they find themselves possessing far less than other children in the church, not to speak of comparing themselves with the children of the world. So, when I began gathering testimonies for this book, I asked Joy and our grown children for any special memories of God's blessing on them. Sandra and Cheryl both recalled the same experience.

We had nearly completed our second year in Troy. We had moved from one church building to another and had even purchased a parsonage. A number of people were giving every free moment to the work of God and others were exceedingly generous. Brother Paul was helping me adapt the building to the needs of the congregation, while working to grow the bus ministry. I was, of course, busy with the usual pastoral duties.

---

37   Proverbs 22:6

Many of us had to wear several hats. Paul, for example, had the responsibility for the bus ministry, but also for the leadership of the entire junior church program. And now he was about to put on a third hat. For he, Tom Muckle, and Ara Shahinian had all secured their bus driver's licenses, and were faithfully driving the buses that brought in a multitude of unsaved children.

But since we were often short of drivers, Paul initially had to call on me to help fill the gap. Like the other drivers, I would board a bus an hour before church, and Paul would send me on one of the easier routes to south Troy to pick up a load of kids and take them to the high school.

The bus captains were not babysitters. It could take up to an hour to pick up the children and get them to the high school, and that again that much more time to return them to their homes, and they had to minister to the children both going and coming. During those round trips, they taught the children Christian choruses, had Scripture memory contests, and acted out Bible stories that the children would remember for the rest of their lives.

In this way, they significantly contributed to the Bible teaching provided during church. What's more, when they visited the children's homes on Saturdays, and spoke with their parents, they had occasions to listen to their problems, to counsel and to pray with them.

Brother Paul had oversight of the entire bus program, and every Saturday morning, he jump-started the ministry. At 8 am, the entire staff—including bus drivers, captains, teachers, and Sunday School workers—met in the basement of the church for a fantastic "Bus Breakfast." It was prepared by several dedicated women who wanted to make a contribution.

We feasted on bacon, sausage, eggs, pancakes, toast, juice, cake, and coffee, while various workers stood to share their testimonies and their problems, and others suggested solutions. It was a time to encourage one another, to tally up our successes and face our failures, and to spend time in prayer. Only then did the captains leave to walk their routes.

When Sunday came, I had to focus continually on the safe operation of my own bus. It was impossible to give any thought to the morning service. I was too busy steering the bus down narrow streets that were lined on both sides with parked cars, while the bus captain pointed out each place I needed to stop to pick up children. When the captain wasn't guiding me, he would lead the boisterous singing and loud story telling. It was not an atmosphere conducive to sermon preparation or prayer.

Hopefully, before the morning service was scheduled to begin, I would already have dropped off the kids at the high school. Then I'd rush to the church to join the ever-faithful Heather Flora, who would play the piano while I led the worship service. The moment we finished singing, she hurried out of the building to help teach the kids at the high school, and I would be left alone to preach to our small but surprisingly growing group of adults. After the closing prayer, I too would run out the door, climb into the driver's seat, and take that same busload of kids home.

Our second year in Troy, when we were operating up to five buses, our income doubled to $42,000. This barely covered our mortgage, utilities, the fleet of buses, and other programs, including a new Christian elementary school, which required the administrators to be trained in Texas, plus special furniture, curriculum, and much more. Somewhere in there, my salary was increased and I quit my job driving bus for the public schools.

About then, the church was paying a meager fifty dollars a week to my close associate, Paul Morrissette, and even less to Pastor Lee and Peggy Hach, who came on board to lead our Christian school. Paul and the Hachs were amazing. Lee and Peggy moved into the parsonage with us. Paul left his high-paying job as a union sheet metal worker, and with his wife Pauline and their two beautiful little girls, trusted the Lord while giving themselves generously to the work of God. We were all rich in friends and fellowship, but poor in the wealth of this world.

It was about then that we were particularly blessed when a young woman began attending the services and brought with her many members of her extended family. They had been faithful members of their historic church, but had become disenchanted. They were seeking the spiritual freedom that comes through a personal relationship with Christ.

Like survivors from other ethnic and religious groups that emigrated to America, they found that they fared best when they kept close community and remained faithful and loyal to one another, to their priest, and to their historic church. But when this woman shared with her extended family what she considered something special about our beliefs, many of her kindred came to investigate. And that's where this testimony begins.

It was nearly Christmas, and our two daughters, ages 8 and 11, were very excited, while our two sons were just toddlers. I was so wrapped up in my work at the church that when Joy asked one morning what we could give the kids for Christmas, I had to confess that we had no money for gifts. I tried to explain to the girls, and they were momentarily crushed.

They then decided to make it a matter of prayer, and Joy and I joined them in asking for a miracle.

I returned to the church, leaving our hopeless situation in God's hands. I was about to be embarrassed as I discovered once again that Jesus loves the little children. He will do abundantly above that which they ask or think.

A few days before Christmas, we received an invitation to visit one of our newest families, and though I wanted to beg off for what I considered more important responsibilities, Joy insisted that we take time to visit. When we arrived, they said they wouldn't keep us long, but instead stacked beautifully wrapped Christmas gifts in our arms, a dramatic answer to our daughter's prayers. How grateful I was for the love of those people.

But my memory is short, for as I was writing this chapter, Sandy sent me an email stating that there was more, much more to the story. These are her words: "Two days before Christmas, presents started arriving by the box load. Cheryl and I counted eleven presents each that Christmas!"

Then Sandy, who is now the mother of four adult children and two adoptees, added these words: "They came mostly in waves on December 23rd to our front door — over and over the doorbell rang and there was another family with more boxfuls of beautifully wrapped gifts — the Shahinians, the Garabedians, the Khachadorians, the Vozzys — am I missing anyone? Cheryl and I were overjoyed and overwhelmed with excitement, and lovingly placed them around the tree and counted them all — over 100 gifts for our family of 6! Matthew was a toddler that year. And yes, exactly eleven gifts for each of us big sisters. It was a Christmas I will never forget. Bless those Armenian brothers and sisters!!"

As I read Sandy's words about the love that these folks displayed nearly fifty years ago, I was swept with nostalgia. I still remember our daughters leading me by the hands and standing amazed as they pointed out the heaps of beautifully wrapped gifts beneath our tree. I was near tears as I saw the glow on their faces.

To our daughters, it was truly an answer to prayer. For me, the greatest gift was to witness how our brothers and sisters were rich in the love of Christ, and like the Wise Men who brought gifts to little Jesus, demonstrating once again that *"Jesus loves the little children."*[38]

---

38   See https://hymnary.org/text/standing_by_a_purpose_true

Chapter 37

"A Matter of Degrees"

"But Simon's wife's mother lay sick with a fever, and they told Him (Jesus) about her at once. So He came and took her by the hand and lifted her up, and immediately the fever left her."
Mark 1:30-31

Most of us do not become upset if the temperature of our coffee varies a few degrees, but when a loved one's temperature rises dramatically, those few degrees can become a matter of grave concern. Our firstborn son was about six months old when he began exhibiting symptoms of cold or flu, and when Joy called from the nursery with concern in her voice, I hurried to her side. Our ordinarily cheerful and effervescent baby lay on the changing table, his entire body a cherry red. When I touched his forehead, his skin seemed burning hot and dry to the touch. His pupils were dilated, his breathing shallow, his little arms and legs outstretched, and his fingers clenched.

Joy showed me the thermometer. The normal temperature range for a little guy like that is between 96 and 100 degrees, and even though she struggled to cool his fever, his temperature was 105. He was docile, and merely whimpered when she sponged his hot little body with a cool wet cloth.

For a moment, we stood there struggling with indecision. Should we wrap him up and rush him to the emergency room or should we try sponging him again? Neither of us could bear to watch him lying there shivering, caught in the grip of that raging fever. But it was the still small voice in our hearts that prevailed. We found ourselves clasping hands, closing our eyes, and praying together for a miracle.

When we opened our eyes, we were startled to discover that Jamie's skin was a healthy pink, his eyes clear and shining, and he was smiling. We again checked his temperature. It was normal! During that brief but intense prayer, our son's temperature dropped from 105 to 98.6. The instantaneous change was so radical that we were stunned by the evidence of God's loving care.

Let others argue over the theology. We were there, and *"... we cannot stop speaking about what we have seen and heard"* (Acts 4:20). This was one of those situations where it was truly "...better felt than telt." It happened so quickly that it might be easily spurned, but so might the account of Jesus healing Peter's mother-in-law when she lay sick with a fever (Matthew 8:14).

That instantaneous drop of six or seven degrees in Jamie's temperature left a vivid impression on Joy and me. We continue to thank our Lord, not simply for healing our precious baby, but for blessing us with this additional evidence of his love, presence and power.

"...And lo, I am with you always, even until the end of the world" (Matthew 28:20).

CHAPTER 38

Heather, Stanley, and Kevin

"And the things that thou hast heard of me among many witnesses, the same commit thou to faithful men, who shall be able to teach others also."

2 Timothy 2:2, KJV

The command to teach others to share the gospel is meant for all Christians; for you and for me. But before we commit these truths to others, we must learn and live them ourselves. We are not to be observers. We are to be very active participants, and that means becoming richly involved in the work of God, so we may teach others what we have learned. Then they, in turn, teach others, *ad infinitum* until Jesus returns.

That has always been one of my goals, but my ambition has far exceeded my grasp. If I were to compare myself to the apostle Paul, I would fall far short in every way. Perhaps the great Apostle was having similar thoughts about his own worthiness when he wrote, *"But with me it is a very small thing that I should be judged by you or by a human court. In fact, I do not even judge myself"* (1 Corinthians 4:3). God is our Judge!

Yet, Paul and I have at least one thing in common. We both thanked God for the men and women whom the Lord sent our way, those with whom we were privileged to serve. Paul didn't hesitate to praise those who faithfully labored with him; those young believers like Silas and Timothy, who went on to become giants of the faith.

Several of my co-workers, whose shoes I am not worthy to tie, have gone on to become great servants of the Lord. I'll mention a few here and apologize up front for failing to mention many others who deserve similar praise. The truth is, if I tried to recall all of them, I could not.

If you are among that number, please blame my failure on age and infirmity, and not on any lack of appreciation for your wonderful service. I confess that I can't count the number of times I have hurt someone's feelings by failing to recognize their achievements. But it is better that some are recognized, rather than that all are neglected. Far better still that, where I fail to praise, God will not.

As I near the end of this life, I, want to applaud the efforts of those who began their service for Christ while we labored together in the same vineyard. I've already mentioned Paul Morrissette and a number of others, especially Lee and Peggy Hach. Now I write about a few more.

When I first met these three, none of us had an inkling of what the Lord had planned for us. There was little in their backgrounds or educations that would suggest the directions their lives would ultimately take. They were all young adults, but two of them were also young in the faith and just beginning significant spiritual growth. But they readily acknowledged that fact and threw themselves into God's work with zeal and humility, trusting the Lord to give them wisdom and see them through.

Each of them persistently adhered to what the Lord had revealed to them as they adhered to his holy Word, and did not allow the world's mockery to deter them. They began to recognize their total dependence on God and happily embraced the Apostle Paul's words: "*... God has chosen the foolish things of the world to put to shame the wise, and God has chosen the weak things of the world to put to shame the things which are mighty*" (1 Corinthians 1:27).

The Apostle Paul was, of course, being a little ironic. Compared to the lost people of this world, the children of God are anything but foolish. Paul told us, "*You are all sons of light and sons of the day. We are not of the night nor of darkness*" (1 Thessalonians 5:5). Yet, in a real sense, those of us who wholeheartedly follow Jesus soon realize that we are not sufficient to the tasks that he lays before us unless we rely on Him. It's then that we learn that "*I can do all things through Christ who strengthens me*" (Philippians 4:13).

When we begin to recognize the preciousness of every human soul, from the unborn in the womb to the gray haired sage, we become increasingly concerned about how one wrong word or one flawed act might stumble them. Paul showed the need for sensitivity for the best interests of others when he wrote to the Corinthians, *"I was with you in weakness, in fear, and in much trembling"* (1 Corinthians 2:3). He didn't want to fail! We are all totally dependent on the Lord for wisdom and power, or we will fail.

The three individuals of whom I write might not have liked being considered foolish by the people of this world; but in their humility, they acknowledged their need to grow and their absolute dependence on Jesus Christ. So when they took his hand, their grip was firm. They were beginning to know the Savior in whom they had believed and were becoming persuaded that He was able to keep that which they had committed unto Him. They proved it by clinging to Him through thick and thin.

Their remarkable growth in faith was like an upward spiral. They were learning that the reward for faithfulness in small matters resulted in larger responsibilities being thrust upon them. With those added responsibilities came greater authority and power to accomplish the work.

We used to joke, "If you do a good job caring for the monkey that God gives you, he will reward you with a gorilla." Greater responsibilities require more authority. Jesus revealed this truth in His Parable of the Talents, when he said: *"Well done, thou good and faithful servant: thou hast been faithful over a few things, I will make thee ruler over many things"* (Matthew 25:21, KJV).

Consider your own life. If you look at yourself in a mirror, you really have no idea what God can make of you. You will tend to compare yourself with others based on your outward appearance or how others evaluate you, but God looks on your heart. He sees things you don't, the things that really matter. You were created in his moral image, and therefore you have incredible worth and infinite potential.

The three individuals about whom I write had no idea what God was going to do in and through them, much less that the lives of multitudes would be changed because of them. Perhaps these before and after pictures will help you comprehend the miraculous changes that God wrought in their lives. And once you grasp that fact, I pray that you will commit yourself to experiencing a similar miracle. All you need to do is trust and obey God.

Earlier I mentioned that I never seemed to have enough time, money, or energy. I was spread pretty thin and I always felt I had far more responsibilities than my limited knowledge, talents, and faith could equal. Yet almost everyone in our little church was similarly challenged. As a result, many were spending almost every free hour at the church or out on the streets, contributing their labor to one ministry or another. Carol Muckle joked that she had been spending so much time at the church that, when she finally reached home, she tried to unlock her front door with the key to the church.

Not only were we always short of cash, our growth was so rapid that we were always short of workers. This was another point of criticism from the detractors who seemed to delight in our deficiencies. They often used it as an excuse not to come alongside to help lift those burdens.

For example, a typical class in a suburban Sunday School today might number between two and ten students, and be led by one or even two teachers. Compare that with Shirley Sexton's class where she labored to instill the great truths of God to a classroom of fifty unruly bus kids. While she was doing that, I was preaching to a handful of adults in the morning service. Is it any wonder that Norm and Jeanette Hoogkamp had questioned my claim that we had between two and three hundred children in Sunday School?

But that's where most of the members of our adult congregation were, ministering to those children at the nearby high school. And each of those adults was growing in stature and wisdom, and in favor with God and man because they were attempting to teach those precious children that Jesus had given His life for them.These kids were already steeped in the cauldron of this world's sin.

On the morning of the Hoogkamps first visit, I remember asking myself how I was going to preach to a group that was the size of a small Bible study. It was extraordinary, for while most members couldn't attend the preaching service on Sunday mornings, virtually everyone attended both Sunday and Wednesday evening services. Ours was the only church I've ever attended that had as many people out for midweek as for Sunday morning. They weren't just hungry for the Word of God. They had discovered that it was the Bread of Life to them, and they couldn't function without that spiritual nourishment.

Our Sunday School workers would be in the auditorium on Sunday night, and again on Wednesday evening, and they expected me to feed them enough of God's Word to help them go and grow. I remember one occasion when a fine young man, Guy Vozzy, stood at the conclusion of an evening service to complain that my message was too short. I was rightly embarrassed, and I determined that I would never fall short again.

And what about those hundreds of children? Anything we could offer was far better than the nothing they would receive without our ministry. The 19th Century evangelist, Dwight L. Moody, would have loved our program. After one of his evangelistic meetings, he was asked, "How many people were saved tonight?" He replied, "Two and a half." His inquirer said, "You mean two adults and one child?" Moody replied, "No. Two children and one adult!" Moody understood that children have their entire lives ahead of them. And, because those two began receiving God's Word as children, they were unlikely to become as poisoned by the world as that one newly redeemed adult.

I couldn't keep up with everything going on around me, and I knew that I had to rely on the Lord to keep things under control. There were so many new and creative ideas being introduced that I concluded that it was my responsibility to delegate and then get out of the way. So, I tried to prayerfully evaluate the character of the workers, and in turn trust them to prayerfully win and recruit helpers and make decisions about their programs. The beauty of entrusting these overwhelming labors to new converts was that they were in the flush of God's love, and their faith had not yet been tainted by "mature" Christians who had actually never grown very much in faith.

I was trying to keep a bird's eye view on the exploding ministry. Thank God I rarely had time or inclination to be a micromanager. When I did intrude, I tended to muck up the works and quench the moving of the Spirit. But often, because I was overwhelmed, I stood back and got to see the Lord unlock the incredible genius that resides in every yielded believer.

All I asked of them was that everyone would check with me before instituting something new. That way we could make certain it wasn't contrary to Scripture and that their plans and activities didn't clash with the activities of others. Most importantly, we needed to pray together.

During that period, I was privileged to watch a score of individuals blossom spiritually as they seized every opportunity to serve God. It was a glorious experience to observe their growing joy as the Spirit moved in their lives. But if I occasionally noted someone becoming envious of another's success, or becoming discouraged because of their own seeming failure, I intervened, though not always wisely.

My job was to provide them with spiritual meat, and to counsel, encourage, and pray with them, while trying to make sure that everything was done decently and in order. Sadly, I too often failed. The Lord laid the burden for the initial period of growth on just a few of us, but many others soon became involved. Three people in particular came onto the scene within a few months of my arrival in Troy. There is no question in my mind that these three were called and anointed by the Lord for lifetime service.

If I initially seem to sound critical of some aspect of their personalities, it is not to demean them. Rather, it is to provide a "before" and "after" picture. Unless there is a before problem and an after solution, there is no miracle. These three individuals yielded their lives to the Lord, and He changed them from "average," typical "run of the mill" Christians to mighty servants of God. And just a decade later, after the Lord had called us all to different fields, these three in particular pressed on to a higher calling.

In a world that promotes hatred, strife, and division, it is the miracle of Christ's love that explains how these three unique individuals, each from a different background—race, religion, culture, ethnicity, and education—became life-long friends and effective co-laborers. And that's not to speak of the fact that two of them have now been happily married for over fifty years. The great apostle Paul expressed it best:

> For ye are all the children of God by faith in Christ Jesus. For as many of you as have been baptized into Christ have put on Christ. There is neither Jew nor Greek, there is neither bond nor free, there is neither male nor female: for ye are all one in Christ Jesus. And if ye be Christ's, then are ye Abraham's seed, and heirs according to the promise. (Galatians 3:26-29)

The bond that they still share in Christ, and the incredible body of work that they have accomplished, is evidence of God's miraculous and loving guidance and power. I was privileged to be there when the Holy Spirit brought us all together in early 1974. Though my memory of events occurring half a century ago may be somewhat flawed, I can only hope that anyone who was involved will make allowances and forgive any errors.

Heather Flora is the first of those who became intensely involved at our church, and ultimately found herself committed to a life of full-time ministry. Heather's father, Henry, recently went to be with the Lord, having lived 105 fruitful years. He was my adult Sunday School teacher in 1969, before I entered Bible college at age 30, and he introduced Joy and me to his daughter Heather one Sunday morning while she was home for a visit.

I don't recall meeting Heather again until about five years later, just a short time after we arrived in Troy, when she visited our church. I didn't recognize her, and she had to introduce herself. Joy describes her as a strawberry-blond and still remembers her as a remarkably friendly person. I don't recall the color of Heather's hair, but I do remember her as an exceptional individual whose keen intellect was hidden behind her winsome personality.

Heather had a hunger to serve Jesus and she would not hesitate to express her righteous indignation if she thought she saw an injustice done. I would know! Through the years, I have been properly upbraided several times. I still bear vivid memories of her "correction in righteousness." Yet no one ever had a dearer, kinder, and more loyal co-worker and friend.

Perhaps it was during Heather's first visit to the church that I happened to remark that the congregation needed to pray for God to send us a pianist. Heather immediately stood and asked, "Don't you know that I play the piano?" That night Heather became our church pianist, and continued ministering at nearly every service during the ten years I was privileged to pastor in Troy. Heather completed her training as a Registered Nurse and used her skills to heal the sick. But she also used her knowledge and resources to support those who ministered with her. Medicine was to Heather what tent-making was to the Apostle Paul. It provided the means to serve God and bless those in need.

Shortly after she arrived, I was beginning a midweek teaching series on the non-Christian cults. That first Wednesday evening a young man stood up and questioned the value of my teaching about false religions. The gist of his argument was that I ought to concentrate on the truths of the Bible, not the errors of the cults.

It was certainly a meaningful thought, but I pointed out that many people were being seduced into joining cults because they weren't familiar with their insidious methods, false teachings, and quasi-Christian claims. I was teaching the congregation to use the Scriptures to expose and refute them. I considered it vital that we understand the characteristics of the cults.

It is not customary for a member of a Christian congregation to interrupt a pastor when he is preaching. On the other hand, a Christian Bible teacher generally encourages questions for clarification and enrichment. But it's almost unheard of for a teacher to be criticized. So the moment that he interrupted me, and began debating the benefits of teaching about the cults, I realized that I had lost my audience, and I found it necessary to terminate the study,

Apart from any damage to my pride, which wasn't relevant, we were a new church, a small gathering, and I was concerned that his words might confuse and stumble young believers or even cause a church split. So I was immediately on guard. In truth, he was more like Jesus' two young disciples, the outspoken James and John, whom he named "Sons of thunder."[39]

I was sensitive to the danger of church splits, as I had already witnessed a couple. But the young man who interrupted me believed that I lacked focus. He was intent on getting more Bible doctrine into people's hearts. He was sincerely concerned that our teaching time was not being wisely used. I could see that he was still upset at what he considered my inept leadership, and he had upset a few of those present.

While people were saying their goodbyes to one another, Heather spoke to me. Even today, I think of her as a type of Barnabus, a daughter of consolation; a peacemaker. She told me that she had witnessed the young man expressing similar indignation at other Christian meetings. Though he might be overzealous, she considered him well-meaning. She was right. I would later come to realize that Stanley was simply a new Christian who, like all of us, including me, had a little growing to do.

In an effort to make peace, she introduced us. It was not a propitious encounter because we were both bristling. At the moment, the only way this young pastor wanted to remember Stanley Birnbaum was from afar. It seemed obvious to me that he felt the same way, but the Lord was about to surprise both of us.

As people began leaving the church that night, rain was pouring down, so Stanley was looking for a ride home. The city of Troy runs for several miles up and down the east shore of the Hudson River, and while our church was nearer the north end of the city, he lived some distance south. Heather again revealed her compassion by offering to drive him home.

Stanley—or Shmuel, as he is known to the fellowship he founded decades ago in Israel—was a very interesting young man. He had been one of the half-million people, many of them "hippies," who attended the infamous Woodstock Music Festival in August of 1969. He received Christ during the Jesus Revolution, and because he is Jewish, became what many were calling a Messianic Jew. At some point he dropped out of a philoso-

---

39   Mark 3:17

phy program at the state university in Albany and ultimately took a job as a reporter for a local Christian newspaper.

His employment as a reporter was the reason for our second meeting, a meeting that I would have been quite happy to avoid. In line with his job, he called me a few days after our first tumultuous meeting, and said he wanted to interview me about my plans for our little church. As busy as I was, I had no alternative but to say yes. Having been a businessman and a candidate for office, I understood the importance of good publicity to any enterprise, including a struggling young church.

I don't recall which church members were at our apartment the morning that Stanley arrived. I do remember that my wonderful wife Joy, the inveterate peacemaker, wanted to pour oil on the troubled waters of our relationship. So, she prepared an impressive breakfast.

Regrettably, Stan arrived late, so the food was cold. As it turned out, everything about the interview seemed cold to me, including the eggs. Despite that, Stanley remembers eating everything on his plate, even the bacon.

I recall that our time together turned out to be more of a discussion than an interview, for he spent nearly as much time expressing his personal opinions as eliciting mine. He didn't hesitate to compare our little church negatively with another new church he was writing about for the same article. When he departed, I was left with the impression that his article would be less than flattering to our church. As it turned out, it was essentially fair and balanced.

That same day, unknown to me, the Lord was acting behind the scenes to alter both of our destinies. Stanley recently sent me an email describing what happened to him.

"I was walking home from the grocery store on the evening after our breakfast interview which I came late to. Wrecked Joy's great food. Eggs were cold, and (during my walk) the Lord clearly said to join with you. ... It was, outside of salvation, one of the most significant moments of my life. Everything started with that move."

Consider these remarkable events. First, Stanley visited our midweek Bible study, weighed me in the balance and found me wanting. Then he came for breakfast and interviewed me for his Christian newspaper. Then, that same evening, the Lord clearly told him to join with me. Those two initial meetings would not be the only times that the two of us would come to judge one another a bit harshly.

Average Guy Meets Extraordinary God

Despite that, God opened up a decade of mutual service and a lifetime of friendship. Following his fateful conversation with the Lord, Stanley immediately began looking for places in our church where he could be useful. With his keen intelligence and undying compassion for the lost, he was a natural soul-winner. At any hour you might find him roaming the streets of Troy, chatting about Jesus to anyone he happened to meet. Over the course of the following year, he was instrumental in leading about a thousand people to a saving knowledge of Jesus Christ, while helping others in the church to overcome their natural timidity to testify of Christ's love.

As a bus captain, however, Stanley faced other obstacles, and he was at first very discouraged in his seeming inability to secure riders. But with the prayerful help of others, we all celebrated when he brought his first bus load of thirty riders to church. The impact of each individual on others, and the subsequent growth of the church, never ceased to amaze me.

Heather's brother, Steve, for example, became excited when she told him what was going on in Troy. He read a term paper I wrote in college, "The Multiple-Staff Ministry," and decided to visit for the summer. But while I felt his efforts and subsequent spiritual growth would be best manifested by working through the church, he felt that God was leading him to sponsor a Christian rock concert in Troy.

Steve held his "Jesus Christ Solid Rock Concert" during the 4th of July holidays, at the historic Troy Music Hall. To do so he had to overcome incredible opposition. The city leaders were opposed to anything that might attract rowdy crowds. Memories of Woodstock, as well as other rock concerts that had resulted in property damage, injuries, and even deaths fostered resistance.

Steve persevered. To this day I regret failing to help him more. I was terribly limited in time and financial resources for the growing church, and felt unable to provide sufficient attention, let alone financial help. I've always wondered what project I might have forsaken, or who I might have neglected, to help Steve more. The point is, I failed him.

Yet that makes Steve's accomplishment all the more impressive. He was forced to wear numerous "hats." He took on the roles of theatrical promoter, lawyer, musician, and publicist. He raised money for an insurance policy, and he somehow succeeded in putting on the concert. Though it might not seem so to some observers, he had an enormous impact on the work of God; an impact that would endure for eternity.

Here's one example. Like Andrew, who brought his brother Peter to Jesus, so Heather brought her brother Steve to Troy. Steve in turn pointed others, like Kevin Nicholas, to the work of the Lord. Steve encouraged Kevin to visit our little fellowship. This seemingly unimportant connection resulted in countless people receiving Christ and is just one example of the fruit produced by Steve Flora's efforts.

Only God knows who else was impacted by Steve's concert, or the personal sacrifices he made to produce Troy's "Jesus Christ Solid Rock Concert." There had undoubtedly been Christian concerts at the famed Troy Music Hall during the 19th century. However, it was quite another thing for someone, a century later, to bring a Christian rock concert to what had become a secular stronghold.

Steve can take consolation in the words of the great Apostle Paul: *"Therefore, my dear brothers and sisters, stand firm. Let nothing move you. Always give yourselves fully to the work of the Lord, because you know that your labor in the Lord is not in vain"* (1 Corinthians 15:58). Steve's work had enduring value.

What he did in sending Kevin Nicholas to our church started Kevin on a life-long voyage of service that would see him crossing many oceans. He began an adventure that would last a lifetime and a quest that would see thousands of lives impacted for Christ. Kevin, an affable young African American, was completing his undergraduate work in computer science at the prestigious Rensselaer Polytechnic Institute (RPI), the oldest continuously operating technological university in the English-speaking world.

In a recent email, Kevin himself told me that he first met Steve Flora at the "Jesus Christ Solid Rock Concert," on Saturday, July 6th, 1974. The next day, Kevin boarded one of our Sunday School buses as it stopped at RPI. He sat with the children who were on their way to "Troy's Largest Sunday School."

In his email, Kevin numbered what he considered to be serious steps in his Christian walk:

"1. Met Steve Flora at the Jesus Rock concert at Troy Music Hall. Saturday, July 6, 1974.
2. Caught the bus at RPI to go to the church for the first time on Sunday, July 7, 1974.
3. I was baptized at Grafton State Park during church picnic on Saturday, August 10th.

4. I first sensed the call to missions the next day, which was August 11th."

In 1976, Kevin received his computer science degree from RPI and immediately started receiving offers for high-paying jobs. But the Lord had other things in mind, ideas which Kevin quickly embraced. Kevin had become a bus captain, Sunday School teacher, occasional soloist, pianist, and much more, and ultimately became an instructor in our Christian school. From the moment Kevin was baptized, God was tugging at his heart. From then on, the lives of all three of these individuals—Heather, Stanley, and Kevin—changed so rapidly that it is difficult to put events in order.

In September 1975, Stan came to me and confided that he felt a leading to enroll at Northeast Bible College, but financial considerations seemed to rule out the possibility. As I prayed with him, I felt led to offer him my last ten dollars as "seed faith money." Evidently, he'd laid down a fleece because this gift provided the assurance he needed to enroll.

I invited Hobart Grazier (1917-1984), one of my two favorite instructors from Bible college, to teach for a week at our church, and Kevin was especially blessed. He wrote, "At that time I felt that the Lord was calling me to go to Bible College and within the week I was on my way to NBC with Stanley."

Yet, every weekend, without fail, Kevin and Stanley drove round trip from Green Lane, Pennsylvania, to Troy, New York, so that that they could serve as bus captains and church workers. They left campus immediately after class on Friday and drove 235 miles to Troy. I have no idea where they rested their weary heads in Troy, but folks in the church felt honored to shelter and feed them. And somehow, week after week, they received gifts of the money they needed to buy gasoline for the 470 mile, 8-hour, round trip. At some point, I believe Brother Paul argued for the church to underwrite their expenses.

On Saturday mornings they would attend the Bus Breakfasts, then walk their routes. They somehow prepared Sunday School lessons, and taught "their kids," both on route to and from church, but also in the Junior Church programs on Sunday morning. When they finished their Sunday ministries, someone in the church fed them, and then they made the 235-mile trek back to Green Lane.

When their little college relocated in 1977, their one-way trip grew to 250 miles each way. They had a number of near accidents when one or the other would fall asleep at the wheel. They also frequently fell asleep during classes.

Were they admired at the college for their sacrificial labors and their zeal to win souls? On the contrary, they were called crazy by some, including one or more professors. But they were instrumental in keeping the Troy bus ministry and Sunday school program alive. No one will know, short of Heaven, how many souls were saved because of their sacrifices.

Kevin's email continues…"At a mission conference at the college, I first learned about Wycliffe Bible Translators. As I was studying Greek at the time I was thinking that this would be the group I would join to do translation." Kevin continued, in *"July, Stanley & Heather got married."*

That was a very special day for me, as well. The wedding took place at the church where Heather's family attended. It was the church where I was baptized, and from which Joy and I set off for Bible college. I was privileged to officiate.

The night before the wedding, my family was invited to stay at the Heather's parents' home. Stanley asked me to prepare a brief salvation message, keeping in mind that many of his Jewish relatives would attend. So I carefully wrote it out, rehearsed it, and had him critique it. He thought it was fine. It took just five minutes to deliver, but in retrospect, I imagine it seemed like an eternity to Stan's relatives.

In late 1976, I resigned from the denomination and left the Troy church, after which I opened a new fellowship in Albany. About half the congregation followed me those additional seven miles south where we rented a vacant school building from the Albany Diocese. Then Stanley went soul-winning along the streets that surrounded the school we were renting, and he just happened to lead the priest's cousins to the Lord. As soon as the priest learned of it, he gave us thirty days to vacate the building. We were again homeless.

Our daughter, Cheryl, had been receiving piano lessons in Troy from a godly lady named Hilda Golding. Hilda was a life-long member of the Presbyterian church in north Troy, but it was down to a handful of elderly members. It was about to close, so she encouraged me to try to rent the building. As a result, by God's grace, we moved back to north Troy. Once again, we were paying two hundred dollars a month for rent and would wind up purchasing a church for a relative pittance.

Since we were moving our Christian school back to Troy, and expanding it through twelfth grade, Kevin decided not to return to college, but to become one of the teachers. The school prospered, largely because of the sacrifice of our workers, but also because of the involvement of parents like Dr. Ted and Elizabeth Hughes and Rev Ted and Debby Kellis. How proud they were when their three sons, in bright red blazers, won a national competition performing "The Hallelujah Chorus" on their stringed instruments before thousands!

Students and staff, Capital Christian Academy, about 1980
(Heather, Stanley, Kevin, and Frank are at the right rear)

By now, you may be wondering how these biographical sketches fit in with a book of miracles. Consider this. The greatest miracles are those that God works in the hearts and minds of those who follow Him, as evidenced by the wonders He accomplishes in and through them to build His Church.

Heather, Stanley, and Kevin were destined to have remarkable futures. In 1983, I left Capital Christian, and my family moved to Texas, where Joy and I worked for a Christian publisher. Stanley Birnbaum—the young man who had once criticized me for teaching a Wednesday night Bible study on the cults—succeeded me as pastor. His wife Heather, along with Kevin Nicholas, continued in their roles in the work of the church and of our Christian school (K-12).

Stanley and Heather later moved on to lead a Messianic fellowship in Albany. In August of 1988, Kevin went to Tijuana, Mexico, where for three months he studied Cross-Cultural ministry. Kevin later traveled to the Philippines to serve as a missionary, and in February 1996, he joined Wycliffe Bible Translators. That November, he returned to the Philippines as a Wycliffe member to provide computer support. On February 19, 2001, he met Gertrude. They became engaged on April 11th, and on September 22nd they were married.

In 2005, Kevin entered the Dallas Theological Seminary, graduating in 2008 with an MA in Biblical Studies and Cross-Cultural Ministry. In

January of 2009, Kevin and Gertrude traveled to Papua New Guinea as Wycliffe missionaries to work with the Notsi people, translating the New Testament into their language. As I write this, that translation is almost ready to go to print.

In the meantime, Stanley and Heather Birnbaum, with their children, moved to Bat Yam, Israel, where they established a ministry. Heather worked part-time as a nurse to help support the family while they struggled to learn the language and sought to reach the people of Israel with the good news of Messiah. Over two decades later, on October 7, 2023, Hamas attacked Israel. I emailed our concerns and prayers to Stanley, now known as Shmuel, and he responded with these words: "Thanks. We are all OK. I will write later in more detail. It is a terrible time for our country. Blessings, Stan"

As I write this, the war is nearly two years old. While a frightening number of people around the world have exposed their anti-Semitism, Shmuel and Heather have been busy distributing thousands of dollars in needed items to those made homeless by the war. So my two young friends—Stan and Heather—who started as Sunday school workers at a small pioneer work in Troy, New York, have gone on to become ministers for the Messiah at the very eye of the spiritual hurricane.

And what of Kevin? Kevin and Gertrude continue their missionary labors in the far Pacific, having remained faithful to God's work. Throughout the last 49 years, the Lord has never failed to lead, guide, and provide all their needs.

In my view, these three in particular are living miracles. They are examples of the greatest Bible heroes who were anointed by God because they were faithful. Each of them could readily share numerous accounts of miracles that they have personally witnessed in their service to Christ.

CHAPTER 39

In the Nick of Time

*"It shall come to pass that before they call, I will answer;
and while they are still speaking, I will hear."*

Isaiah 65:24

I've already mentioned that in 1977, I resigned from the denomination and opened a new church in a vacant Catholic school we rented near the state capital in Albany. No matter how justified I may have felt in my decision to leave the denomination, it proved a difficult burden to our people. My decision to surrender the real estate to the denomination—both the church structure and the parsonage—which had been purchased with money raised during my tenure, proved a difficult burden to those who followed me. We had to start over, but the Lord ultimately compensated us for our sacrifices.

I had been influenced by late night phone calls from a young friend who was assisting a pastor in Schenectady. He repeatedly encouraged me to leave the denomination, at the same time expressing his frustrations with his own role in his church. After I resigned from the denomination, I was surprised to learn that he had replaced me at the Troy church.

I left the denomination just as their newly elected district superintendent was taking office. This made my separation more difficult because he was assuming numerous responsibilities and we had poor communications. Additionally, he had been more than my associate, he had been my friend and frequently testified that I had predicted he would one day be elected superintendent.

Nonetheless, forty-five years later, he and I began regularly chatting on the phone, with his wife occasionally joining in. We would speak at length about their early days in ministry, share the stories of our courtships and early pastoral struggles, and he even sang snatches of hymns he loved. On a more serious note, he revealed his concerns over the spiritual decline of pastors and churches everywhere. I, in turn, shared thoughts from my books. We always prayed together. When he passed away, I experienced a great sense of loss, but also great happiness because our personal fellowship had been restored.

Those from our congregation who didn't follow us to Albany, but instead continued to occupy our former church building, remained with the denomination for only a brief period. After our split, their new pastor made it clear that they had no use for either a bus ministry or a Christian school. Since these had been at the heart of our efforts to evangelize and educate, their board voted to give us their two school buses and the furnishings for the Christian school. Then, ironically, the new pastor of the church we left behind also pulled out of the denomination. Unlike me, he claimed the valuable real estate for his new church.

In the confusion and financial stress that were a result of my resignation, I failed to arrange support for both Paul and Pauline Morrissette and housing for Pastor Lee and Peggy Hach. Paul was struggling to continue our bus ministry, while our deeply committed and gifted friends, Lee and Peggy, continued blessing the children in our Christian school.

Lee and Peggy had lived with our family in the parsonage, and we had become close friends. After I left the denomination, the assistant superintendent sent a letter immediately evicting us. Later, other denominational leaders refused to believe that he would send such a letter, but when I produced the original signed copy, they apologized. By then, however, the Hachs, like us, were moving on with no money and nowhere to go.

Paul and Pauline saved the day. They had a vacant apartment in their home that they could have rented, but they instead moved the Hachs in, gratis. That enabled Lee and Peggy to continue operating our Christian school through the end of the school year, at great personal sacrifice. And they were generous! Lee had even sold his beloved Porsche sports car and contributed the money to the church prior to my resignation.

When I learned of Paul's generosity in providing them with a home, a burden was lifted from my heart, but I was left with a cloud of shame because I had failed all my faithful co-workers. I don't even remember whether the new church was able to continue paying the Hachs the trifle they'd been receiving. Though, I suspect that Paul and Pauline helped with their expenses. Then, to my everlasting sorrow, the Hachs left the church and returned to their Hudson Valley home.

In the meantime, someone had located a vacant school owned by the Roman Catholic Diocese of Albany. We foolishly agreed to pay a whopping four hundred dollars a month to rent what proved to be an impossible to heat concrete and brick mausoleum. We incorporated our new fellowship under the name Capital Christian Church and moved into the building. That was a regrettable choice because some people associated our non-denominational church with the Church of Christ.

Brother Paul somehow kept both of the buses running. Tom Muckle and Ara Shahinian continued faithfully driving kids from Troy to Albany every Sunday. And we actually had a few people join the church, including Linda Bennett and her friend—the young woman who would serve as our church secretary for the next five or six years—Judie Muscatello.

Despite all our difficulties, the hearts of our people were not dampened for our mission to reach the lost. For example, Stan Birnbaum went soul-winning in the vicinity of our rented school. As I mentioned earlier, led a woman to the Lord who was a cousin of the priest who had rented us the building.

What's the old saying? "No good deed goes unpunished!" As soon as the priest learned of his cousin's newfound faith in Christ, he gave us thirty days to vacate the school. We again found ourselves without a place for worship and education, but just in the nick of time. Just before we found ourselves out on the street, God provided a new home. He didn't simply provide an adequate place to gather, but provided a facility which was above anything we could ask or think.

In Chapter 28, I shared how we sold a decrepit church building without my having given any thought to where we might relocate. God then provided us with a beautifully maintained, fully equipped church building. We rented that building for only two-hundred dollars a month, ultimately purchasing the structure for just twenty thousand dollars.

Then, just two years later, after I resigned from the denomination and we had relinquished the property, I led our "half tribe of Manasseh" to the other side of the Hudson. There, we signed an unbreakable lease on a building that we soon learned we couldn't afford to heat. Following that bad news, Stanley Birnbaum took the message of salvation to a lost soul, and our landlord broke the lease for us.

It was a mixed blessing. Yes, the priest's cousin had made a personal confession of faith, and in his anger, the priest freed us from the burden of an unbreakable lease. But now we again found ourselves without a place to meet. For the second time, our fellowship had nowhere to go, and just a few weeks to locate and move into a new home.

Would God deliver us again? We could only hope we would again rejoice in the truth that, *"All things work together for good to those who love God, to those who are the called according to his purpose"* (Romans 8:28). We explored every possibility and spent much time in prayer. Then one of our members called a local Christian radio station and mentioned our need for a new church home.

Capital Christian Church, Troy, New York, 1978

One of their listeners was Hilda Golding, an elderly lady who had once given our daughter Cheryl piano lessons. Hilda reached me by phone and told me that she was a life-long member of the Presbyterian church located across the street from her home in north Troy. She went on to say that their congregation was down to a few elderly people, and that the denomination was planning to close the church.

On her advice, I called the Presbytery of Albany to learn whether they might rent the church building to us. It was located on the corner of 5th Avenue and 101st Street, and the presbyter set up an appointment for us to walk through the stately old brick building. It consisted of two wings, at right angles to one another—a "sanctuary" plus a separate auditorium—plus two large classrooms, a kitchen, a cluster of offices, and lavatories. In all, it totaled about ten thousand square feet, about three times the floor area of the building we had surrendered when we left the denomination.

It too was fully furnished. It contained pews, a Steinway baby grand piano, and a completely equipped kitchen, with a commercial range and steam table. Both auditoriums had thirty-foot-high cathedral ceilings, and the sanctuary had magnificent stained-glass windows that ran along three walls, with several that depicted stories from the Bible.

The Presbytery of Albany encouraged us to move in immediately, renting us the building for just two-hundred dollars per month. After a couple of years, we negotiated its purchase for twenty-five thousand dollars. That church would easily have cost a million dollars to duplicate in 1977.

Cynics might argue that our purchase of the first church for twenty-thousand dollars was coincidental, a case of our being in the right place at the right time. A second similar purchase, just blocks from the first, is far more difficult to rationalize. That was the second time that God had provided a wonderful facility for our ministry, "just in the nick of time." The first incident might be called providence. Does twice constitute a miracle?

When I later resigned Capital Christian to join the staff of a Christian education publisher, we had been gathering in that building for about seven years. The fellowship would remain there for decades.

CHAPTER 40

Break the TV Habit

"But sanctify the Lord God in your hearts, and always be ready to give a defense to everyone who asks you a reason for the hope that is in you, with meekness and fear."
1 Corinthians 12:10

When church pastors gather, they inevitably share their experiences. One or two may simply expose their own pride by boasting, but the truly godly men want to encourage others. So, they humbly offer testimonies of the wonderful things that the Lord has done in their lives and work. One or two may share their defeats and ask for prayer. Most remain silent.

I have attended numerous conferences, and I know that some pastors return home discouraged because they compare themselves unfavorably with others. It's difficult to look to the Lord for personal affirmation when someone next to you is flaunting the blessings God has heaped on him. This is especially true for the pastor who plants a new church.

The missionary pastors of yesterday, who struggled to rebuild a crumbling inner-city church, revive a troubled country congregation, or plant a new fellowship, were often overworked, underpaid, and short of physical and human resources. These men are increasingly rare. Those who are willing to boldly stand on the front lines, endure defeats more often than victories, carry incredible burdens, and suffer unseen wounds, have all but disappeared.

Sadly, these hard-working and sacrificial servants are often looked down on and even sneered at by associates who have successful and lucrative ministries. It's ironic, because some of those men that have it easy may imagine themselves particularly gifted, while in fact they are particularly blessed. Their seeming success may be the result of God's mercy rather than the fruit of their labors.

Tragically, some of those great successes become so puffed up that, like King Nebuchadnezzar, they vainly imagine, *"Is this not the great Babylon, that I have built...?"*[40] Easy success can result in great pride, followed by a great fall. The media constantly reminds us of prominent church leaders who succumbed to the temptations of this world and the lusts of the flesh. We read almost daily of another highly visible preacher who turned his eyes away from Jesus, yielded to sinful temptations, and is now disgraced.

Don't imagine for a moment that the trials faced by church planting missionaries are any less severe than those faced by church magnates. For these faithful few experience many of the same temptations as the wealthy and influential. What's more, because of their true value and effectiveness, the devil is just as eager to snare them. I know because I was one of them, but as this account will reveal, I lacked the faith of many.

I recall one dark rainy night in the late 1970s when the enemy was tempting me. I was driving home from a pastor's conference, traveling west on the Massachusetts Turnpike toward Troy, musing over my failures as a pastor. As I reasoned that my balance sheet was heavy on failures, I became increasingly discouraged.

I wasn't any different from others who, from time to time, become disappointed in themselves, their congregations, and even in our Lord. But that's a dangerous place to be. It's so easy to forget that we are not to lean on our own understanding, but continually trust in God.

The keynote speaker at the conference had exhorted us to return to our churches and urge our people to get rid of their television sets. Why? Because television wastes so much time and the programming is often outright evil.

As I drove down that dark and rainy highway, I weighed the pros and cons of the speaker's arguments. There was no question that most of my congregation was addicted to what we called the "boob tube." What hope did I have to persuade them to stop watching TV? Those who owned

---

40   Daniel 4:30

TV sets were drawn to them like steel filings to a magnet. I knew that my own relatively dedicated congregation was apt to reject my appeal, and that a cry to get rid of TV sets might cause me to lose influence and repel potential visitors.

Yet I had their long-term welfare to consider. I began to calculate how many hours a week my own family was wasting in front of our thirteen-inch black and white television set. I was shocked. Instead of doing household chores, homework, playing outside, or studying God's Word, they might be wasting up to twenty hours per week! So even if I couldn't inspire people to get rid of their TV sets, it might be worth investing a Sunday morning sermon to encourage them to cut back.

I thought about our fine congregation. For the most part they wanted to grow in faith, and I realized that they couldn't do so if they were wasting hours each day being subtly indoctrinated by worldly TV programming. One didn't have to be a Christian to realize how destructive TV was to intellectual growth and character, and they weren't even facing the perversion that is heaped on us today, of which so many have become desensitized.

Even those who attended every service—Sunday School, Sunday morning and evening worship, and Wednesday Bible study—received little more than three hours of real teaching a week. But at the other end of the scale, most of them were watching that many hours of television every day, totaling twenty-one hours every week! And what preacher or teacher could begin to compete with TV's sophisticated, costly, and colorful productions that targeted the minds and hearts of viewers?

"It's a good thing," I reflected, "that God's Word does not return to Him void!" As I drove on, my thoughts grew darker. I was already discouraged about the slow growth of our church, both numerically and qualitatively. I realized that any effort to influence their TV habits might actually have a negative impact, possibly even causing people to leave the church.

Worse, I realized that I myself was double-minded about the idea. I'm ashamed to admit it, but I realized that I might suffer withdrawal symptoms if I got rid of our family TV set. There were a few programs that seemed decent enough, shows that I enjoyed. So I began to rationalize. "Would I be throwing out the baby with the bath water?"

Then I realized that my obvious addiction was a strong argument for getting rid of my own TV set. When it occurred to me that my wife and I might be using our TV set as a babysitter for our two little boys, or that my own children might not want to get rid of it, I had additional reasons for breaking the habit. Then it occurred to me that my children might be mocked by other children for what was considered my radical decision, and as it turned out, they were.

These contrary arguments rang back and forth in my mind. Hey! I was the pastor. If I could imagine my family being divided over these issues, it seemed a forlorn hope that a single member of our church would emulate my actions and get rid of their TV set for their own good. It was no small thing to ask people to create a void in their lives that had formerly been filled by hours of canned entertainment—situation comedies, sporting events, soap operas, movies, political propaganda, all the news that's fit to tint—much less that I would fail to suggest a viable alternative.

Television had become such a powerful national pastime that millions now sat transfixed in front of their TV sets while eating their TV dinners off TV trays. Housewives were addicted to daytime soap operas, men to Sunday football, and entire families to evening situation comedies and movie reruns. There had been The Early Show, The Late Show, and even The Late, Late Show.

I wouldn't simply be asking our congregation to cease watching TV cold turkey. I'd be exhorting them to destroy the state-of-the-art electronics in which they took pride, and for which they may have invested over a month's pay! Then I realized that, if television played that large a role in people's lives, our relationship with it needed to be seriously reevaluated.

But why by me? So I asked myself, "Why not just remain silent and not upset the status quo?" But our Lord had other plans, and we rarely see the beginning from the end. It's natural that we tend to put ourselves at the center of our own little universes, though it can be a dangerous thing. For a Christian ought *"...not to think of himself more highly than he ought to think; but to think soberly, according as God hath dealt to every man the measure of faith"* (Romans 12:3).

The truth was that the networks were filling our heads with a lot of garbage. So having acknowledged the problem, I couldn't turn away from dealing with it. And whether I wanted to get rid of our TV or not was no longer the issue. If it was God's will, then I must do it!

It was obvious that the Holy Spirit was dealing with me, for I was then reminded that even a television set can become an idol. As I meditated on the issue, it became a matter of my personal submission and obedience to the Lord. I had to take a stand. Like Joshua, who proclaimed,

"As for me and my house, we will serve the LORD" (Joshua 24:15), I realized that I must do what the Lord wanted and trust him to deal with everyone else involved. Once I came to that conclusion, I actually grew excited at the prospect.

That pastor's conference, focusing on the evils of television programming, was just one of many being conducted across America at that time. Although thousands of pastors had been exhorted to tell their congregations to get rid of their television sets, this was the first time that I had heard the challenge. And where else would I have heard it? Media in general, and the TV networks in particular, had an inherent need to protect their own interests, and were engaged in an unspoken effort to silence all critics, particularly the people of God. They certainly weren't going to publicize what might amount to a boycott against their own industry.

As I drove through that dismal night, it came to me that I should exhort our people to unplug and even dispose of their TV sets. But objections continued to flood my mind. "People will mock us," I thought. "They'll say I'm crazy. My own congregation might split if I take such a stand. For that matter, can I go cold turkey and throw out a TV set that cost a good part of my meager salary as a pastor? I won't even sell it, for that would be hypocritical; I would simply be encouraging someone else to use it."

So if I exhorted others to break the TV habit, I'd have to practice what I preached. If I didn't, I would indeed be the hypocrite. But was I ready to get rid of our TV set? And would my own family resist my efforts?

It occurred to me that a few people might actually be attracted to our church by my taking such a stand. Although, that seemed unlikely. On the other hand, I might lose members. But wasn't that up to the Lord? Their loss might be a healthy thing for the fellowship. Jesus commanded, *"Seek ye first the kingdom of God,"*[41] and he warned, *"A little leaven leavens the whole lump."*[42]

And then the possibility of reduced offerings came to mind, and I was ashamed! One of the worst things that can happen to a pastor is to begin looking at his congregation with dollars signs in his eyes! The bottom line was that I wanted to help my congregation grow in faith, and they couldn't do that if they were wasting hours each day being subtly indoc-

---

41   Matthew 6:33
42   Galatians 5:9

trinated by worldly and even satanically inspired programming.

The arguments cannonaded back and forth in my mind. But one thought persisted. If television played that large a role in people's lives, our relationship with it needed to be seriously reevaluated. So as I drove, I prayed. And by the time I arrived home that night, I knew what I must do.

I was somehow reminded that I might know a bit more about public relations than most pastors. After all, before I'd entered the ministry, I'd operated a business with a hefty advertising budget and I had continually searched for means to enhance my firm's image in the eyes of the public. Apart from that, I'd run for the state senate, and I had learned something about preparing press releases to raise public interest in a cause.

When I arrived home, I broached the subject to the staff of our small church, and to my surprise, there was some positive feedback. Of course, not everyone in the church would be enthusiastic. There were those who pretended to be holier than thou, but would hang on to their TVs, just as they clung to hidden habits that were far more sinister. But I finally put all those conflicting thoughts aside and decided to deal with the issue on the following Sunday.

I produced a press release that went out to newspapers and local TV stations, and one talented lady in our congregation painted a large banner that hung across the platform at the front of the auditorium: "Break the TV Habit." When that fateful Sunday morning arrived, Paul Morrissette suggested we bring nearly a hundred children from our junior churches into the auditorium for this unique service. The bus kids wouldn't sit still for a sermon, so I decided to deal with the TV issue first, then send them back to their own auditorium before preaching the morning sermon.

We moved the podium to the side of the platform so that everyone's view would be unobstructed. Then my family's television set was placed on a table at the middle of the platform, a "false idol" taking the place of my pulpit. As we were making these arrangements, someone excitedly told me that a TV crew and a newspaper photographer were making their way into the auditorium.

At that point, the children became impatient, so I made only a few introductory remarks. Then I picked up my family's little portable TV with one hand, and an eight pound sledgehammer with the other. I had covered the screen with a blanket so that no one would be hurt by flying glass if the CRT exploded, and we had a fire extinguisher nearby. The kids wanted me to remove the blanket so that they could see the screen implode. I explained that it was too dangerous, but that I'd remove it so that they could see the damage done.

Then about a hundred kids, accompanied by a number of adults, started counting: "One, Two, ... THREE!" I didn't like the idea that the event was being turned into a spectacle, but I had little choice, so I swung the hammer.

There was a very satisfying crash... and I was suddenly holding a TV set with a smashed cathode ray tube that would never again display a broadcast. The laughing children were ushered from the auditorium, the pulpit was again centered in front of the banner that read, "Break the TV Habit," and I picked up my Bible to preach my morn-

Troy Record newspaper photo of
Pastor Frank Becker breaking his TV set

ing message to an overexcited crowd. But just as I was about to begin speaking, someone came up on the platform and interrupted me. "Pastor, you've got a phone call."

No one had ever before interrupted the morning message, and I wasn't about to leave the platform to take a phone call. But the person was insistent. "It's the manager of another TV station." So I excused myself, and the worship leader led another song, as I made my way to the nearest phone.

When I said, "Hello," an excited voice demanded, "Did you break your TV yet?"

When I replied, "Yes," he said, "Oh, d-mn!"

Then, "Can you do it again?"

I replied, "No, I don't think so."

But my secretary interrupted me, saying that she'd run home and get her TV set. And while we again began rearranging the platform, the congregation didn't seem at all put out. They found the entire matter unusual and entertaining. And suddenly there was another TV camera crew in the audience.

Average Guy Meets Extraordinary God

As I recall, we ushered the children back in, but they were far more unruly this time. And there was a much more coordinated and louder "One, Two, THREE," as I smashed a second TV set before the TV camera. And that night, Dan Rather closed the "CBS Sunday Evening News" with a clip of Pastor Frank Becker, standing in front of a poster that said, "Break the TV Habit," and swinging a sledgehammer through the screen of a TV set. What were the satirical words of this since-disgraced CBS commentator as he closed out the CBS Evening news? "Well, there goes another point on the Nielsen Ratings."

What was not immediately obvious was that the Lord truly had His hand in all these matters. While the pastors of huge churches across America may have been seeking to encourage their people to break the TV habit, it was our little church, just north of the New York State capitol, that was given national attention during America's number one evening news program. Our little church did indeed receive a great deal of attention, both positive and negative, from our "Break the TV Habit" campaign.

The next day, I received a phone call from my younger brother, Bob, who was Vice-President of Advertising at Eckerd Drugs of Florida. He had seen me on the CBS affiliate in Clearwater. Bob thought it was a hoot that his brother was on national TV and promised to get me a copy of the Beta tape.

A miracle? Maybe not. But subsequent events seemed to reveal that it was far more than a mere happenstance.

Chapter 41

"Tell us why...."

"Now to Him who is able to do exceedingly abundantly above all that we ask or think, according to the power that works in us, to Him be glory in the church by Christ Jesus to all generations, forever and ever."

Ephesians 3:20-21

That Sunday morning, when the station manager of the CBS affiliate in Albany called me on the phone to learn whether I had already broken my television set, his response, his frustrated cursing, and his plea for me to do it again, revealed several things. The producer had no real interest in my reasons for breaking my TV set. That was made clear by the fact that his camera crew simply filmed me breaking it and immediately left.

Their reporter never asked me a single question because they didn't care why I did it. They simply wanted to focus on the sensational aspects, and by mocking yet another hare-brained pastor with their "Man Bites Dog" story, they found something that the network would latch on to. They simply wanted to gain audience share by exposing yet another nutty Christian. And the producer inched closer to a better job in a bigger market.

I have already made it clear that I was initially dubious about the benefits of holding a "Break the TV Habit" Sunday, so I may appear to have been working at cross-purposes. On the one hand, I put out a press release inviting the local newspapers and TV stations to attend. On the other hand, I was afraid that the notoriety might damage our church.

I wanted to believe that I was obeying God and therefore hoped that my actions would do no harm. I didn't really expect that my "object lesson" would add members to our church, but I hoped it might get my congregation thinking about the real issues. I initially took solace in the fact that I would only be breaking the TV set in front of our congregation, and that most of the people in Troy were unlikely to get even a whiff of any notoriety. Yes, I realized that word might spread, and that the shallow and ignorant would consider me a bit crazy, but I had to take the chance.

So when the station manager of the CBS affiliate called the church and asked me to reenact the spectacle so that his tardy camera crew could film it, I felt compelled to go ahead. One station had already taped it, so I reasoned, "In for a penny, in for a pound." Or, as another old saying goes, "I might as well be hanged for a sheep as a lamb."

These were, after all, just local TV outlets, and the Albany-Schenectady-Troy market ranked only 59th among the nation's major metropolitan areas. Although Albany is the capital of New York State, ours was just a little church in a nondescript rust belt city seven miles north of the state capital. Nobody would notice what happened here and since Sunday is generally a slow news day, if we happened to make the local news, few would see it. It would be largely ignored because we were just a little independent, non-denominational church with absolutely no influence.

Besides, I felt justified in taking a whack at the television broadcast industry. After all, Newton R. Minnow, head of the Federal Communications Commission, had recently labeled television a "vast wasteland." And while many Christians considered television to be a morally corrupting influence, most remained indifferent. They didn't think that TV was particularly good, but they didn't consider it particularly bad either.

My misconceptions were swept away that same Sunday evening when a member of our church—someone who had obviously not smashed his own TV set—called to tell me that he had just seen me on the CBS Sunday Evening News. He told me that Dan Rather had closed out his nationwide news program with a clip of me smashing the TV set with a sledgehammer. At that time, Rather was considered America's number one newsman, the respected anchor of the CBS Sunday Evening News. But he was later disgraced because of a botched investigation into then-President George W. Bush's military record. As the camera showed me holding up the broken TV set, what were his sarcastic closing words? "Well, there goes another point on the Nielsen ratings."

During the 1950s, television had become immensely popular, causing many to argue that radio had lost its following and would ultimately disappear. For a while it looked as though it would. By the late 70s, however, virtually every new car was equipped with an AM radio, and people were tuning in during drive time, while multitudes listened to portable radios in their homes and offices. Radio was more portable than television and still enjoyed a huge audience.

At the same time, stations that broadcasted Christian programmings were riding a wave of popularity across America. I wasn't aware of the scope of this phenomenon, but I had been told that one local station had a significant Christian audience. So,I had begun paying fifteen hard-earned dollars each week to air a five-minute weekday program I called Reflections. The program brought a few visitors to our church, but my future in radio didn't look promising.

After Dan Rather provided me with notoriety on a national stage, I concluded that the future looked truly dismal. For one thing, it seemed clear that the arguments in my sermon had not swayed those church members who called me, because they were obviously still watching television. I did not learn until later that several of our families had gotten rid of their TV sets. Worse, in my view, my little gesture had been elevated from an unimportant local event to the level of a national sensation.

Despite that, I never began to imagine the extent of the fallout from my actions. Whatever may have been going on in the hearts and minds of people across America, I was about to learn that God had his own agenda. Behind the scenes, a few other local viewers were having more serious thoughts, and the Lord was doing something unusual. "Doors" were being opened and closed, and God was about to demonstrate, as the Apostle Paul wrote, that he *"... is able to do exceedingly abundantly above all that we ask or think"* (Ephesians 3:20).

I knew nothing of God's plans, but I had a hopeful thought: The world might ignore or deride my actions, but thinking Christians, like those who conducted the pastor's conference, might applaud them. It also occurred to me that few pastors ever received national media attention unless they'd committed some illegal or illicit act. My emotions were nonetheless tossed like the waves of the sea by the rapidly changing events. I didn't know what to conclude, so I simply prayed for God's grace.

One of our ministries was a Christian school, kindergarten through 12th grade, so there was a lot of activity in the building every weekday. But on the Monday morning following my appearance on national TV, most conversations centered around my breaking the TV set. Unable to focus on regular church business, I found an excuse to get out of the office. Each week, I recorded five of my "Reflections" programs, and I decided to take the tape to WHAZ, the local Christian radio station.

It was a chilly, overcast afternoon, and the leaden sky and blustery wind matched my mood. The station's facilities were temporarily housed on the second floor of an old brick building in downtown Troy. I didn't know anyone at the station, and I wanted to get in and out as quickly as possible.

I made my way upstairs and found my way to the reception area. After handing my tape to the receptionist, I headed back for the exit. The floor plan was something of a maze, and as I was making my way out, I found myself walking past a couple of broadcast studios.

Intent on my own thoughts, I was brought up short when I heard a loud knocking. It is, of course, forbidden to make noise near an open microphone, but when I turned to see the source of the racket, I found myself staring through a plate glass window into a broadcast studio. I saw a smiling, middle-aged man sitting before a microphone. He was wearing a headset and knocking on the glass with one hand while waving to me with the other. He seemed to be beckoning to me to enter the studio, but the "On the Air" sign above the door was lit, and I knew that it was forbidden to open the door of a studio when that sign is illuminated.

It seemed clear that he just wanted to get me in there to talk about my breaking the TV. I was in no mood to be further embarrassed, so I forced a smile, waved back, and turned to continue on my way. But I found my path blocked by a secretary. She told me that "Larry" would really like to interview me. Then the door was opened, the on-air personality stuck his head out, and asked, "Are you Pastor Becker?"

I nodded, and he said, "Why don't you come in and tell our listeners why you broke your TV set?"

I had been in a number of radio studios through the years, both in relation to the business I'd managed and during my run for the state senate, and I'd pretty much gotten over the false glamour attached to being on the air. In my mood, I had no desire to speak to a live audience. Still, it was a legitimate question, and the on-air personality seemed friendly enough. So, I didn't feel as though I was being blind-sided by someone who wanted to embarrass me.

He was sitting in front of a control panel and waved me over to a chair across the counter from him. Then he handed me a headset, swung a microphone in front of me, and introduced me to his audience. He said that he had Pastor Frank Becker with him, that he had seen me on the CBS Sunday Evening News, and he wanted me to tell them why I broke my television set. I hesitated, feeling oddly reserved, and just as I finally leaned toward the mic, someone outside the studio tapped lightly on the outside of the studio window to get our attention.

From the look on the broadcaster's face, this too was unprecedented. I looked up to see the same woman gesturing to my host and pointing at his telephone. One of those buttons was illuminated, indicating that he had a call, but when he shook his head in refusal, she seemed insistent. So, he told me to hold on while he took a call.

I was wearing the headset, so I couldn't hear what was being said. After a moment, my host turned a dial and flipped a switch, and I heard the caller's voice. He didn't mention my TV set. He wanted to ask a question about a Bible passage, and he specifically wanted "Pastor Becker" to answer it.

My head was still swimming a bit from being called into the studio, and I had just begun framing my reply about why I broke my TV set. But the host encouraged me to reply to the caller, so I did. When I finished, and the caller had thanked me and hung up, I was again prepared to discuss the evils of television. But then another button lit up on the phone, and then a second, and a third. And for the remainder of that hour, the two of us replied to questions about the Bible from caller after caller.

And as the host was closing the program, and thanking me for coming in, he asked if I would please return the next day to tell the people why I'd broken my TV set. I really didn't want to return. My days were too short, and my hours were filled with numerous responsibilities as a pastor and school administrator, not to speak of husband and father, so returning to answer that question seemed a little silly. But he was insistent, and since I didn't want to risk having my own little five-minute radio show canceled, I agreed.

But when I returned to the church, I learned that a staff member had been listening to the program, and others had gathered around. They thought it was incredible that I'd been on the air. They thought I'd done a good job and considered it a great opportunity for me to return the next day.

On Tuesday I arrived in time for the opening of the two-hour program and brought notes to defend why I broke my TV set. But the two-hour program was a repetition of the preceding day. All the buttons on the phone lit up before the program began, and the host encouraged me to answer most of the questions. Again, I did not have the opportunity to discuss why I broke the TV set. The host, Larry Foss—whom I had just learned was the station manager—told the audience that he hoped I'd return the third day to finally explain why I had broken my television set.

On returning to the church, I told my staff that I was frustrated with this business, but they didn't understand my attitude at all. They considered it a fantastic opportunity. "Pastor, look at the exposure you're getting, and how you're ministering!"

So I went back for the third time on Wednesday. But this time I was not to be deterred. All the buttons on the phone were again lit up when the program opened, but the moment the host was finished with his introduction and opened my mic, I said, "Now I'm finally going to tell why I broke my TV set." And I tried. But after a few sentences, Larry interrupted me to say that we had a lot of callers who wanted to speak with me. As far as my motives for breaking the TV set were concerned, I realized that either nobody cared, or they were already aware and satisfied with whatever I might have said. So, for the third day in a row, I wound up speaking with callers for the entire two-hour program.

After the close of the show that day, Larry Foss told me that he had been trying to start a talk show since he'd arrived at the station, but rarely received a call. He made it clear that he considered it miraculous how people were calling in every day to speak with me. He asked me whether I'd consider co-hosting the two-hour program with him every weekday.

Oh, no, I thought. This is too much! So I told him that I'd have to pray about it. It would be very demanding, but when I returned to the church, my staff and others were ecstatic. When I mentioned the opportunity to the congregation during the Wednesday evening Bible study, they were thrilled. They considered it a wonderful opportunity from God. But I wondered how I could satisfy my responsibilities as a pastor and also commit three to four hours each day to preparation, travel, and on-air time as a radio talk show host. Somehow, I did.

It was a novel experience hearing Larry introduce me each day with the words, "Frank is no ordinary pastor, and his is no ordinary church." Literally overnight I went from breaking a TV set, with nationwide notoriety, to co-hosting a daily radio talk show in New York's Capital District. At first, I did not understand or appreciate the fact that, of the scores of highly qualified pastors in New York's Capital District, I was the one who became the co-host on "Teletalk," commenting on everything from Bible content to the Christian's role in an increasingly antagonistic world system. During the years that followed, I would interview contemporary Christian notables like Pastor Jerry Fallwell, Word of Life's Jack Wyrtzen, ACE's Donald R. Howard, Christian Law Association's David R. Gibbs, and Bob Jones, Jr, president of Bob Jones University.

And what about "Reflections?" I kept the program up for a couple of weeks, but composing and recording the broadcasts consumed too much time. Then Larry Foss suggested that, since the station wasn't paying me, the management would continue broadcasting "Reflections" at their expense, and my wife, Joy, could host it. And she did! Her five-minute show became one of the three most popular shows on WHAZ. Our two-hour afternoon talk show, "Teletalk," was number one, followed by the morning primetime broadcast of Jerry Falwell's half hour program, then Joy's "Reflections," which lasted only 5 minutes and was lost in an 11:04 mid-morning time slot. She continued doing a superb job for several years, until she returned to college.

Clearly, God did this thing. After allowing me to make myself "... *a spectacle unto the world*" (1 Corinthians 4:9), He led me, kicking and dragging my heels, into talk radio. The order of events and their rapid sequence still defies my comprehension. Little more than twenty-four hours after breaking those two TV sets, I was, for all intents and purposes, co-hosting a Christian radio talk show!

And, why me? Before I broke my TV set, hundreds of fine men across America, successful pastors of large churches, had encouraged their congregations to break the TV habit. So why was it that this small city pastor wound up in front of the CBS national audience?

That national exposure resulted in monumental changes in my life, in the lives of my family and in the work of our church. I remember stopping at a store about fifty miles from Troy, and when I asked a clerk a question, someone nearby shouted, "I know that voice!" I was a mini-celebrity. Yes, the fellowship grew, and a number of people joined us who ultimately committed their lives to full-time Christian service. From testimonies we have heard through the years, the lives of many listeners were changed too. Those changes can only be explained in the context of God's special providence and miraculous intervention.

"Now to Him who is able to do exceedingly abundantly above all that we ask or think, according to the power that works in us, to Him be glory in the church by Christ Jesus to all generations, forever and ever."

Ephesians 3:20-21

CHAPTER 42

Judie, Joe, and Donna

"But sanctify the Lord God in your hearts, and always be ready to give a defense to everyone who asks you a reason for the hope that is in you, with meekness and fear."

1 Peter 3:15

A number of people joined our fellowship because they heard about my breaking the TV set. As a result, God led them to spend the rest of their lives laboring for him. But they would never have heard of our church if it weren't for the actions of one unsung hero. If it weren't for her decisive actions, I would not have appeared on Dan Rather's CBS Sunday Evening News, nor been the co-host of a Christian talk show. Such is the wonder of God working in the lives of those sold out for him.

It was our church secretary, Judie Muscatello, who persuaded me to answer the phone call from that CBS producer that fatal Sunday morning. After which, she encouraged me to repeat that sensational act. Then, she ran home to get her TV set so that the tardy CBS camera crew could film my breaking a second TV, thus making the story available for national exposure.

Judie's television set represented a significant investment to her. The church paid her a mere thirty-five dollars a week for her unstinting labors. She not only served as secretary for, the church, but for our Christian school, and for myself. Yet, without hesitation, she left the church that morning, ran down the street to her apartment, and brought back her TV set. She was, in a sense, about to sacrifice an idol on the altar of faith.

But her story doesn't end there. The New Testament tells us that Andrew brought Peter to Jesus. Well, Judie's sacrifice ultimately resulted in the attention of millions being brought to our Lord via national television.

Among them were Joe and Donna Flynn. That Monday afternoon, when Larry Foss put me on the air at WHAZ to explain why I'd broken my TV set, Joe was one of those who called in. The following Sunday, he and his wife Donna visited our church. They remained with the church for decades. Joe later served as pastor for over twenty years. He and Donna also managed a weekly "soup kitchen" in downtown Troy, where 80 to 150 people were fed hot meals, and souls were saved.

Heather, Rich, Stan, and Kevin, along with countless others were slumbering coals that the Holy Spirit blew upon to produce incandescent light, carrying them far and wide to kindle righteousness and love in the hearts of multitudes.

CHAPTER 43

The Dog Whisperer

"Save Me from the lion's mouth and from the horns of the wild oxen!"
Psalm 22:21

Soon after Donna and Joe Flynn joined the church, Donna's sister, Betty, began attending. I picked up bits and pieces of her story over time. Betty didn't speak to me of her marital problems until her husband's behavior seemed to be threatening their family's welfare. Unlike many women who complained about their marriages, Betty didn't broadcast her problems. She was determined to stick by her man.

At the same time, her husband Don evidently heard some things about me that made him wonder whether I might actually be a sincere man, the "real deal." He told Betty that he wouldn't come to the church. However, if I was willing to meet him, I could come to their home one Saturday morning.

Their house was on a country road, and if memory serves, a waist high hedge bordered both sides of the front walk, hemming in any visitors. I parked on the shoulder, and had just started down the sidewalk when a big German Shepherd slipped out the front door of the house. He bared his teeth, I saw the fur rose on the back of his neck, and his threatening bark turned to a menacing growl as he started down the walk toward me.

A dog had recently bitten our son on the face, so I held no illusions about my danger. I scarcely had time to think, much less pray. I found myself kneeling, forcing a confident smile, and holding out my hands, palms up, as though to say, "You have nothing to fear from me."

And the running dog stopped abruptly just short of where I knelt, then walked slowly toward me. He sniffed my hand, and brought his grinning mouth close to my face. I reached slowly around his head and began scratching him behind his ears. As I stood to my feet, I heard Betty scolding the dog. She had come out the front door in time to see the aborted attack and was ordering the dog to return to the house.

After he went back inside and she closed the door, she apologized, both for the dog's attack and for the fact that her husband had changed his mind and didn't want to see me that day. The next time she came to church, she told me about the conversation she had with her husband following my brief visit. She was furious with him because he admitted that he had intentionally left the front door ajar so that the dog would attack me. He was actually watching from an upstairs window to see what would happen. She told me that the dog had already bitten their postman and driven off others.

And then she told me that her husband was shocked by the dog's behavior, that instead of mauling me or chasing me away, he had allowed me to pet him. From what she told me, I gathered that the dog never allowed strangers to touch him. Her husband was mystified by the dog's instant change in behavior and was convinced that I must be a special man of God.

That incident cracked open a door of friendship between us. Don even visited the church on special occasions. I have a photo of he and Betty, taken while they were renewing their wedding vows during a New Year's Eve celebration.

Was I frightened when the dog attacked? Probably. Up until now, thank God, I haven't faced a situation where the Lord had to stop the mouth of a lion or turn the attack of a wild ox in order to save my life. Am I a "dog whisperer?" Hardly. But I do know that God's intercession that day turned a ravening dog to a friendly pet and turned the heart of his master from hatred or suspicion to friendship and respect. Do I recommend that you try to make friends with a dog that is attacking you? Nope!

CHAPTER 44

"He is Able to Deliver Thee"

"He also brought me up out of a horrible pit, out of the miry clay, and set my feet upon a rock, and established my steps."
Psalm 40:2

This incident is instructive because it again contrasts my human weakness with the grace, mercy, and power of God. There may be a time in your life when you discover that you have stumbled and fallen into a deep and slimy pit, and your efforts to crawl back out seem futile. If such should happen, turn your eyes upon Jesus, for He has saved multitudes. If you trust Him, He will save you!

The slide began when I came up with a number of reasons for why I should resign my role as pastor, and move our reluctant family nearly two thousand miles—far from the good and the familiar—to join a Christian education ministry in Texas. On occasion, I've been tempted to admit that my family was right in their opposition to that move, but out of that debacle God ultimately brought forth numerous testimonies.

The idea that I might have made a terrible mistake wasn't based simply on the fact that our new jobs lacked the variety, challenges, and blessings that we had known in the pastorate. Although, that was certainly true. But shortly after our move to Texas, it became clear to me that we had fallen into a "pit." As a result of my decision, we experienced numerous trials, and the directions our lives took was radically changed.

Soon after our arrival, I began to suspect that Joy had been right. I had foolishly failed to heed her cries. I sensed that there was something terribly wrong at the Christian education publisher we had joined, something insidious. The least of it was that we found ourselves entrapped in what I had mistakenly judged to be a ministry, but soon realized was tantamount to a cult.

Then I began receiving hints that the founder and leader of the ministry, the man whom I'd earlier come to respect as a giant of the faith, was involved in egregious sin. I'm not going to discuss the squalid side of this situation. I will however, as the Bible so often does, attempt to show its impact on others.

Here's how our involvement began. During the late 1970s, I began listening to the hype surrounding several biblically conservative individuals who appeared to be turning the world upside down for Jesus Christ. Like most pastors, I was eager to learn and benefit from anyone who had fresh approaches to ministering God's eternal Word. I observed one man who was achieving amazing things in the area of Christian education, and whose success seemed to indicate that he had been anointed by God.

But, like many others, I made the mistake of trusting too much in a mere mortal. I failed to remember that we are not to trust the arm of flesh, but are always to rely on our Lord. I soon came to understand that someone may be anointed by God to introduce a new and effective kind of ministry, but that is no assurance that the man himself will not become a proud victim of his God-given success.

I had forgotten that those who begin with good motives may slip into a practice of sin that damages their ministries and impacts the lives of those around them. Biblical examples include the account of the deluded King Nebuchadnezzar who foolishly boasted that he had built great Babylon, and King David, who dallied with Bathsheba to the detriment of his family and brought permanent damage to his kingdom. Contemporary examples are so numerous that most of us are familiar with at least one fallen Christian leader.

All of us need to understand that leaders who have been gloriously elevated by God, may also be subject to more and greater temptations. Because of their success, the eyes of the world turn upon them, and they become prime targets for the enemy. Satan seems to concentrate his attacks on such individuals because, when he seduces one of these highly visible Christians, the eyes of the entire world become focused failures.

Similarly, when the founder and leader of the program we joined fell into sin, countless thousands suffered. Early on in his ministry, I have no doubt that the difficulties he faced forced him to lean heavily on the Lord every moment. But as the success that God granted him began to attract hordes of supporters and sycophants, and his bank accounts swelled so that he could satisfy every earthly desire, the enemy saw an opportunity.

Success is a heady thing, and any of us, in a similar situation, might also find ourselves puffed up with pride. It's so easy to forget Peter's admonition, *"Therefore humble yourselves under the mighty hand of God, that He may exalt you in due time,"* (1 Peter 5:6).

But we tend to become addicted to praise, so much so that we surround ourselves with "yes men." Blinded by the limelight, we are prone to relax our spiritual grip on Christ. We might even be tempted to look at the ministry Christ had given us, and ask, *"Is not this great Babylon, that I have built ... by my mighty power and for the honor of my majesty?"* (Daniel 4:30).

And, perhaps because of overwork, or with a perverse sense of pride, self-justification, and even entitlement, we might believe the serpent's lie that we have somehow earned license to stray beyond the limits permitted to other lesser Christians. We might even justify toying with sin, and, too late, discover that we have strayed far from God's law of love.

I had assumed that the man I followed was a giant of the faith. For a while I guess he was, because the success of his ministry was phenomenal. So, I had come to expect from him more than any man should be expected to deliver. We must never forget that only Jesus Christ deserves our complete trust.

The crisis began to unfold shortly after our arrival in Texas. I first realized that something was wrong after I wrote a small check as a donation to what I thought was a ministry. Except, it wasn't really a "ministry."

My donation was returned with a cryptic note that stated it was their policy to refuse donations. Although everyone I knew assumed it was a Christian ministry, it was not! It was a "for-profit corporation." Yes, it produced curriculum, and it offered assistance to Christian schools, but it was a business that had earned its founder and president millions.

It's not necessarily wrong for a publisher to focus his efforts on serving churches. He may indeed be facilitating the work of God. But if he exploits his employees by implying that they are Christian missionaries and manipulates them so that they sacrifice their own welfare while unwittingly helping him grow rich, he stands condemned.

There were about 200 employees on the headquarters staff, and many of them were deeply dedicated to Christ. Most of them blindly followed the founder and president. And they were highly motivated, despite being paid far less than they would earn in the marketplace. They were proud of the sacrifices they made to contribute to the Kingdom, whether they prepared meals in the cafeteria or wrote curriculum.

Toward the end of our year there, rumors began to circulate. A middle manager I respected warned me that something evil was in the wind, and Joy and I would be wise to resign and leave as soon as possible. Then, something happened that shook the entire staff.

Upon arriving at the facilities early one Saturday morning, the teenagers who were paid minimum wage to pack publications for shipment were told to return home immediately. Before they left the campus, however, they noticed graffiti had been spray-painted on the outside wall of the administration building. After a closer look, they realized that the words condemned our revered founder and president for having committed flagrant sin.

When one of the vice-presidents noticed the teenagers staring at the words, he took them aside and swore them to secrecy. Most of them obeyed him, even keeping the event a secret from their own parents, indicating how powerful was the grip of that cult-like program on their minds. Like teenagers in the Hitler Youth, forty years earlier, these kids had been so brainwashed that they were now more loyal to their "Fuehrer" than to their loving own parents. But word got around that morning, and a number of employees slipped past the traffic barriers that the managers had erected, where they stood off to the side watching as one of the vice-presidents climbed a ladder to try to pressure wash the paint off the wall before others saw it.

About that time, the Wall Street Journal ran an article discussing accusations of sexual improprieties that had been made against the founder. Then a high-level manager told me that the founder had actually tape-recorded a confession, including a plea for forgiveness, and it had been duplicated, packaged, and addressed to each pastor or administrator of the 5,000 church schools that subscribed to the program. But at the last moment, the corporate executive committee decided not to mail the confession.

I've always thought that their change of mind was a terrible error. In my judgment, their attempt to keep the events secret would backfire. Hadn't they learned anything from the Bible that they dared insist was their sole rule for life? Such cover-ups are rarely successful. These men thought they would weather the immediate storm, but they were wrong. The Bible warns, *"... take note, you have sinned against the LORD; and be sure your sin will find you out"* (Numbers 32:23).

My own manager gathered the members of our group and ordered us not to gossip about the situation. He made an incredibly ironic statement about our founder, a man who had been accused of adultery: "We need to put this to bed."

Ultimately, the program took a serious blow, with hundreds of churches withdrawing and turning to competitive Christian publishers for their curriculum. But the company survived, and now, forty years later, is still producing materials for church and home schooling. The founder and president, however, was disgraced, divorced, and driven out of the program.

At the time that these events occurred, we'd been in the program for almost a year. Layoffs and a great exodus of disillusioned employees would soon follow. As soon as we were faced with these revelations, we decided to leave. Like most employees, we had no savings and were living hand to mouth.

I had cautioned my wife that the company could legally deduct any money that had been advanced to us upon our arrival the preceding July. These included moving expenses and corporate uniforms. Yes, every man and woman, boy and girl, had to wear the appropriate company uniforms, whether employees or students in the schools. And if we didn't stay for the entire 52 weeks, we had to pay it all back, even for worn out uniforms we had donned every weekday for fifty-one weeks. Joy could no longer bear the hypocrisy, and insisted that we leave as soon as possible. So, we pulled out at the end of our 51st week. Since we didn't stay, they took our pay.

Before we escaped, however, we were told that the founder wasn't pleased to see us go. He had plans for me. Before we resigned, I had completed the preparation of a computer literacy manual, writing in record time. I had even written drafts for two successive manuals. That booklet, "Introduction to the Computer," sold over 5,000 copies in its first month, a record. It was the first package of curriculum that they published on which they printed the author's name.

The night before we left Texas, still ignorant of the fact that we would not receive our final pay checks, we attended a company function. The founder sent someone to ask if I'd be willing to speak with him alone. I agreed, and he took that occasion to ask me not to leave. As he spoke,

I remained silent. It was as though my tongue was stuck to the roof of my mouth. Finally he told me, "I love you, Brother Becker." Even then, I found myself unable to open my mouth. I didn't feel very charitable toward him and simply nodded my head in acknowledgment. Then I turned and walked away. I never saw him again.

Not only did they withhold our last two weeks' pay—money on which we counted to pay for our move back to New York—they also billed us hundreds more. And though I knew their treatment was grossly unfair, I later sent them a check for the amount they said we were short, plus two years' interest. We had, by God's grace, made our escape, and I was not about to let these fallen men, all of whom have since passed away, claim that we were anything less than honest.

If I had told the founder that we were willing to stay on, we might have gotten our paychecks. But that would have been dishonest. So, we departed with barely enough money to complete the journey and knew we would have nothing with which to rent an apartment or buy groceries once we arrived back in New York.

As it was, we had to borrow money to complete the trip. Our only hope was that we would have enough cash to make it to Lake George. There, a friend promised to put us up if we'd join his family in cleaning and maintaining a motel he had contracted to buy. Evidently the Lord had some things he wanted to reveal to us, things we would never have experienced if we had money in our pockets.

If I hadn't been so feverishly involved in preparations to get back to New York State or if I had time and inclination to count the cost, I might have been crushed by our circumstances. This was another occasion where someone might ask whether we were stepping out in faith or it was just a matter of "ignorance is bliss." Joy and I believed that it was a matter of spiritual necessity.

Think of it! I had gone from church pastor to curriculum writer, and now I was to be a motel maintenance man. But if we succeeded in reaching New York, and my friend was unable to keep his commitment, we would have no money for food or a place to live. As it turned out, we were not able to stay at his motel. The next couple of years were filled with one challenge after another, but through it all the Lord never failed us.

When departing for New York, I was at the wheel of a rented moving van and Joy was driving our old station wagon. We had no savings, no credit, and very little cash. We ultimately reached our friend's motel with almost empty gas tanks. This was the beginning of one of the most discouraging, yet equally rewarding periods of our lives.

You may wonder how we profited in all of this, or where the miracles are. The fact is that all of us believe we learned valuable lessons while at that publishing house and gained important knowledge that the Lord would use to guide and help us in the years ahead. After our departure, we repeatedly saw God's hand moving in our lives.

Keep in mind, it was not the founder's fault that we joined his company. It was my decision, and from the first, Joy had lovingly resisted. Even today, she only grudgingly admits that a little good may have come out of it, and I occasionally confess that the only benefit I saw is what God taught us.

He not only helped us survive, but to prosper through one of the more difficult periods of our lives. Sadly, we Christians often have to find ourselves wallowing in a miry pit and up to our noses in effluent, before we are prepared to confess our needs and seek God's deliverance. Sometimes the end of the story is the real reason for the story.

Before we reached the Texas border, we faced the first test in our attempt to break away from what I think of now as a spiritual swamp. I was driving the 24-foot moving van when Joy, who was following in our old station wagon, began flashing her headlights. We pulled onto wide a sandy shoulder, and I climbed down to see what she wanted.

Steam was rising from under the car's hood and it was obvious that the engine was leaking coolant. The question in my mind was, "Had all the antifreeze leaked out, overheating the engine and leaving it irreparably damaged?" It wouldn't have been the first engine I had destroyed by running it without coolant, thus warping the heads and causing the pistons to seize up. Hardly daring to imagine how desperate our plight might be, our family of six gathered around the old station wagon and prayed for a miracle.

After the engine cooled down, I concluded that the water pump might be leaking and need to be replaced. I had no way of ascertaining whether the heads on the V-8 engine were warped, but if so, any efforts I might make would be in vain. If that happened, we couldn't afford to replace it. The car was old and would either be junked or abandoned. I could take two members of the family with me in the cab of the truck, but I didn't know how I'd get the other three "home."

Hoping that the engine was not damaged and that I merely needed to replace the water pump, I drove the U-Haul back to the last town.

There I found an auto parts store and picked up a replacement. That rebuilt water pump cost only about twelve dollars, but adjusting for inflation, that was a lot of money in 1984. It took a serious bite out of our available cash.

Through the years, I had learned something about auto repairs, so I dug out my toolbox and changed the water pump myself, right there on the shoulder of the highway. Then I topped off the radiator and we went on our way. We praised God because we had no more problems with the engine.

Then Joy again had to stop our little convoy because the turn signal control arm snapped off when she pressed it to signal a turn. The control arm was a hollow plastic tube that enclosed the wires that controlled the turn signals, windshield wipers, and high and low headlight beams. Down the center of that hollow arm was a supporting rod that had fatigued and finally snapped off right next to the steering column.

If we had to have a dealer replace something that old and complex, it would undoubtedly take time and probably be very expensive. We couldn't afford the repairs, much less an extra night in a motel. But we had to get the turn signals, high and low beams, and windshield wipers working, or it would be too dangerous to continue.

Again, we prayed, and as we approached a local Walmart, I had a strange feeling that I might be able to find something there to solve the problem. It was one of Sam Walton's original rural stores, and it wasn't very big. None of us had a clue as to what we might use to repair the problem, but everyone was cheered by how the Lord helped us with the water pump crisis, so we enthusiastically set out to find something that would take care of the problem.

We began wandering around the store, ending up in its small hardware, plumbing, and electrical department. Several of our children pointed out items that they hoped might be useful, but nothing looked remotely like a solution. After a few minutes, one of our children said we were wasting our time, and we ought to get back on the road. Someone else suggested we pray, so we did. This was a smaller Walmart and only stocked the most popular and sought after items, so I too was growing discouraged.

But while glancing doubtfully over some plumbing parts, my eyes fell on a brass rod. It was about an eighth inch thick, seven inches long, and was threaded at both ends. It was designed to screw into a toilet ball cock flotation assembly. I was so desperate that I wondered if it might possibly screw into the place where the signal arm had broken off, and, if so, whether its diameter and thread type would be correct. But it was the best possible solution we had seen, so I bought it.

When we returned to the car, I was almost struck dumb when I un-screwed the short broken rod from the steering column, and discovered that the threads on the brass rod I had just purchased fit perfectly. Joy no longer had functioning windshield washers, but she could operate the windshield wipers, raise and lower the headlight beams, and signal turns. I merely had to wrap masking tape around the outer end of the brass rod in order to pad the sharp threads.

This was certainly one for the record. The substitution of a toilet re-pair part for a sophisticated automobile turn signal arm required another entry in my catalog of weird, wild, and wonderful faith experiences. This seemed like far more of a miracle than the changing of the water pump, and enabled Joy to safely drive the remaining 1,500 miles. And in the years ahead, whenever we thought of a car's turn signal, we would joke, "left flush, right flush," and give thanks to God for delivering us.

THE WANDERING YEARS:

THE PRESERVING HAND OF GOD

Chapter 45

Wandering Is for the Birds!

"Like a bird that wanders from its nest Is a man who wanders from his place."

Proverbs 27:8

Wandering is for the birds! We know. We moved a dozen times over the next seventeen years, while I accepted every opportunity to preach, and invested heavily in a ministry to encourage the spread of New Testament house churches. While God was moving the clockwork of history inexorably forward, the underground church movement was indeed flourishing. The world was racing toward its own destruction, and I persisted because I remain convinced that persecution will ultimately force the church back to its scriptural roots.

In order to support our family, I built, rehabbed and flipped houses. Then the Lord enabled me to become an award-winning technical writer and manager. Joy earned her master's degree, wrote for educational publishers, and finally found the work she loved, teaching high school English. We experienced much stress, but finally moved to the great state of Texas, and it has been our home for the past twenty-two years.

"I have been young, and now am old; Yet I have not seen the righteous forsaken, Nor his descendants begging bread" (Psalm 37:25). Has our sojourning ended? One thing is certain. We've learned that we can count on God's faithfulness.

CHAPTER 46

"Except the Lord
Build the House..."

"Except the Lord build the house, they labor in vain who build it."
Psalm 127:1

Six years after we fled that publishing house in Texas, I was hired as a contractor to manage a technical publishing project at General Electric Power Generation, in Schenectady, New York. We finished the project well ahead of schedule, and GE offered me a job. The manager said that the hiring decision was not based merely on my success converting textbooks to electronic media, but largely because I had designed and built a house. He correctly believed that it takes numerous skills to carry so large a project from conception to completion.

But he had no idea of the incredible challenges that my family and I had actually faced in the building of our home, nor how the Lord brought us through. Yes, every member of our family worked hard and persevered through difficult times, but it was the Lord that truly built that house. It took a miracle. Actually, it took a whole bunch of miracles!

I'd better start at the beginning. Within days of our return to New York from Texas in 1984, we found ourselves living in a campground in the central Hudson Valley, not far from where Joy and I grew up. Our "home" was an 18-year-old canvas tent trailer. It originally retailed for $595 and was the cheapest thing on the market. We also had a tent for the boys, but the campground owner didn't like our equipment because

"

he catered to people with shiny trailers and elegant motor homes, so he moved us to a remote area amid a piney wood.

It was one of the wettest summers on record, and the six of us were forced to sleep in the crowded fold-out, canvas-roofed camper. We stored our meager possessions in the separate tent. Only later did we discover that it leaked and our daughter's good clothes were turned green with mold.

For two weeks, we cooked and ate at a picnic table. We had no phone, no mailing address, and no money. One morning I had just enough coins to buy milk. We were homeless, and these were desperate times. Although I was searching for a job and my wife was struggling to make a home in primitive surroundings, our pre-teen sons were having a wonderful time swimming and playing about the campground.

I had a friend in Kingston who ran a tire store. He and I had both run for state office years earlier, and he "paid" me a couple of hundred dollars for working in his store for a day or two. It really amounted to a much appreciated gift.

Then an amazing thing happened. My mother somehow learned of our plight, located me, and sent word that she and my stepfather were on their way to New York from their Florida home. We met them on a parcel of land that my late father had bought decades before.

The land is located just north of Hyde Park—the site of the F.D. Roosevelt Home and Library—so you might assume that it was a valuable parcel. Indeed, a few attractive homes had been built nearby. But our land fronted on a narrow winding country lane that was then known as "Trailer Row."

Although the parcel was seventeen acres, it was only two hundred feet wide at the entrance. Though it widened as we hiked south. Serpentine in shape, it was heavily wooded with stately oaks, white birch, and walnut trees. A rugged driveway zigzagged up and down over rock and rill almost to the rear of the property, a half mile south.

It was a beautiful parcel, but difficult to build upon. Because of the property's location, its odd shape, and rough topography, my stepfather had been unable to sell it. It was valued at only twelve thousand dollars. During our brief meeting, he handed me the deed, transferring ownership of the seventeen acres to me.

But it was not pure altruism on his part. He was a very shrewd southern red neck businessman who had no use for preachers, and especially no affection for this stepson who once had both an African American and a Messianic Christian as his associate pastors. He wanted to give Joy and me the land so that he and my mother would no longer have to pay taxes on what he considered a white elephant.

It was a wise move on his part. The taxes in Hyde Park, New York, and anywhere in New York State were, and are, excessive, even on a "trailer row." My mom also loaned us some money, so we experienced a little financial breathing space for a short time. Breathing space, yes. Living space, no!

Although we had moved our tent camper back under the pines to a remote corner, the owner gave us our walking papers. We were being evicted from the campground and had nowhere to go. Our furniture and personal possessions were stored in a garage at our friend's motel in Lake George, over a hundred miles north, and our only asset was the 17 acre parcel.

Despite that, I was excited, for I had immediately concluded that the land was a gift from God. I was suddenly determined to build a house on it. Of course, we'd have to raise the money. In the meantime, I had the zany idea that maybe we could hide our tent trailer back in the trees and camp there while figuring things out.

My head must have been in the stars because my feet were definitely not planted firmly on the ground. The English poet, Thomas Gray, who coined the phrase, "Ignorance is bliss," certainly understood unrealistic ambitions such as mine. A better phrase for my pipe dream might have been, "Pie in the sky." Or, as Lee Hach, my former associate pastor and principal of our Christian school had quipped years before, "If wishes were fishes, we'd all live in the sea." My Aunt Katherine's expression, "Going off half-cocked" comes to mind.

As I look back, I cannot imagine how Joy and I, with four children, ages nine to nineteen, dared undertake such a project, much less imagine we could complete it. But Joy has always been a woman of great courage, and where the Lord leads, she has always been ready to follow. Since then, she's added a great deal of wisdom to her faith, so she is perhaps a bit more cautious today, especially in differentiating between God's leading and mine.

Never were our Lord's words more pertinent, nor blithely ignored: *"For which of you—intending to build a tower—does not sit down first and count the cost—whether he has enough to finish it...."* (Luke 14:28). Did we have enough money to finish building a house? We didn't even have any money to begin it! It seems to me that I took the last dollar out of my wallet, and we prayed over it, that the Lord would treat it as seed money, multiplying it many times over, to see us through. And somehow it did.

But I was undeterred. I felt somewhat like I did that time we were finishing Bible college, when I began packing books in preparation for the move to the church that had not even called me. It was not reason! As Jonathan Swift wrote, "You cannot reason a person out of a position he did not reason himself into in the first place."[43] I simply believed that it was just going to happen! And not a single member of our family ever expressed any doubt. Some people might say that we were presumptuous, but inasmuch as God saw the project through to completion. I like to think we were exercising faith.

During the following year, I was so busy from dawn to dark that I had no time to keep a diary of our victories and defeats, so I am relying on a memory that has faded over the past forty years, often leaning on the recollections of my wife and children.

I remember visiting a bank in Rhinebeck, where the manager all but sneered at me when I suggested he might provide a mortgage loan to build the house. We had no home address, no job, no credit, and no proven experience as a builder! It was incredible. In little more than a year, I had gone from being the respected pastor of a great church to being a man despised by the world. But we consoled ourselves with the fact that it wasn't the world that would build our house. *Except the Lord build the house, they labor in vain who build it* (Psalm 127:1).

Joy and I had seen the Lord do many wondrous things during our marriage and we were determined to trust God and press on. Our first Sunday, we drove ten miles south to visit our home church. I had been saved at the age of eight, but this was where I became a serious disciple of the Lord Jesus, and Henry had been my first adult Sunday School teacher. It was here that I made my commitment to enter the ministry. After we left for Bible college, Henry helped us financially.

When he learned of our homeless predicament, he and his wonderful wife, Lois, told us they were, coincidentally, about to leave for a two-week vacation at "The Camp of the Woods," and offered to let us live in their home. What wonderful brethren to trust us so. It was a blessing to

---

43   See https://quotefancy.com/quote/1014491/Jonathan-Swift-You-cannot-reason-a-person-out-of-a-position-he-did-not-reason-himself

get out of those leaky tents and into their lovely home, even though we knew it was only for a short time.

During the day, we began working on our property, cutting down twenty-year old clumps of four-inch-thick sumac that had grown in the driveway, and clearing the site atop a knoll where my father had once parked a double-wide. We discovered that there was a drilled water well within a few feet of the planned foundation, and amazingly, no one had stolen the valuable submersible pump. In addition, there was a utility pole nearby with electrical cables strung to it. We even found the connection to the existing septic system. The discovery of these improvements was heartening because they easily saved us twenty thousand dollars in site preparation.

And we had other encouragement. The father of my childhood friend, Bill Adams, Sr. still lived in Hyde Park and was so enthused with our bold plan that he helped us clear the area. A professional contractor, Bill proved himself a stalwart mentor throughout the building process, offering sound advice, loaning us tools, and even interceding with the building inspector.

The construction of an owner-built home is always carefully watched by building and electrical inspectors. After I received our building permit, Mr. Adams' excellent reputation brought us credibility and helped smooth our path. Nor had Henry Flora ceased acting on our behalf. While he was at The Camp of the Woods, he interceded with the new pastor of the church. When we left the Flora's house at the end of their two-week vacation, we were permitted to live in a furnished parsonage for nearly six months, paying only for utilities.

I remember sitting at the dining table each night, revising the plans for the two-story, four bedroom, two bath house I had designed, estimating materials required, and planning the following days' work. At first, however, there were no materials because there was no money. That was September 1994, and every member of our family—Matthew and Jamieson, ages 9 and 10, plus Cheryl and Sandra, both college age, as well as Joy and myself—worked daily on the house.

I lacked a transit to set the forms and level the foundation, so I improvised by using a fifty-foot garden hose filled with water to set up the batter boards outside the corners. We spent over a hundred dollars to rent a small backhoe, but the engine failed to generate sufficient power. So, we wound up digging the ditches for the footings with picks and shovels.

Average Guy Meets Extraordinary God

The parcel was unique. Bedrock lay just inches below the surface, so once we scraped away the topsoil, we had an immovable base on which to pour shallow footings and set any concrete blocks. But when we began scraping away that topsoil, we discovered that two trenches ran diagonally across our planned foundation, deep into the bedrock on which we planned to build the house. They had been scored in the bedrock by the enormous weight of an ancient glacier which had dragged boulders across our little knoll, clawing and polishing those two deep parallel trenches in the bedrock. Each of them was several feet deep, and four or five feet wide at the surface, narrowing to just inches at their bottoms.

They posed a problem because I needed to run level rows of concrete blocks for the footings over the irregular surface. Bill Adams suggested that we simply build plywood forms and have the cement truck fill the irregular trenches with concrete. His idea resulted in a level foundation and brought our new floor the desired foot above ground level.

A ready-mix truck arrived, and we poured the footings. I began laying the blocks, The second morning, ten-year old Jamieson pointed out that we had run out of mortar, and I lacked the two dollars we needed to buy a single bag of mortar. He insisted we pray, I searched my pockets, and found the money we needed to pick up a sack of mortar at Crispell's Hardware.

We somehow soldiered on, finished the footings, and anchored the 2x8 sill plates atop the foundation. Then we began framing the first-floor walls, using 2x6 studs in order to install thicker insulation. We did it all using old fashioned hand saws and hammers. We had no electricity, so even if we had the power tools, we couldn't run a skill saw or a pneumatic nail gun. It was another failing on my part. When I finally had the money, I should have had the electric company run in power to a temporary meter so that we could at least run saws and drills. According to industry estimates, an average-sized home contains approximately 20,000 nails of at least ten different types, and I suffered from tendinitis because I drove at least half of them.

Most houses are built over many months by crews with special skills. We were doing it all, learning as we worked. But all of our activity would have been in vain if my former church secretary, Judie—the same woman who sacrificed her TV set so that the local CBS TV crew could record my breaking it—hadn't somehow reached us to ask about our plans. She and her husband Bob had postponed their plans to build an energy efficient house, and she asked how much money we needed to finish ours. I had no idea how much it would cost to build the house, so I simply picked a number out of thin air, underestimating the final cost by more than half.

A few days later, she and Bob showed up at our building site with a cashier's check for ten-thousand dollars. They would not take our land as collateral, and even refused a promissory note. The loan was done on a handshake and the love of God. They said they were led by the Lord to loan us the money for as long as we needed it.

Without Bob and Judie's loving help, construction would have stopped at the foundation. Their loan was the first of several, without which our enterprise would have failed. Their timely assistance staggers the imagination, and is simply one more example of how the Lord made things happen.

Now it seemed that we were off to the races, but when we deposited the check in a new account at the Hyde Park Savings Bank, they held it for ten days, even though it was a cashier's check written on a major Albany bank. Such problems were characteristic of our entire venture. We learned to pray often and had no choice but to wait on the Lord, not always patiently.

As the first-floor walls went up, I had an "off the wall" idea, or should I call it an epiphany. What if we could get our hands on beams like the ones that years before were contributed to our church in Troy to build a playground for our Christian school? That was about 1977, and the City of Troy was tearing down houses built before the Civil War. A wrecking crew dropped off half a dozen beams in our church yard. They were about 4 inches thick, 12 inches wide and at least twenty feet long.

Now I had the zany idea that perhaps I could somehow find similar wooden beams in my hometown and convert my design to a modified post and beam house. So, at my insistence, we got into the old station wagon. I led in a brief prayer, and we headed for town. My family obviously thought I was a bit addled. At best, we were wasting time, and they were impatient to return to work. But it was a break from the tiring labor, so no one complained much.

I reasoned that I might visit the fine old men who operated a lumber yard at which my father did business during World War II. He was loyal to them because they had trusted him with credit during the Great Depression. I somehow imagined myself bargaining with them for some massive beams that might lay forgotten in one of their ancient sheds.

But when we arrived at the place where the huge old lumber yard had stood, there were just acres of dusty concrete slabs that had once served as the floors of the buildings. And those fine old men had long since gone to their reward. Discouraged, and with my family urging me to return to Hyde Park, I became fascinated with other changes that had taken place in the area.

So, I decided to spend a few minutes exploring. We were passing an old Railway Express warehouse when I noticed that workers were in the process of removing the roof. And then I saw one of the beams that supported the roof. I became excited and pulled the car to the curb so that I could watch. And I was right. These were the beams I'd imagined. But as I watched, reality set in. Based on what we had already paid for lumber, I suddenly realized I could never afford them, let alone get them back to Hyde Park.

One of our children said, *"Come on, Dad. Let's go!"* But as I put the car in gear to pull away, one of the workers approached us. He asked me whether I was interested in buying the beams, and the more I revealed my negative attitude, the more he insisted we could make a deal.

The beams were ideal. They had been sawn from solid fir, were four inches thick, fourteen inches wide, and forty feet long, and there was not a single knot in any of them. They had supported the roof of that building for over a hundred years and were incredibly straight and unbowed. They were perfectly suited to my purpose. When the foreman offered to deliver seven of those beams to our property in Hyde Park that same afternoon for a total of three-hundred and fifty dollars, I couldn't refuse.

It's been nearly forty years since we bought those beams, so as I was writing these words, I checked the advertised price for similar beams today. The closest size I could find on the Web were just 32 feet long, not an incredible 40 feet, and they were priced at thirty dollars per lineal foot. At that price, our seven forty-foot beams would cost about twelve hundred dollars each.

We paid fifty dollars each, including delivery. What can we say then? Because of the way we were led to the Wells Fargo building to discover these unique beams, is it presumptuous of me to conclude that the Lord had presented us with yet another incredible act of providence?

When the beams were delivered, my wife and children began the thankless task of removing scores of nails from their upper edges. After I cut the beams to length, the six of us raised a thirty-two-footer that ran down the center of the house, above the first story walls. It took all our combined strength to lift one end of that beam at a time, and we almost dropped it. I wish we had a photo of the six of us, ages nine to forty-three, as we struggled together to raise that beam. The other beams were twenty-four feet, and we found them a bit easier to handle.

In the meantime, our dear friend in Lake George had encouraged me to visit his longtime friend, the pastor of a church in Hyde Park. His congregation blessed us by bringing meals to the building site each evening. Our house was to be a "salt box," with a long steep roof on the north side, and when I started raising the heavy twenty-four-foot rafters, I became pretty shaky. The peak of that roof seemed awfully high to me.

It was then that the pastor of the Hyde Park church, himself a professional carpenter, showed up unexpectedly with a highly skilled friend. The two of them erected the framing for the roof, nailed down the sheathing, and even applied most of the siding to the outside walls.

After the house was framed, Cheryl began laying the brick floor that is still in use today, nearly 40 years later. And after the roof was on, and we had run the electrical wiring through the walls, Sandy began installing the fiberglass insulation that our dear friends, Bill and Linda Womer, the founders and directors of Christian Music Ministries, somehow secured for us.

To help buy our groceries and gasoline for the car, Joy took a job as a secretary with a commercial real estate appraiser. Cheryl put off college for a year to help with the work, and Sandy remained with us in order to home-school her brothers. She took them on field trips each week, and helped them advance academically far beyond their contemporaries in the public schools. And I continued building.

Each night found us falling into bed exhausted. Each day seemed to find us with too little cash to buy needed materials, or unable to find just the right part required for a given job. But we kept on. For the first couple of months, we had no electric power to run saws or drills and did most of the work with hand saws and augers, the old-fashioned way.

I was no Aholiab or Aminidab. I was a would-be carpenter, an amateur, but constant prayer was answered with sufficient skill and resources to move from task to task. My Uncle Larry stopped by and joked that he could build a house with the nails I dropped. We successfully laid a foundation that was square and level. The walls that our family built were plumb and square. When I didn't know how to lay out the stringers for the staircase so that the risers would be exactly the same height step to step, Bill Adams loaned me measuring devices with which I managed to get it precisely right.

We were praying pretty much continually, and we somehow endured. I studied manuals on plumbing and wiring. I was able to install the electrical entry system, the interior wiring, and all the plumbing. We received the approvals of the town building inspector for basic construction, and the Underwriters Laboratory inspector for the electrical entry system and internal wiring.

It was about that time that Bill Adams learned that Bennett College, in Millbrook, had closed its doors. We were able to pick up some closet and bureau drawer assemblies that had been recently installed in dormitories that would now be converted to rental apartments. Bill wanted a set of these cabinets for a cabin he was building in the Adirondacks and we wanted five sets for our kitchen and the four bedrooms. We also picked up large sliding-glass windows. Bill owned a pickup truck, and we made several trips to Millbrook to retrieve everything. It was a challenge to lift those heavy cabinets to our second floor.

The electrical inspector failed me on my first inspection because I didn't tie off all the ground wires in the electrical outlet boxes. I finished up, and the electric company allowed me to use an old utility pole saving us a thousand dollars. I installed the entry system, but we didn't realize he'd made the final inspection until we pulled into the driveway one night, and discovered the lights were on.

The inspector had passed us, and the electric company had installed the meter. The timing was amazing because a new assistant pastor was due to move into the parsonage, so we had only until the end of the month to vacate. Now we could secure our certificate of occupancy and move immediately.

Imagine it. At the very moment we found ourselves homeless, Henry and Lois Flora offered us their beautiful home for two weeks. Then he arranged for us to dwell in a vacant church parsonage for six months. The folks at the Hyde Park Baptist Church provided numerous home-cooked meals, and the pastor and his friend contributed several days of labor to help finish the exterior of the house.

Folks from the church we had founded in Troy came to help one Saturday with the work. When we were without a car, John and Susan Bassani came to our rescue. The construction of the roof was done by the Hyde Park pastor and his associate. The installation of dry wall and roof shingles was completed with the help of my late brother-in-law, John MacNiven, and his son, Michael. None of it would have been possible without Bob & Judie's loan, secured only with a handshake! Later there were loans of $5,000 each from two elderly Christian ladies, and $3,000 from a fine pastor in Lake George. It's impossible to tally the value of the labor contributed by friends, family, and former parishioners.

Though there was much finish work to do, including interior doors, trim, painting, and more, we were able to move out of the parsonage and into our new home just as time ran out. The completion of that house is a testimony to God's providence, with some events and their timing defying imagination, and arguably qualifying as miracles.

We who had been homeless now had a home. More than that, we understood far better how the Lord increases our faith as we exercise and build on the faith we already have.

*Our owner-built home in
Hyde Park, New York*

Over the past thirty-seven years, that house has been altered. Its six walk-through sliding-glass windows were replaced by much smaller ones, the paint changed from pale blue to tan, and even the wide brick sidewalk was removed. Zillow recently estimated its value at over four-hundred thousand dollars.

Several Bible passages came alive for us while we labored, but especially this one: *"Not that I speak in regard to need, for I have learned in whatever state I am, to be content"* (Philippians 4:10). Let me encourage you with these words: *"... my God shall provide all of your needs according to His riches in glory by Christ Jesus"* (Philippians 4:19).

CHAPTER 47

Joy's Testimony

"... grant to Your servants that with all boldness they may speak Your word, by stretching out Your hand to heal, and that signs and wonders may be done through the name of Your holy Servant Jesus."

Acts 4:29-30

I can remember the time that God touched my damaged hand and instantly healed me. But I can't explain it. I feel a little as the blind man must have felt when he testified about Jesus: *"Whether He is a sinner or not I do not know. One thing I know: that though I was blind, now I see"* (John 9:25).

To both Frank and me, what happened was inexplicable. But it really happened! One minute, I was in terrible pain and nauseated from the throbbing in my hand, and moments later, I was pain free, no swelling, nothing!

It happened at our daughter's house on the second floor. Frank was going up the folding staircase into the attic to do some repairs. I was watching him climb as I held the rickety ladder for him and hoped for a swift fix of the problem in the darkness above. Suddenly my hand was struck a blow so severe that the pain seemed to take my breath from me. Frank had dropped a heavy tool and it struck my wrist. I immediately felt a crushing amount of pain. I staggered to a couch, hoping to get some ice on the bruise while I recovered.

I could already see a huge knob, over a half inch high and an inch wide, where the tool had struck my hand. The red aura around the perimeter was growing with what was the beginning of the bruising. The pain was excruciating, but prayers were immediately offered and ice applied. Since I had previously broken a wrist, and since my bones were already fragile, I was sure I had broken a bone.

I was musing and praying, trying to focus on God, and I knew He was there. Suddenly I realized that I had no pain. I looked down, and "the knob," was gone. The swelling was down, the discoloration was gone, and it seemed unreal to view my hand. It was healed. I was okay! I was so, so excited to see what God had done that I immediately wrote it down, and told God that I knew this was His doing. I would never forget it. It was His witness to me on that day that He cares for everyone and everything and wanted to bless me especially.

I stand in amazement because I knew we serve the risen Savior, but never had I personally experienced this kind of thing. God stretched forth His hand to heal me. May I be faithful to boldly proclaim His word!

CHAPTER 48

Crash, bang...

"Whoever walks blamelessly will be saved, but he who is perverse in his ways will suddenly fall."

Proverbs 28:18

———————————

When I recently asked our grown children to share any memories of God's providence, our son Matthew reminded me of an accident in which our entire family was involved. Matthew was nine when this accident occurred, and he still attributes our survival to the mercies of God. It occurred one icy winter morning, shortly after we moved into our new home in Hyde Park.

"I remember," he wrote, "the accident on Fallkill Road, how we passed directly between two trees that took the mirrors off." That accident was the result of my foolishness. Like most accidents, ought never to have happened.

We left our new house one Sunday morning, planning to drive to church. There had been a late spring ice storm, followed by an inch or two of snow. The trees were glorious, their ice-covered branches radiant in the rising sun. It was as though we lived in a crystal forest.

Access to our house was along a winding, snow-covered road. It was crowned slightly in the middle, and the snow hid a layer of clear hard ice, what some call "black ice." The moment I pulled our car out of our gravel driveway and onto the road, I knew we were in trouble.

Average Guy Meets Extraordinary God

We were moving at a walking pace and had gone only a short distance before I lost control. With the car stopped, and my foot on the brake, it slid sideways toward the edge of the road. I stayed behind the wheel while everyone else got out to slide our two-ton station wagon around in a circle on the slick surface. After they got it turned around, we headed back toward home, about a hundred yards away.

The road was relatively straight and level here, and the family wanted to return home, reasoning that, if we couldn't go to church, we shouldn't attempt to go anywhere else. But I insisted that we continue on to our little country store to pick up the Sunday paper. "Once we reach the state highway," I argued, "it will be clear and salted, so all we have to do is drive the short distance to 9-G, and we will be okay. The store is only a short distance south of the intersection."

So, instead of making the safe and easy turn into our driveway, I started down the quarter mile of winding road that led to the highway. But, as Matthew so vividly recalls, we didn't make it. We were entering the final broad curve where Fallkill Road joins the state highway at an acute angle, when the car seemed to take on a mind of its own. It no longer responded to the wheel, and we began careening toward the right, toward a row of trees that bordered the right side of the road.

I followed the recommended procedure and steered in the direction of the slide, but was unable to regain control. It didn't take much imagination to picture what would happen if our car wrapped itself around one of the trees that seemed to be rushing at us. By now I had the brake pedal pressed to the floor, my hands locked futilely on the wheel, and I found myself uttering one of the shortest, most sincere prayers of my life.

At the last moment, just before we drove head on into one of the trees, the front wheels seemed to grip the gravel that lay on the shoulder of the road. The car lurched to the left and seemed to move on its own volition toward a narrow gap between two trees. Crash, bang...there was one jarring shock after another.

The rear of the car slammed back and forth, bouncing from the tree on the left to the tree on the right. Then, so fast I couldn't take it in. We were sliding down a snow-covered lawn toward the row of trees that bordered the state highway. But before we reached the far edge of the lawn, the car finally skidded to a stop.

We got out, looked over the damage and thanked the Lord no one was hurt. We lost both outside mirrors, ripped off the rear bumper, and broke the left rear window. Though we were all in a state of shock, we were okay. God had delivered us from my foolish decision. I was able to start the car, turn it around, and drive back onto our country road.

The irony was that the ice was now melted, and we were able to make it back home with no trouble. I am reminded of Deuteronomy 6:16. *"Thou shalt not tempt the Lord thy God."* There is no question in my mind that the Lord preserved us that day. I've come to love this phrase, which is repeated many times and in many places in The Holy Bible: "His mercy endureth forever."[44]

----

44   Psalms 136

CHAPTER 49

"You must be perplexed…"

"But the natural man does not receive the things of the Spirit of God, for they are foolishness to him; nor can he know them, because they are spiritually discerned."

1 Corinthians 2:14

Thanksgiving morning, 1990, was bitter cold, overcast, and depressing. It was a good day to remain indoors and relax by a laughing fire with a cup of hot cocoa in hand. Instead, I knelt on the frozen gravel surface of our driveway beneath a gray and dismal sky, buffeted by a biting wind that presaged heavy snows, my numb fingers struggling to replace the brake pads on our daughter's ancient Honda.

I was just gathering my tools when someone called from the front door that they were about to put our Thanksgiving dinner on the table. This was one of my two favorite feasts of the year, and I should have been eager to join my family. However, I was suddenly overcome with dizziness, mild nausea, and a sense of exhaustion. So while they dined, I simply climbed into bed and fell asleep.

The next morning, after Joy left for work, I felt much worse. With snow beginning to fall, our daughter Sandra drove me to Schenectady's Ellis Hospital. By the time we reached the emergency room, the area was in the grip of a full-blown blizzard. The waiting room was packed with people who had succumbed to the current flu epidemic.

Average Guy Meets Extraordinary God

The staff was overwhelmed by the number of patients, so Sandy and I were forced to sit in the cold entrance foyer. It was nearly two hours before a nurse checked my vitals. She wasn't impressed, as my temperature was only slightly elevated. But because I was coughing violently, she took pity and installed me on a gurney a few feet from an outside door. She drew blood for the overworked lab, covered me with a light blanket, and left me in my daughter's care. Every time that sliding door opened, we were whipped by icy air and blown snow. I couldn't stop shivering.

Finally, after several hours, the nurse returned. She told us that they had planned to send me home, but when the lab reported that my white blood count was over 30,000, they decided to admit me. The initial diagnosis was pneumonia, so they put me in a room with another pneumonia patient.

As soon as I was settled in, we agreed that Sandy should try to get home before the snow became too deep. Then my roommate and his visitors lit up cigarettes, and I began coughing. It was twenty-four hours before the staff forbade any further smoking in our room.

We had a daytime nurse who was not only highly competent, but somehow brought cheer to a dismal situation. A woman of color, she was worth more than a dozen pickle-puss co-workers. She proved that a merry heart does indeed make a good medicine.

On the second day of my hospitalization, Sandy brought me an ice cream sundae from Friendly's. She was faithful to visit every day until she was no longer permitted to visit me. For the most part I seemed to move in and out of consciousness. Though I remember a parade of specialists stopping to query me about how I felt.

I think it was the third day in that dismal room that my favorite nurse came bustling in, but she was no longer smiling. If I had been feeling more awake, I would have been far more shocked by her words. "Those (expletive deleted) say you have TB!" she shouted. She went on to explain that my blood tests indicated that I had tuberculosis, and the staff was in the process of moving someone less dangerous out of the hospital's isolation ward so that they could move me in.

A short time after I received this ominous news, my beloved wife brought our two teenage sons to visit for the first and last time. I was propped up on pillows, an oxygen tube clipped to my nose, with IVs inserted in both wrists. It was 1990, and at fifty years of age I must have looked like death warmed over. I told them what I'd just learned, and in no more than two seconds, Joy's face turned ashen and seemed to grow old before my eyes. The boys looked stricken too, and as I watched their faces, it was obvious that they were not only shocked, but unable to hide their feelings at my ghastly appearance.

The nurse came in, and my family stammered their goodbyes and left. On their way home, the boys told their mother that they didn't want to return. Their decision was academic, as the hospital was about to forbid visitors.

I did not have time to brood over their reactions because over the next few hours several specialists visited my room. I remember visits by a pulmonologist, a lung specialist, a cardiologist, and an oncologist. I think there were one or two more, but I was too ill to do much more than try to answer their brief questions.

After they left, I was placed on a gurney and moved to the isolation ward. It was a large room with just one bed, but it had a private bath that I wouldn't visit for another week. There was a large window in the outside wall, and an anteroom where doctors and nurses could look in on me through a window. There they were required to don robes, masks, and gloves before entering my room.

My first morning after entering isolation I received a visit from a woman who said she was the head nurse with the New York State Department of Health. She made it clear that TB was considered a major threat to the populace and questioned me at length as to where I had been and who I had been with, trying to determine where I might have picked up this highly infectious disease. She wanted to know whether I had visited a jail or prison, and whether I had a homosexual relationship.

I was at first shocked, then angry. Then she asked whether I would be willing to remain in my home for a full year while undergoing treatment, and I told her that I would. As she ended the interview, she told me that—had I answered otherwise—I would have been incarcerated.

Well, there I was, propped up in that bed, as weak as a baby kitten, denied visitors, and helpless to change my hopeless estate. They were pumping what they described as the three most powerful antibiotics into me in an attempt to defeat the infection, but I wasn't responding. The diagnoses were now double pneumonia and tuberculosis. I ate little, slept a lot, and—as is common with hospitals—was awakened every few hours to have my vitals checked, or to have an IV removed and reinserted elsewhere. Sometimes I fell back asleep while they were inserting needles.

Average Guy Meets Extraordinary God

The morning after the woman from the health department visited, I had another visitor. This was a young man who looked remarkably like the TV character, "Doogie Howser, MD," and my first impression wasn't far from the truth. He identified himself as the chief bacteriologist at Albany Medical Center and explained that the state health department had sent him to Schenectady to review my case.

He told me that he had been downstairs with the head of the hospital laboratory, and they had examined my latest blood samples. Then he told me, "We don't know what you have, but you don't have TB!" Was that good news, or bad? It reminded me of the joke about the guy who had just seen his mother-in-law drive off a cliff in his brand-new Cadillac.

I asked myself, "If I don't have tuberculosis, what do I have?"

And Doctor Doogie immediately justified my concern. "We don't know what you have, but it's highly contagious."

A day or so later, I got some good news. I was told that I'd begun to respond to the drugs, and my body was slowly beating off the pneumonia. Yet my lungs remained full of something strange and highly infectious. I was shown an X-ray and it looked like there were little white feathery things floating around in my lungs. It was sort of like the old "angel hair" that people used to put on their Christmas trees.

A day or so later, my new pulmonologist had me taken by wheelchair to her office where I got to see Joy for the first time in days. The doctor suggested eight or ten deadly diseases that might be threatening my life. I remember just a couple of them: Hodgkin's disease and a couple of kinds of cancer. Most of them were fatal, especially thirty years ago.

As she went down the list, Joy turned pale and excused herself. She escaped into the hallway, and if our good friend, Bill Womer, hadn't been there to catch her, she would have fallen to the floor because she fainted dead away. She was more touched by the feeling of my infirmity than I was. It was odd, but throughout my hospital stay I felt oddly removed and indifferent, as though I were a spectator watching someone else in a TV drama.

But the pulmonologist wasn't indifferent. She insisted I have a bronchoscopy. The next day I lay on an operating table in a crowded room, with at least four people in gowns, masks, and hats hovering over me. They used a Q-tip about eight inches long to put Novocain down my nose, which is not one of my favorite memories. It was followed by their forcing a tube down my throat into my lungs, definitely not a favorite! Then they inserted a video camera to examine the lobes. I was actually able to view the inside of my right lung on a TV screen. Though I soon became nauseous.

Then the oncologist did something that caused such pain in my right lung that I involuntarily screamed. When she stopped, I asked what she was doing, and she replied that she was trying to pinch away a bit of scar tissue for biopsy. "But don't worry," she assured me. "You don't have any nerves there."

I closed my eyes, and she evidently pinched the "nerveless" scar tissue again, because I again screamed in pain. Then we had a bit of a debate.

"There may not be any nerves there," I said, "but it sure hurts when you do that."

"Show me where," she challenged.

I reached my hand up, and put my index finger down on my chest, and they all seemed surprised that I was pointing at the exact spot where she was working. So, they terminated the procedure. From what I later learned, they never did get a sample to study.

Then she sent me to an oncologist who sat me down in a chair on the front porch of his little office building, and carefully examined my fingernails. He told me that they looked very healthy, and that if I had cancer, the color of the flesh beneath the nails might have changed. He told me that he had reviewed all of the notes made by other specialists, and that he didn't think I had cancer. But since I had signed a release, he was going to take some bone marrow. I didn't know what that entailed, and being sort of in a twilight state, I submitted.

That was another memorable experience. In retrospect, my advice would be, "If you can avoid it, do so!" He inserted a long thick square needle in my hip and pushed it through the bone in order to draw out enough marrow to fill a couple of Petri dishes. As it turns out, that marrow would be very valuable, not just to check me for metastatic cancer, but for experimentation. If not infected, it could be used to help other cancer victims.

That's the last major procedure I remember. After that, I remained in my room feeling a bit lonely and forsaken. But one night, a pastor I knew slipped into the isolation room, followed in minutes by two others. One of them, Pastor Jay Francis, founder of the extensive worldwide IAM Ministries, read a brief passage from the Bible. They anointed me with oil to symbolize the presence of the Holy Spirit, then the three of them prayed for my healing. Without further comment, they slipped out of the room.

The next day, my nurse stood in the little annex room and watched through the window as I did fifty jumping jacks. Fifty! She just shook her head in amazement.

And that day or the next, the hospital bacteriologist came by to tell me that my latest blood tests indicated that whatever was in my lungs was now inert and not infectious. He said that they wanted me to remain in my room for a few more days while I regained strength. The doctor told me that I'd had a particularly bad case of pneumonia and that it would take several months for my lungs to clear. However, it would take at least a year to regain my strength. In fact, it took only one month for my lungs to clear, and in three months I was feeling my old self.

A week after returning home, I went for a required follow-up visit to my personal physician. I'll never forget the first words he spoke:

"You must be perplexed that all those specialists couldn't tell you what you almost died from."

My sincere reply? "I'm not perplexed. The Lord healed me."

Don't get me wrong. The staff at Ellis Hospital was great. I appreciate those who practice medicine and still adhere to the Hippocratic Oath; who don't practice abortion or euthanasia. And in my case, they were certainly used of God. But too many doctors don't respect life, and in the case of those who abort the unborn and alter the sex of children, the Bible teaches that their lack of understanding will ultimately bring them great sorrow, for "*the natural man does not receive the things of the Spirit of God, for they are foolishness to him; nor can he know them, because they are spiritually discerned*" (1 Corinthians 2:14).

As for me, I'm not at all perplexed that all those specialists couldn't tell me what I almost died from. I'm reveling in the fact that the Lord of glory healed me!

CHAPTER 50

His Eye Is On the Olive Plants

"Your wife shall be like a fruitful vine in the very heart of your house, your children like olive plants all around your table."
Psalm 128:3

It was 1992, and Hurricane Andrew had reached south Florida. Andrew was the most destructive hurricane to ever hit Florida, both in terms of structural damage and cost. That is, until Hurricane Irma struck 25 years later.

Our eighteen-year-old son, Jamie, was driving from New York to Florida on what he called his "coming of age" road trip. He was in a lightly populated area in north Florida, driving his old Chevette toward the on-coming hurricane, determined to reach Tampa. It was night, and the skies around him were roiled with dark clouds, and punctuated by distant flares of lightning. His car was buffeted by gusting winds and sporadic rain. His memory of the accident today doesn't square with our memories of what he told us by phone during the course of the incident. But we are doing our best to get it right.

Visibility was very poor, and when the highway suddenly divided, he tried to pull to the right to avoid a curb that seemed to appear out of no-where. The car began to skid, and as he fought to maintain control, it slid across the berm, then rolled over as it went down into a drainage ditch. His first fear, he later told us, was that the ditch would be filled with water.

The car landed on its wheels. Miraculously uninjured, he was able to exit the vehicle. He then began surveying the damage. The rear side windows on each side had popped out, and the roof was slightly caved in. The battery had come loose from its mountings, two of the four tires were flat, and tree roots or vines were entangled in one wheel. It was impossible for him to drive the car out of the ditch.

He was able to call us from a nearby pay phone. Over the next few hours we made several phone calls in an effort to assist him. When I reached the state police, we were told that the nearest officer was eighty miles south, involved with another accident. Due to the hurricane, no one was available to come to his assistance.

But the auto club agreed to send a driver to help him. When the man arrived, he towed Jamie's car out of the ditch. He then left our son and his wrecked Chevette on the side of the road, tires flat, in the face of the approaching hurricane.

Again, we called the auto club, and they grudgingly sent a flatbed truck. This time, the driver loaded the car onto the back of the flat bed. Our son was allowed to ride up front with the driver and his girlfriend.

His car was taken to an auto center in Gainesville. I arranged to pay for the necessary repairs to get him back on the road. Then I called my brother Bob, who lived in Clearwater, and he agreed to drive to Gainesville, so that he could follow Jamie back to Tampa.

I can't imagine the trauma that our son experienced as his car rolled over, hanging momentarily from his seat belt, wrestling with the fear of severe injury and drowning. Not to speak of his waiting alone for hours in the wind and the rain, trying to figure out what to do. Others have died of shock in similar situations.

It was certainly a difficult night for his mother and me, as we sought to come to the aid of our son who was over a thousand miles from home. It made us realize once again how our Heavenly Father must feel when we find ourselves in seemingly impossible situations. When I think of Jamie's car rolling down into that drainage ditch, it certainly makes me appreciate David's words: *"He also brought me up out of a horrible pit, out of the miry clay, and set my feet upon a rock, and established my steps"* (Psalm 40:2). By God's grace, our son survived that threat to his life, and today he and his wonderful wife, Jennifer, have children of their own.

CHAPTER 51

By the Grace of God...

"And He said to me, 'My grace is sufficient for you, for My strength is made perfect in weakness.' Therefore most gladly I will rather boast in my infirmities, that the power of Christ may rest upon me."

2 Corinthians 12:9

By God's grace, Joy and I were able to remain productive during our wandering years. She went on to write curriculum for both Christian and secular publishing houses. Then, she taught high school English for fourteen years. Additionally, her first book, *Break Out!*, was just published. In addition, she spends hours each day responding to emails from individuals around the world who want to know more about Jesus Christ. Joy also goes house to house in our neighborhood, visiting the elderly, the infirm, and shut-ins to offer them comfort and encouragement, and to witness about Jesus.

For my part, I founded Cross Trainers Ministries nearly twenty years ago to disciple individuals and promote the planting of house churches. As the attacks on God's people have increased around the world, the Biblical approach to church growth and survival is being embraced in many countries. Cross Trainers Ministries also supported several pastors in India and provided funds to buy land and erect a new orphanage in Hyderabad—The Joy Becker Home.

Average Guy Meets Extraordinary God

Cheryl Bliss,
composer, musician, and vocalist

While in my sixties, I tried to teach myself to paint.

In 2011, I emailed Paige Patterson, then president of the Southwestern Baptist Theological Seminary, asking whether he'd look over my latest book. Dr. Patterson, a Biblical conservative, has labored liberally to save the Church from moral and theological corruption. He is a battle-scarred veteran of the holy wars, a leader who continues to fight for an honest approach to God's Word, encouraging churches and Christian leaders not to compromise Scriptural values.

At the time I wrote him, he was on a speaking tour in Europe. He nevertheless invited me to send him the manuscript of my new book, *The Depression Proof Church: The Biblical Answer to the Church in Crisis.* The title, of course, refers to those rare churches that are free of the typical problems—economic, emotional, and spiritual. Dr. Patterson responded with a glowing endorsement. It was remarkable because it is a near miraculous event for an unknown author to get the ear of a busy and outstanding Christian leader, much less win his endorsement.

Paige Patterson was one of the early targets of the "cancel culture," the mob that tears apart reputations, demeans accomplishments, and attempts to bury the memories of outstanding people. Dr. Patterson was subsequently removed from his position for an alleged failure in leadership that supposedly occurred decades before. He received vindication in the court room when a federal judge dismissed the claims, a major blow in a high-profile lawsuit. Paige Patterson remains a true hero of the faith and continues to fight the good fight.

And me? As might be expected, I have slowed down a bit since 2019, when I began receiving treatment for two kinds of cancer, as well as the implant of a stent. But I asked the Lord to give me time and strength to finish this, my tenth book, and He did. One of my greatest joys has been the opportunity to occasionally preach God's Word.

And what's my counsel to you as I near the end of my exciting and wonder-filled eighty-four years? *"Whatever your hand finds to do, do it with all your might"* (Ecclesiastes 9:10). *"... In all things showing yourself to be a pattern of good works; in doctrine showing integrity, reverence, incorruptibility"* (Titus 2:7).

ALMOST HOME:

THE REASSURING HAND OF GOD

CHAPTER 52

Flying "Premiere Classe"

"Now to Him who is able to do exceedingly abundantly above all that we ask or think, according to the power that works in us, to Him be glory in the church by Christ Jesus to all generations, forever and ever."

Ephesians 3:20-21

The Bible makes it very clear that we are not to envy the wicked. We are told repeatedly that righteousness promises blessing. Therefore, the most important thing is to keep our eyes on the greatest prize—eternal life with our Savior, Jesus Christ. But once in a while, most of us find ourselves hungering for a bit of earthly comfort.

Like the Lord Jesus, the Apostle Paul was alternately honored and cursed. He suffered far more than any other apostle: experiencing shipwrecks, imprisonments, beatings, hunger, stonings, and, finally, beheading. Yet he also walked with kings and won some of their closest and most trusted associates to the Lord. King Herod Agrippa told Paul, *"You almost persuade me to become a Christian"* (Acts 26:28). As a result, Paul was able to assure us that he had seen life from both sides. He wrote: *"I know how to be abased, and I know how to abound. Everywhere and in all things I have learned both to be full and to be hungry, both to abound and to suffer need"* (Philippians 4:12).

Most Americans enjoy far greater comforts than did any of the ancient kings. We fill our glasses with ice by pressing buttons on our refrigerator doors. At our local grocers, we can select from a tremendous variety of meats, vegetables, fruits, and exotic foods. We can either prepare our own meals, order in, or dine out. Many sleep on mattresses that are fourteen inches thick and live in homes that are shielded from rain, sun, dust and insects, with remote controlled air conditioning. We drive around at incredible speeds, seated on padded upholstery, wearing an unimaginable variety of clothing that we keep clean with modern appliances. And yet, most Americans are not content.

Like Paul, Joy and I have been both full and hungry, abounding and suffering need. But we have come to appreciate the "simple comforts." We too have an ice maker, a home with windows and screens, a comfortable mattress, and air-conditioning to maintain a satisfactory temperature. But it is, admittedly, a small house, and at my age, and with my debilities, these things are more in the line of lifesaving, rather than merely pleasurable.

But once in a while, the Lord does something special in our lives; something to emphasize His love, something to take us out of the everyday and the ordinary, something so dramatic and unusual that it leaves a lasting memory.

To the rich and famous, such pleasures may seem so common and mundane as to be beneath their notice, but to those of us who have never experienced anything like them, they highlight what it's' like when an average guy meets an extraordinary God.

In 2014, our four children, along with their life-long mates and our fifteen grandchildren, threw us a party to celebrate our 50th wedding anniversary. But it wasn't until two years later that Joy and I finally took our anniversary vacation, flying economy to Paris, France. The last day of our journey found us back at Charles DeGaulle Airport, waiting to board our plane for the ten hour flight back to Houston.

I thought about that long trip home in those narrow, uncomfortable seats, and wondered whether I might somehow surprise Joy by upgrading to seats further forward, perhaps with a few inches more leg room. At 76, I too would be glad for a more comfortable seat.

So I said a little prayer, excused myself, and made my way to a kiosk where a harried looking woman in a blue uniform sat speaking in voluble French with the man who stood in line in front of me. When she was free, I briefly explained that my wife and I were celebrating our 50th anniversary, and asked, without much confidence, whether there might be some chance that we could upgrade to seats with a little more legroom.

She didn't scowl, but her response wasn't very encouraging either. She first shook her head, but then seemed to have second thoughts, and said, in English, "Let me see your boarding pass." I handed it to her, she studied it for a moment, then she picked up her phone and dialed a number. She spoke very rapidly in French, became silent for a moment, said a few more words, listened, another moment, then hung up.

Then she asked. "Do you have your wife's boarding pass?" I handed it to her, and she began typing something on her computer. After a moment, she tore up our boarding passes and tossed the scraps in a waste basket.

I didn't want to appear obvious, but as I leaned on the counter, I could see the new boarding passes tumble out of the printer, and I noticed the seat numbers. I couldn't help wonder where on the plane seats 6D and 6E were located. I was excited. It was a huge plane, and it appeared that we were being moved up near the front of the Economy Plus Cabin. I thanked her profusely, and she gave me a sweet motherly smile, then said, "Have a nice trip."

As I returned to our waiting area, a smiling attendant came to lead us to a different waiting area. We had hardly seated ourselves when we were told that we they were ready to board us. All the attendants seemed to have funny little grins on their faces, as though they shared a secret.

When we boarded the huge aircraft, we were shown to a pair of seats that stood alone, in a closed off area with just six other passengers. I looked over the privacy wall in front of us, and a few paces away, not quite facing us, were two identical chairs set at an angle. I learned that this smaller seating area was part of the huge First Class cabin.

The entire First Class cabin had only twenty-eight of these private little "islands" placed at angles to one another to provide optimum privacy. The Economy Plus cabin, where I had hoped to be moved, had the same floor area as the First Class cabin. But, it seated nearly four times as many passengers, all shoulder to shoulder in rows of three.

Joy's chair and mine were next to one another. We were almost in a cocoon, with aisles on each side, and a low wall in front. We each had our own large screen TVs and storage cubicles. The chairs folded down to make flat beds, and I would later enjoy seven hours of sleep with a real pillow and blanket.

We were treated like celebrities. First, a lovely attendant knelt down, introduced herself, and told us how happy they were to have on board a couple that had been married fifty years. She asked if she could return later to chat with us. Then she offered us our choice of beverages, a delicious steak dinner, and the suggestion that we should feel free at any time to go upstairs to the sandwich board. Downstairs, of course, were rows of private lavatories.

That same hostess came to visit us several times to make certain we had everything we could wish for. She was really impressed that we had remained married for so long and wanted to know our secret. She told us that her parents had been married for over thirty years, and she went on to share her own life story. It was a wonderful opportunity to share God's love.

It was an incredible journey for us, though it would probably seem blasé to the wealthy and the powerful business executives who regularly travel First Class. I would love to repeat the experience, but those round-trip tickets now start at about $8,000 each, a total of $16,000. I somehow doubt that they would again upgrade us from Economy Class to what the French call "Premiere Classe."

That was clearly the hand of God. But who knows? Two months ago, we celebrated our 60th wedding anniversary, and the Lord isn't finished with us yet!

So, keep these two things in mind. If you are walking with Jesus Christ, anything is possible. And once you get to heaven, everything will be far superior to "Premiere Classe!" *"But as it is written: 'Eye has not seen, nor ear heard, nor have entered into the heart of man the things which God has prepared for those who love Him'"* (1 Corinthians 2:9).

Chapter 53

What's Your Story?

"Most assuredly, I say to you, he who believes in Me, the works that I do he will do also; and greater works than these he will do, because I go to My Father. And whatever you ask in My name, that I will do, that the Father may be glorified in the Son. If you ask anything in My name, I will do it"

John 14:12-14

Some people mock these words of Jesus, but wisdom is indeed justified by her children. The things Joy and I have seen and experienced leave us no alternative but to happily believe them. If you haven't received Jesus as your Lord and Savior, you are among the doubters.

You may read testimonies like ours, and even witness acts of Providence, but somehow you rationalize them away. If so, you shouldn't expect to receive God's blessings for yourself, or for your loved ones. For, this requires that you place faith in Him, and doubting is the antithesis of faith.

If, on the other hand, you have trusted Jesus for your eternal salvation, but have not seen His hand moving in your life, then you evidently haven't been growing in faith. He has promised to resurrect you from the dead and give you eternal life. Therefore, you shouldn't find it difficult to trust Him for a far smaller miracle now and then.

Too many Christians fail to call upon the name of the Lord because they feel undeserving or because they lack faith. Faith is a residual benefit of walking with God. It's an outgrowth of trusting and complying with His Word, the Bible. When you begin to trust and obey, you also begin to witness amazing things and they increase your faith for even bigger things.

But if you have not asked Jesus to be your Lord and Savior, you really need to do so today. It's questionable as to whether you will ever again feel so inclined. *"For He says: 'In an acceptable time I have heard you, and in the day of salvation I have helped you.' Behold, now is the accepted time; behold, now is the day of salvation"* (2 Corinthians 6:2).

God warns, *"My Spirit shall not always strive with men"* (Genesis 6:3). So, if the Spirit of God is dealing with you right now, you need to respond immediately. How do you go about it?

First, acknowledge why you feel no connection with God, and identify the cause of your separation. It's your sin! Romans 3:23 explains, *"for all have sinned and fall short of the glory of God."*

You are not alone in this. We have all missed the mark. You may have repeatedly resolved to give something up, to cease some practice, to change your life, and you've failed. In the midst of your struggle, you find yourself hurting the ones you care about.

Acknowledge that you are helpless to cease sinning, much less compensate for your sins. You ought always to have lived a sinless life. You can't add a single minute after your death to undo the wrongs or compensate for the damage you've done to yourself and others. So, you are guilty. You have a debt you cannot pay. Jesus warned, *"But I say to you that for every idle word men may speak, they will give account of it in the day of judgment"* (Matthew 12:36). Ask yourself, "How many sins does it take to make me a sinner?" Romans 6:23 warns, *"For the wages of sin is death, but the gift of God is eternal life through Christ Jesus our Lord."*

Next, recognize that the Son of God, Jesus Christ, who is both perfect God and perfect man, died on the cross in your place, to pay a debt He did not owe: yours! When you accept Christ's forgiveness, the slate will be wiped clean. He paid your debt. You will no longer be destined to suffer eternal pain and sorrow.

Why not speak to God right now? Keep in mind that your confession must come from the depths of your being. Admit that you are a sinner and tell him that you are truly sorry. Romans 10:9-10 states, *"that if you confess with your mouth the Lord Jesus and believe in your heart that God has raised Him from the dead, you will be saved. For with the heart one believes unto righteousness, and with the mouth confession is made unto salvation."*

Can you imagine being forgiven and cleansed of every sin you've ever committed? It's unimaginably easy, but you must mean it! Look at God's promise! Romans 10:11 goes on to proclaim, *"Whoever believes on Him will not be put to shame."* The Bible assures us, *"Therefore, if anyone is in Christ, he is a new creation; old things have passed away; behold, all things have become new"* (2 Corinthians 5:17).

Why would Jesus suffer and die on the cross for you? The explanation is found in John 3:16: *"For God so loved the world that he gave his only begotten son, that whoever believes in Him shall not perish but have eternal life."*

Yes, my experiences may encourage you to look into the matter, but you cannot base your salvation on my experience or opinions, but on the eternal Word of God.

You may ask, "What if you're wrong, Becker? What if there is no Heaven or Hell?"

If there is no God, no Heaven, and no Hell, if there is no "white light at the end of the tunnel," and our bodies perish, and conscious thought ceases when we die, we would simply cease to experience. Isn't the fact of your conscious ability to consider these things sufficient to reveal you are created in God's image?

Everywhere we look, we see evidence of God's existence. But, it's not scientific proof. The Psalmist wrote, *"The heavens declare the glory of God; and the firmament sheweth his handiwork"* (Psalm 19:1, KJV). Yes, the heavens provide evidence, but not absolute proof. Why?

We need to keep in mind that God doesn't want us to have absolute proof. We have our greatest evidence of His existence and His love in the historical record of the life, death, and resurrection of Jesus Christ. Yet multitudes still question. And that's God's plan.

If everyone believed in God simply because of historical or scientific evidence, rather than through faith, then, even the most vile and obdurate might be saved. It was because of that very possibility that Jesus spoke in parables. And when Christ's disciples asked him why he spoke in such a confusing fashion, He replied:*"For the hearts of this people have grown dull. Their ears are hard of hearing, and their eyes they have closed, lest they should see with their eyes and hear with their ears, lest they should understand with their hearts and turn, so that I should heal them"* (Matthew 13:15). For *"faith is the substance of things hoped for, the evidence of things not seen"* (Hebrews 11:1).

Many today accept the theory that our universe was born as the result of a "Big Bang." Since it appears to be a complex scientific issue, most people readily accept the theory without examining the premises on which the faulty hypothesis is based. They instead submit to the idea that an awesome quantity of gases filled the vast space we now call the universe, then somehow exploded, and after countless ages, ultimately produced our world.

The Big Bang Theory is just that, a theory. But it is very attractive because, like Darwin's theory of evolution, it does away with the need for a Creator. It instead enables us to consider our beginnings as impersonal—free of any ethical, moral, or spiritual implications or obligations.

A skeptic may ask you, "Who created God?" You should ask them, "Who created the gasses that produced your Big Bang?" Numerous recent scientific discoveries overturn many evolutionary theories and support Creation as revealed in Holy Scripture. And as science continues to unravel the mysteries of time and space, the veracity of the Holy Bible is increasingly corroborated. From a scientific standpoint, it's becoming easier to accept the reality that the Creator as First Cause for everything that exists.

Why, then, are people predisposed to accept the Big Bang theory rather than the reality of creation and a Creator? It's simple. We are rebels at heart. We want to go our own way, rule our own lives, and not be held accountable for our actions or for their impact on others. Our stubborn pride resists our submitting ourselves to an unseen God. We deny ourselves the possibility of eternal life because we want to live in the moment. In short, we walk by sight and not by faith.

The Big Bangers dismiss the Creator, Jesus Christ, and live their brief lives for the pitiful pleasures they can seize from the world. They care not how their eternal spirits are corroded as they harm others in order to satisfy their own fleshly appetites and attain their own vain ambitions. Their view of the future is tainted, for they believe that when they die, they will not be judged for their sins, but will simply face oblivion.

But they are wrong! The Bible is true, and unless they turn to God, they will experience the judgment of a just God whose righteousness must be satisfied. We Christians, on the better side of the argument, enjoy help for today, and have hope for tomorrow. And that's the message of this book. The Lord's invisible presence has repeatedly produced visible blessings in my life.

Consider this, if I'm wrong, and I am not, then the life I've lived has still been far superior to that of my unsaved friends. My life has been filled with wonders that, apart from God, would be inexplicable. It has been a continual demonstration of God's presence, power, and love, yielding me increasing peace and joy. So even if there were no Heaven, my walk with Jesus Christ has been worth it all! But the icing on the cake is that I will indeed dwell in the house of the Lord forever.

On the other hand, if you are wrong, and you continue rejecting the Son of God who loves you and gave His life for you, you will spend forever and ever in torment. Sound unfair? He's given you every opportunity to do the right thing! He's doing so right now!

If you receive Jesus Christ as your personal Savior, you will begin an exciting time of personal development. You will grow in faith as you study God's Word, as you pray, and as you fellowship with God's people. You will develop new interests and abilities, and your life will take on new meaning. The peace of God which passes understanding will enter your heart and mind.

When you bow and pray right now, you can anticipate unique and amazing experiences. So don't wait. Start this moment. Trust Jesus!

It's as easy as sincerely saying these words to him: "Jesus, I acknowledge that you are the Son of God. I know that you came to earth to die for my sins. Please come into my heart, and make me a new creature. Take my guilt and fear, fill my life with peace and joy, and be my Savior and Lord forever. Amen."

CHAPTER 54

The Best Is Yet to Come!

"Until now you have asked nothing in My name. Ask, and you will receive, that your joy may be full."

John 16:24

Through the course of this book, I have tried to offer encouragement by describing incidents that reveal the presence and power of God in the lives of believers today. You might wonder which of these I consider most impressive. Many chapters touch on God's call to salvation and service, but in terms of deliverance, the chapters entitled, "Daddy, I can't swim" and "I guess we overreacted" stand out. They speak of God's deliverance from earthly perils and bodily illness.

In terms of protection, the account of my hanging through a church ceiling, and the story about the primitive fire alarms, come to mind. There are many amazing testimonies in the chapter entitled, "Except the Lord build the House." But, "Brother Al's Fleece," and "The House at Green Lane," are near the top of my list as evidence of God's provision. "A Morning Prayer" blessed me in a unique way, but as I am in my 85th year, there is one experience that, apart from my eternal salvation, exceeds them all.

In 2019, an oncologist diagnosed me with metastatic prostate cancer, the same disease which, in 1968, took my father's life. But my prostate cancer was not diagnosed until after a carcinoid tumor was discovered blocking my small bowel during abdominal surgery. My oncologist insisted that the prostate cancer had spread, but five years after radiation therapy, there is no evidence of its presence.

Not so for the carcinoid cancer that was discovered during surgery. Those stealthy tumors grow slowly, but they spread from one vital organ to another. What is worse, my very rare tumors produce the hormone serotonin, so I have to deal with a second threat—Serotonin Syndrome. Over the past few years, my serotonin levels have dropped to about twelve times normal, but they can still cause all kinds of debilitating side effects, including heart attack, stroke, and seizure.

On two different occasions, the surgeon who was head of the abdominal transplant department at a Houston medical center was ready to go in and remove tumors from my liver, only to call me back to say, "Surgery is not indicated. In both cases, subsequent PET scans were taken to exactly locate the tumors for surgery, but the tumors were no longer visible." False positives? I wonder.

Radiation therapy, over an extended period, is very stressful to the body. Add that to the physical and emotional stress involved with having to make trips to various specialists as often as five times in a week, and you can imagine the additional stress to an aging heart. Late in 2019, my cardiologists found it necessary to implant a stent in my heart. Then, in 2024, I underwent my third heart catheterization, and they discovered two small irreparably blocked arteries, and a partially blocked carotid artery to my brain.

There's not a lot the oncologists and cardiologists can do about my cancer and heart disease. Apart from a medication for high blood pressure and baby aspirin, about all that my fine doctors can do is keep an eye on me. Too many drugs can speed the growth of the cancer or further damage the heart.

The oncologist tests my blood every six months, orders a CAT scan once a year to check the spread of those demonic tumors, and discusses whether I should begin infusions to deal with carcinoid symptoms that have not appeared. That's because, as carcinoid tumors spread, they have some nasty symptoms. Nearly three years ago, several oncologists recommended that I immediately begin a monthly infusion of Octreotide to treat the anticipated symptoms. The specialists also assured me that, as the cancer progresses, "We will try to keep you as comfortable as possible."

You can imagine how their assurances made me feel. I refused the Octreotide, and to their surprise, after nearly three years, the symptoms they said were imminent have not yet appeared. So apart from the occasional problems from an erratic heart, I'm feeling great!

The caregivers strive to help me keep a positive attitude, but I was told five years ago that the ultimate outcome of my battle with carcinoid cancer is inevitable defeat. Well, those five years are up, and I feel better than I did ten years ago.

In fact, I still work out with weights several times a week and walk every day. I have been privileged to preach at our church a number of times over the past year, and, of course, I'm writing this, my tenth book. To paraphrase Mark Twain, *"The reports of my death are greatly exaggerated."*

That raises the question, how should we Christians respond to life-threatening challenges like mine? The enemy of your soul wants to ensnare you, to cast you into the depths of despair, and cause you the greatest anguish. But the Bible assures you of God's blessings, if you will only believe. *"Jesus said to him, 'If you can believe, all things are possible to him who believes'"* (Mark 9:23).

It has sometimes been a struggle for me, but I'm learning to believe. As the testimonies in this book should indicate, my faith has been increased. But someone will say, "Yes, but you haven't actually experienced the late term horrors of cancer yet!"

But I have! In 2018, I was in and out of the hospital several times with severe abdominal pain, but the cause and location of the problem defied diagnosis. The attacks grew more severe, while the periods between them grew shorter. Finally, I could no longer eat or digest food, and when a score of X-rays, CT scans, and other tests didn't locate the problem—I got a real foretaste of the horror.

Finally, in late March of 2019, I was in the hospital with severe pain, a tube down my nose, and my stomach being pumped. I consumed neither food nor drink for four days. I was not allowed a nibble; not a drop! And the surgeon admitted later that he knew I couldn't survive much longer. So, he studied every X-ray and scan, and on Sunday morning, March 24, 2019, he removed a section of my small intestine that was blocked by a carcinoid tumor, along with a number of infected lymph nodes. Carcinoid tumors are, by definition, metastatic.

And later, I was so crippled with muscle rigidity that I could barely lift a fork. Some doctors misdiagnosed it as arthritis and wanted to give me hormone infusions. But they would have spread my cancer. I can only attribute my healing from that year of pain to the hand of God.

Average Guy Meets Extraordinary God

So, yes, I know something of the horror, and I know what it's like to dwell continually in the valley of the shadow of death. But when the enemy tempted me to deny God, I have, by His grace, been able to answer as Daniel's three friends replied before Nebuchadnezzar had them thrown into the fiery furnace: *"If it be so, our God whom we serve is able to deliver us from the burning fiery furnace, and whether or not He does he will deliver us out of thine hand...."* (Daniel 3:7).

I have even begun to understand the significance of the rhetorical question that the great Apostle Paul asked, *"O death, where is thy sting? O grave, where is thy victory?"* (1 Corinthians 15:55, KJV). And I rejoice in the words of David in Psalm 23:6, *"Surely goodness and mercy shall follow me all the days of my life: and I will dwell in the house of the Lord forever."* Because of my growing understanding, I almost continually enjoy a peace that passes understanding, and a joy indescribable and full of glory.

You might ask, "Why aren't such blessings available to all of us, even to those who don't believe in Jesus?" I assure you that the possibility of a miracle is available to everyone who has received Christ. And miracles are even occasionally available to the unsaved, but only to advance their faith, only to help lead them and others, along the path to salvation. Those who trust Jesus Christ as their personal Lord and Savior immediately become members of God's family. Those who have not believed, and those who have actively rejected him, are not members of his family.

Obviously, God doesn't always answer our prayers for healing. Yes, I have been healed of prostate cancer, and that has encouraged me. As far as my Carcinoid Syndrome is concerned, I have outlived the specialist's predictions. But I have been sustained, not healed.

Then something strange happened. On July 15th, 2024, long after I initially wrote the above paragraph, a radiologist commented on that day's CT scan of my abdomen: "Peritoneal/pleural based nodules, improved since the prior exam." In lay terms, those evil cancerous tumors had inexplicably shrunk! And I had not taken the drug which sometimes shrinks tumors for a short period.

Am I deserving? No! I consider myself a poor example of a deserving Christian. But I like to think I am increasingly committed to the Lord and more fruitful than ever before. There are far greater examples than me. Consider the incredible number of glorious hymns written by the blind Fanny Crosby, just one example of how God can be glorified by someone whose prayers for healing were not answered.

We walk by faith with the unseen God. Yet there is empirical evidence of His presence in our lives. The acts of providence which I've seen and experienced attest to His presence, but the world is blind to this because it has rejected the light of God.

The blessings that have been manifested in my life can only be explained by God's grace. They confirm the conclusion that I will spend eternity with Him in the glories of Heaven. If you have received Jesus Christ as your Savior, have you been experiencing the grace that comes from making him the Lord of your life?

It's a question of faith versus sight. *"For the just shall live by faith"* (Romans 1:17). Take your choice. It's a matter of life or death, eternal life or eternal torment. The long-term outcome is the issue. God has done His part. He gave His only begotten Son. Now it's up to you!

Give it some thought? Pray about it. Your few years on this planet amount to a little more than a hands breadth across the heavens.

If you have the smallest interest in God, He will open your eyes. If you prayerfully read your Bible, He will reveal Himself. The promise remains: *"For I know the thoughts that I think toward you, says the Lord, thoughts of peace and not of evil, to give you a future and a hope. Then you will call upon Me and go and pray to Me, and I will listen to you. And you will seek Me and find Me, when you search for Me with all your heart"* (Jeremiah 29:11-13).

The wonderful things that I have described in this book testify to both the existence of God and to His loving mercy. They don't prove it, but they have certainly encouraged Joy and me. Goodness and mercy have followed us all the days of our lives, and they have increased our confidence that we will someday experience the greatest miracle of all. And whether I die of cancer, of heart disease, as a casualty of war or terrorism, or in a pandemic, I will experience the greatest miracle of all, the resurrection from the dead, and "I will dwell in the house of the Lord forever."[45]

The question is, "Will you?"

Could we with ink the ocean fill,
and were the skies of parchment made;
were ev'ry stalk on earth a quill,

---

45   Psalms 23:6

Average Guy Meets Extraordinary God

and ev'ryone a scribe by trade;
to write the love of God above
would drain the ocean dry;
nor could the scroll contain the whole,
though stretched from sky to sky.

The Love of God
Fredrick M. Lehman

www.ingramcontent.com/pod-product-compliance
Lightning Source LLC
Chambersburg PA
CBHW020903060726
47591CB00004B/1069